John,

Congrat[ulations] [on being?] e the
first perso[n to] to
sign a sec[ond] the
book! I [c...] [...] you
lots. Your contribution to
GSCC has been significant.
It's always good to see you
with us. May He continue
to bless and use you
for His glory.

your brother,

Randy

June 1985

P.S. If you lose this one, let me
know. I'll be happy to sign
another. ☺

Christians In The Wake Of the Sexual Revolution

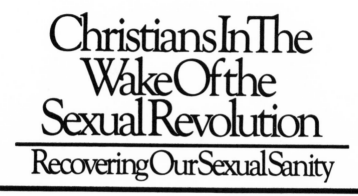

Christians In The Wake Of the Sexual Revolution

Recovering Our Sexual Sanity

RANDY C. ALCORN

MULTNOMAH · PRESS

Portland, Oregon 97266

Unless otherwise indicated, Scripture quotations are from the Holy Bible: New International Version, © 1973, 1978 by the International Bible Society. Used by permission of Zondervan Bible Publishers.

Edited by Rodney L. Morris
Cover design and illustration by Britt Taylor Collins

CHRISTIANS IN THE WAKE OF THE SEXUAL REVOLUTION
© 1985 by Randy C. Alcorn
Published by Multnomah Press
Portland, Oregon 97266

Printed in the United States of America

Library of Congress Cataloging in Publication Data

Alcorn, Randy C.
  Christians in the wake of the sexual revolution.

  Bibliography: p.
  Includes indexes.
  1. Sex—Religious aspects—Christianity.   2. Sexual
ethics—United States.   I. Title.
BT708.A43   1985   241'.66   85-4959
ISBN 0-88070-095-5

85 86 87 88 89 90 91 – 10 9 8 7 6 5 4 3 2 1

To Nanci,
whose loyal love
makes marriage a privilege
and a pleasure.

Contents

Preface

When I started writing this book four years ago, I envisioned a practical "how to" guide for resisting sexual temptation. Though I'd still like to write such a book, this isn't it.

The more I researched and evaluated, the more I became convinced that practical advice about sex must be built on a proper foundation of right thinking about sex. Without this foundation, the practical help can at best engender a superficial morality (superior to immorality, but far less than ideal).

My counseling experience has demonstrated to me that the majority of believers simply do not have this moral foundation upon which to build. We may hear the right words, speak them, and profess to believe them, but the photographic plates of our minds have been exposed so long and so thoroughly to the world that the Word doesn't seem to sink in.

There is much wrong sexual behavior among Christians, to be sure, but *wrong thinking is at the root of the wrong behavior.* Because we fail to identify this wrong thinking and its sources—and fail to eliminate or reject them—we continue to indiscriminately buy the antibiblical sexual propaganda foisted on us by the world, largely through the media. This leads to more wrong thinking and, eventually, more wrong behavior. While I have included much that is practical in this book, I have sought to avoid the stopgap fallacy of telling people how to change their behavior without helping them change their thinking.

I am acutely aware there are many risks in tackling the subject matter of this book. If I handled it with kid gloves and delicately veiled references it would have no impact. Yet by being specific in my illustrations, I run the risk of conjuring up images that present sexual temptations. I may also sometimes appear to be negative in a day when being negative is considered worse than being dishonest. I am consoled that the Bible itself is full of warnings and corrections. To ignore the negative is not only unbiblical and naive, it destines an author to irrelevance, since his readers live in a world that is painfully real.

While I emphasize the beauty of sex as God intended it, I also point out the ugliness of abusing God's gift of sex. Many of the subjects in this book—such as the sexual abuse of children, pornography, and the homosexual movement—are admittedly disturbing, but they cry out for our attention. Scripture says, "It is shameful even to mention what the disobedient do in secret" (Ephesians 5:12). Yet the previous verse tells us "Have nothing to do with the fruitless deeds of darkness, but rather expose them." How can you expose something if you refuse to talk about it?

The one justification for discussing immorality is to expose it for what it is; to condemn, curb, and prevent it—and motivate others to do the same. The Bible speaks clearly and directly about sexual immorality, not to entice us but to tutor us in the path of righteousness. I have tried to follow this example. The result is a book that will not always help you feel good, but will hopefully help you be good.

It might appear to some that I have hung out the church's dirty laundry before the world. But what is the alternative? Silence? A pussyfooting approach that fails to address head-on what is threatening both the life and witness of the holy church of Christ?

God's Word answers by example. It does not showcase spiritual giants or gloss over the vulnerabilities and failures of the saints. On the contrary, Scripture is painfully honest in describing flesh and blood men and women with whom the later twentieth century believer can readily identify. As this book falls into the hands of non-Christians and young Christians, I can only hope they will understand and respect the need for the Christian community to take hard stock of itself in an honest effort to shore up its sagging morality.

This book incorporates elements of history, sociology, and psychology, and attempts to examine them in the light of biblical theology. I have made every effort to avoid a technical treatment in the desire to be read, and equal effort to avoid a superficial treatment in the desire to be right.

No illustrations in this book are fictitious, but I have gone to great lengths to protect the identities of people. Not only names but some details are changed, though the essential factors that bear on each illustration have not been distorted.

I want to acknowledge my debt first to the Lord Jesus, to whom I owe all and to whose glory this book is offered. Thanks and praise go to Nanci, my wife, and Karina and Angie, my daughters. Without their understanding and sacrifices my efforts would have been impossible or worthless.

Special thanks also to Kathy Duncan, whose countless hours of cheerful and flawless typing were God-sent; to Rod Morris, my skillful and meticulous editor; to my friends John Kohlenberger and Kin Millen, who first encouraged me to write on this subject; to Ed and Carol Barker, whose model of ministry never ceases to move me; and to Don and Pat Maxwell, whose friendship Nanci and I appreciate so much.

I also want to thank my fellow elders Stu Weber, Rick Norquist, Alan Hlavka, Garland Gabbert, Arden Meyer, Norm Norquist, Tom Poole, Jim Spinks, and Byron Weber; fellow workers Steve Keels, Steve Tucker, Brian Wheeler, Dave Stout, Karen Stout, Kathy Norquist, Joan Petersen, Bonnie Reid, Linda Brice, Rollie Aden, and Dennis Cate. These men and women provide the camaraderie and spiritual stimulation that makes our ministry at Good Shepherd Community Church such a pleasure. To the good people of Good Shepherd, I also express my heartfelt thanks for the open and warm climate in which many of the insights in this book gestated and materialized.

Edmund Burke's classic observation kept me going when

everything within me wanted to fold under the weight of this project: "All that is necessary for the triumph of evil is that good men do nothing." This book is an attempt to do something.

PART 1

WHERE DOES THE WORLD END AND THE CHURCH BEGIN?

Chapter 1

Sex, the World,
and the Church

*A*sk the enlightened American what he thinks of Christian sexual morality. To him, it's a fossil—an antique that went out with washboards and penny candy. Who believes any more what the Bible says about sex? Old ladies and helpless traditionalists, the same quaint folk who still use push lawn mowers, manual typewriters, and clothes that are years out of style.

The moral ice-age is over. Exit the dogmatic dinosaurs of sexual repression. Enter the sensuous sirens of sexual expression. We live in the age of sexual enlightenment, presumably but a few years from sexual utopia. *So what does this bright new age look like?*

Newspapers publish invitations for sexual partners. A singing telegram service sends male strippers to act out sexual fantasies in private homes. Rows of pornographic tabloids line city streets, available to any child with a curious mind and a few spare quarters. Prostitutes, massage parlors, adult book stores, strip joints, peep shows, female impersonators, gay baths, singles bars, sado-masochist leather shops—they've become as much a part of urban America as skyscrapers and parking meters.

15

"But that's just the big city." My church, believe it or not, is in Boring, Oregon (a town less eventful than its name). Yet a mile away from our church building a tavern features nude dancers. Want ads in a nearby community college's newspaper solicit homosexual partners. The convenience store down the road stocks a dozen pornographic magazines and a rack of porno novels.

There is open season on sex in this country, and you don't have to look far to see it.

Strolling through the Sexual Wasteland

Walking through a new shopping mall, my wife and I stepped into a gift store where children were huddled around battery operated stuffed animals. Ten feet into the store we were surrounded by nude puzzles, sex games, sex gadgets, and sex potions. Family variety stores sell pin-up posters of celebrities in seductive poses, along with "Playmate," "Buns," and "Hunk-A-Month" calendars. Bumper stickers and license plate frames boast of the driver's sexual prowess ("Nurses do it . . . ," "Carpenters do it . . . ") and scorn traditional morality ("Chaste Makes Waste"). Teenage boys wear T-shirts reading "Sex Instructor—First Lesson Free"; teen girls "I am a virgin—this is an old T-shirt."

Stopping at a motel on a business trip, a man is asked "Do you want adult movies? Do you want a woman?" Driving through a city, we stopped near two junior high boys in shorts and tank tops. Next to us a Lincoln Continental drove up, and the male driver beckoned to the boys. "Which one of us do you want?" one of the boys asked. When the man pointed his finger, the other boy hopped into the car. Teen prostitution—a multi-million dollar business in America.

A few blocks from the Bible college I graduated from, a massage parlor is located directly across from a grade school, in full view of the children. A mile up the street, across from a high school, is a topless soft drink bar where students can view nude dancing during lunch hour.

Incest is at epidemic proportions. Whether at day care centers or in prostitution-pornography rings, child molesting makes the papers every week. So do rape, sodomy, and serial sex murders. Organized clubs of transvestites, sado-masochists, and pedophiles have joined homosexuals by coming out of the closet and actively lobbying for their rights.

The new technology has become the tool of this new morality. When I subscribed to a computer newsletter, I was offered software disks featuring nude women. One company sells sex graphics titled "Dirty Old Man," and a program called "Street Life," where the player is a pimp trying to manage several prostitutes and avoid the police.[1] Another company produced three X-rated video games, marketed 750,000 copies, and made plans to issue twelve new games in the next few years. The goal of "Custer's Revenge," the game that captured the media's attention, is to rape an Indian woman tied to a post.

Whole companies are devoted to manufacturing sex toys and instruments. Some flourish from national chains, others from privately sponsored neighborhood parties where sex toys are sold like tupperware. Millions receive by mail color catalogues featuring this paraphernalia, along with every variety of pornography.

A local television news program featured a human interest story on a strip tease performer. The slant was that strip bars create jobs, meet a public need, and cause no harm. The stripper interviewed was a bright, cheerful college student who makes good grades and considers stripping a "challenging profession."

A Lesson from Miss America

Miss America 1984 resigned when *Penthouse* magazine published ten pages of her nude photos, depicting sexual overtures to another nude woman. The whole scenario was an instructive lesson in modern morality.

Miss America practiced modern morality when she sought to promote her career and earn her money by posing nude, and again later when she signed a statement for the pageant saying she had never been involved in any "moral turpitude." The photographer followed the same code of ethics by lying to the girl ("no one will ever see them") and selling the photos to the highest bidder. *Penthouse* showed its true colors (as if there was ever a doubt) by publishing the photos despite knowing they would humiliate the girl, force her to resign, and possibly ruin her career.

The Miss America Pageant demonstrated its own moral hypocrisy by uplifting "traditional virtues" in calling for the girl's resignation (a correct decision), despite the fact that the pageant's most celebrated event is the swimsuit competition, a form of sexual exploitation different only in degree, not in kind, from *Penthouse*'s. The American media demonstrated its moral integrity by reveling over the whole affair for days on end, thereby supplying millions of dollars worth of free advertising for *Penthouse*.

Finally, the American public not only enjoyed soaking up the media's account of this sordid mess but committed its own moral turpitude by buying every one of the month's five million copies (the number of "readers" being far higher), thus rewarding the unprincipled for their immoral decisions and tactics and driving up the price the next time a photographer seeks to similarly exploit a not-so-innocent young woman. Here we see in miniature the supply and demand cycle of America's waning sexual morality.

Sitting at the Feet of the Experts

Anyone with a degree in medicine or psychology (whether earned or bought) has suddenly become a sex expert. Freudians, neo-Freudians, and quasi-Freudians abound, each seeking to corner a big enough share of the sex market to guarantee talk show appearances and early retirement.

Psychiatrist Thomas Szasz has written *Sex By Prescription*, an enlightening book debunking the so-called science of sexology. It *is* hard to take the sexologists too seriously when their professional journals feature articles like "Erotic Messages on Lavatory Walls," "Women Who Seduce Teenagers," and "Sex in Nudist Camps."

Hundreds of sex manuals—making grandiose promises to revolutionize our sex lives—fill the shelves. Some are thinly disguised erotica, others as matter of fact as an encyclopedia for home handymen and almost as inspiring. No sexual stone is left unturned.

Sex therapy is no longer a private affair. Dr. Ruth Westheimer, author of *Dr. Ruth's Guide to Good Sex,* is a media sex therapist with a popular syndicated radio program called "Sexually Speaking." She receives four to six hundred phone calls per hour while on the air and now has her own daily television program, "Good Sex," on which she freely discusses such topics as masturbation, affairs, and oral sex.

The Search for Sex—The New Holy Grail

Harper's Bazaar asks, "Can sex cure arthritis?" The question typifies our age. Surely, sex is the answer to everything.

Television, movies, radio, books, magazines, newspapers, and music all constantly bombard us with sex. Thousands of industries, from cameras to computers—most of which have about as much to do with sex as athletes have to do with rental cars—use sex to sell their products. Even the scientific journals seem preoccupied with sex. I recently saw one article on prehistoric sex and another on insect foreplay.

The American sexual hype borders on the pathological. The search for a new female erogenous zone (the "G-spot") was treated by the media as if it were the search for the Holy Grail. And despite the pain, expense, and possible side-effects, each year more than seventy thousand U.S. women have their breasts surgically enlarged.[2]

Were a future civilization to one day unearth the tell-tale ruins of present day America, it would undoubtedly conclude we spent a third of our time having sex, another third planning it, and the other third talking about it.

Our obsession with sex is so great that anyone who doesn't

share it is considered abnormal. According to *Time*, sex therapists report that one half of their cases focus on the problem of Inhibited Sexual Desire (ISD). They estimate that 20 percent of the population suffers from ISD.

"The biggest surprise so far," says one psychotherapist and sex researcher, "is how well these people are functioning. They look good, feel happy, like their families and are successful in their work."[3] *So what's the problem?* Despite the happy appearance of ISD victims, the psychotherapist feels bound to add this ominous conjecture: "But under the cheerfulness there's a lack of fulfillment." The irony is that most of these people are coming for help (which includes being taught to fantasize about sex) only because their society has intimidated them into believing that eroticism is essential to personal worth and happiness. No one points out that unbridled sexual lust destroys countless more lives than does ISD.

Though the American Psychiatric Association removed homosexuality from its list of disorders in its diagnostic handbook, it recently added ISD. Apparently, any sex is better than no sex.

But is it possible that the sexual revolution itself has robbed people of their sexual desire—intimidated them into backing off from sex because they cannot perform by society's numbers? Among its sexually liberated readership, *Psychology Today* reports an "astonishing" 28 percent of men and 40 percent of women hold back from sexual intimacy "due to a lack of desire." It is a significant exposé of the sexual revolution that, according to this study, "among men, the largest proportion who lack desire (41%) have had *at least seven* extramarital affairs."[4] So much for the lie of liberation.

Sexual Health or Sexual Sickness?

The sexual revolution has fostered a barnyard morality that robs human dignity. It has resulted in people being seen and treated as sexual objects rather than sexual subjects. It has left us a nation of technological giants and moral dwarves. Millions now live under the burden of sexual expectations and pressures to perform in a prescribed manner. Victims of the tyranny of the orgasm, they feel that unless their sexual experience is what they see in the media—where everyone is effortlessly erotic and every encounter is comparable to nuclear fission—they're being robbed, or they're not a real man or a real woman.

Instead of a spontaneous expression of other-oriented marital love, sex has become a self-oriented, goal-oriented obsession—an object of endless analysis, comparison, experimentation, and disappointment. Like the end of the rainbow, the ultimate (apocalyptic?) sexual experience is always sought, but never found.

Our modern sexual openness is endlessly pawned off as healthy, emancipating, and long overdue. But is our preoccupation with sex *really* a sign of sexual health? Who talks most about how they're feeling? Sick people. Who buys the books on car repairs? Those with car problems. Who buys the drain cleaner? Those with clogged drains. Who thinks about, talks about, and buys the most books about sex? Those with sexual problems.

Notice how much of the literature on sex deals with sexual problems, inadequacy, impotence, and dysfunction. This betrays not just a strong interest in sex, but a prevailing difficulty with it. Why do we still need so much help with sex? After twenty years of sexual freedom, where's the sexual utopia promised us in the sixties and seventies? It's not knowledge of sex we lack, but *perspective*.

The sexual freedom established during the past couple of decades has not been accompanied by the increase in happiness that many people assumed would follow from a freeing of sexual mores. . . .

We have been liberated from the taboos of the past only to find ourselves imprisoned in a "freedom" that brings us no closer to our real nature or needs. . . .

[Sex] remains for most men and women a world

through which they move warily, cautiously, self-protectively—not a home but an alien land. . . .

Despite all our rhetoric, all our manuals, all our universal make-believe—the sexual realm is marred by pretense, desperation, and an immense amount of "bad faith," which constitutes a simultaneous betrayal of both the other person and oneself. . . .

[Sex] remains, in the midst of that "revolution" which has provided neither much equality nor liberty nor fraternity, a troublesome but fecund darkness in which, like lost children, we call out to one another in both fear and delight.[5]

The move from the famine of Victorianism to the feast of eroticism hasn't been what it was cracked up to be. Like people who have bought choice real estate that turns out to be swampland, we've bought a lie—and a costly one at that.

The more we say about sex, the more we herald the new liberating sexual doctrines, the more we seem to uncover (or is it produce?) a myriad of sexual problems. The harder we try to drown these sexual problems in a flood of new relationships, erotic magazines, novels, movies, and sex education literature and classes, the louder and more persistently our sexual problems cry out for attention. We have become little more than a nation of sexual misfits. An honest look at our newspapers, magazines, television programs, and a host of other social gauges substantiates this. The more we talk about sex and trump up sexual liberty, the more we forge the chains of our sexual slavery.

The more we have sought fulfillment apart from God, the further into the sexual desert we have wandered. Throats parched, lips cracked and bleeding, we are nomads in search of a sexual oasis that forever eludes us.

We have turned our backs on the Architect, Engineer, and Builder of human sexuality. We have denied his authority and ridiculed his servants. Our glands as our gods, we have discarded his directions, burned his blueprint, trampled on the ashes, and, like rebellious children, stalked off to do sex our own way.

We are just beginning to reap the results.

HOW DIFFERENT IS THE CHURCH?

In 1959 A. W. Tozer wrote,

> The period in which we now live may well go down in history as the Erotic Age. Sex love has been elevated into a cult. Eros has more worshippers among civilized men today than any other god. For millions the erotic has completely displaced the spiritual.[6]

Though he had harsh words for the effects of eros on the world, Tozer's concern was for something far more serious:

> Now if this god would let us Christians alone I for one would let his cult alone. The whole spongy, fetid mess will sink some day under its own weight and become excellent fuel for the fires of hell, a just recompense which is meet, and it becomes us to feel compassion for those who have been caught in its tragic collapse. Tears and silence might be better than words if things were slightly otherwise than they are. But the cult of eros is seriously affecting the church. The pure religion of Christ that flows like a crystal river from the heart of God is being polluted by the unclean waters that trickle from behind the altars of abomination that appear on every high hill and under every green tree from New York to Los Angeles.[7]

If Tozer were still with us, he would be both grieved and outraged to discover the sad truth—that the church's moral life in 1959 was *far* superior to what it is today.

In New Testament times, the sexual purity of God's people

drew a sharp line dividing them from the non-Christian world. Prior to the sexual revolution, this was largely true of the church in America. But things have radically changed. In *Flirting with the World,* John White draws these sobering conclusions: "the sexual behavior of Christians has reached the point of being indistinguishable from that of non-Christians . . . in our sexual behavior we, as a Christian community, are both in the world, and of it."[8]

Christians in Moral Crisis

Substantiating White's claim is this paradox uncovered by a 1984 Gallup poll: "Religion is growing in importance among Americans, but morality is losing ground." That same poll found "very little difference in the behavior of the churched and unchurched on a wide range of items including lying, cheating, and pilferage."[9]

High standards of morality—including sexual morality— used to be inseparable from the Christian faith. No longer. It is increasingly difficult to discern where the world ends and the church begins.

Examples are not hard to come by.

Christians and the Media

My observations and conversations confirm there is little difference between the media habits of Christians and those of their non-Christian neighbors. There are those who feel the freedom to miss an occasional Sunday at church (and I do not criticize them for this), but would never miss an episode of "Dallas," "Dynasty," or some of the other dramatic series, soaps, television movies, and sitcoms peppered with sexual immorality and innuendo. We are hopelessly naive to think that Christians do not watch such programs—or that watching them we are somehow immune to their effects.

A Christian couple confided they subscribed to an adult entertainment network that brought X-rated movies into their living room every night after the children went to bed.

Three high school students, all Christians and from Christian families, spent the evening in one of their homes watching two video movies. Parents also watched snatches of them. Both movies were rated R and contained sexually explicit language and crude sex scenes. The parents shook their heads in disgust a few times but didn't want to "spoil the fun," so said nothing.

I've been in several Christian homes where one look in the bedrooms of the teenage sons reveals the best selling sex symbol posters on the market, rivaling the *Playboy* foldouts of a generation ago.

Like the frog that boiled to death by degrees, many Christian homes have been gradually desensitized to sexual sin. The result is predictable—immorality is more rampant among believers than ever before.

Immorality in the Holy Church of God

A twenty-three-year-old boy announces to his parents, "I'm gay." A man comes home from a business trip to find his seventeen-year-old daughter in bed with a boy she's been dating three weeks. A woman comes home from shopping to find her six-year-old daughter and a teenage neighbor boy naked and fondling each other. A father of two has sex with the sixteen-year-old baby sitter. A high schooler admits to his unsuspecting parents that he is a prostitute. These things didn't just happen; they happened in Christian families. I know, because they came to me for help.

When we hear that 60 to 80 percent of young people engage in sexual intercourse before marriage, most of us assume our own church young people constitute the other 20 to 40 percent. But any youth counselor in touch with reality will tell you this is often not the case.

Jim was a high school sophomore, from a Christian family, active in his youth group. His first sexual experience was at a Christian summer camp. Linda also had premarital sex at a Christian camp—with one of the counselors.

Dave became a Christian as a twenty-two year old. He

made such great spiritual strides that he assumed he would never fall back to his former lifestyle. Yet one day he found himself committing adultery with a woman he'd been witnessing to.

Susan was also a strong Christian. One evening, seemingly without warning, she fell back into sexual sin. Later, in a small group Bible study, she volunteered to the rest of us, "I didn't know I needed to be on guard against immorality. I thought being a Christian made it impossible to go back to that again. When I fell, I was shocked and devastated. I really didn't believe it could happen to me. But it did."

Endowed with exceptional intelligence, attractiveness, and athletic skill, Brian was a leader in the youth group. He charmed the whole church with his exciting testimony. But time brought a gradual erosion of Brian's moral standards. It surfaced in his words, his clothing, his body language, and his choice of friends. Now in his twenties, Brian recently boasted to a friend, "I can get any girl I want in bed with me."

Cindy is a Christian girl whose fiancé broke up with her and dropped out of church, disillusioned with the Christian life. When I asked her why, her matter-of-fact reply took me by surprise—"I think it began when I seduced him." She went on to say, "At first he didn't want to have sex, but I talked him into it. After that, sex was all he could think about. Then he got bitter at me and at God, and now he's really messed up."

Adultery in the Church

Linda, a mother of four in her middle thirties, had just discovered she was pregnant again. But there was a complication. The child's father was the man who lived next door, not her husband. "Should I get an abortion?" she asked with alarming ease and sincerity.

Debbie's situation was similar to Linda's—she was uncertain whether her baby's father was her husband or one of their friends at church with whom she said she had "slipped up."

John and Pat came into my office with the vague diagnosis of "marriage problems." When I met with each separately, John described himself as "a man of strong biblical convictions— which is the only thing keeping me from divorcing Pat." Later John admitted he had been unfaithful to Pat and had carried on "a few affairs" behind her back. "How many affairs?" I asked. "Six," he replied, with a slight blush (they had been married only eight years).

Recently I was asked to confront a man who was resisting a Christian woman's attempt to break off their adulterous affair. I called the man and was surprised when he assured me, despite his adultery, "I want you to know that I'm a Christian, and I regularly pray that Joel [the woman's husband] will come to Christ."

Homosexuality in the Church

Al was a thirty-year-old Bible study leader in another church. One day Al told me that for as long as he can remember, he has been sexually attracted to other men. Al confessed he had given in to his desires for the last two years, having sex with forty different men. He came to me devastated, "sick and tired of living a lie." Al got right with God, and as we met regularly over the next three months he reported real progress.

Then one day Al lost his job. Depressed, he wandered to a shopping mall, a place we'd agreed he should never go alone. Soon he was picked up by two men and had sex with them. Still reeling from his fall, on the way home he picked up a hitchhiker whom he recognized as a homosexual. Before long the two of them were holding hands. As they talked, it came out that the hitchhiker was a Bible college student. Shocked into reality, Al didn't allow the relationship to go further.

Twenty-year-old Stacy told me, "I'm engaged to a Christian, but we have one problem. He's bisexual, and he's had some recent affairs with men."

Other Sexual Perversions in the Church

Nicolle, a young Christian wife, tearfully confessed that her husband had hounded her to go to bed with him and another woman. At first she refused, but in tired frustration she finally gave in. To say the least, she was sorry.

Belinda called late one night and began, "I'm ashamed to even ask this. But what should I do if I think my husband is fooling around with our three-year-old daughter?" Her husband was a professing believer—an alumnus of a fine Christian college.

Fran was raped as a six-year-old by her grandfather, and again when she was eleven by the father of children she was babysitting. Both men were faithful church-goers.

Tom and Betty, parents of four, were active lay leaders in their church. They came to me—on the verge of divorce—because Tom was sexually involved with his sister.

A friend told me that his church just went through a scandal that rocked the community. A fourteen-year-old girl was pregnant by her grandfather—one of the church's elders.

Immorality in the Ministry

"Randy, something terrible has happened here at the church," said my friend, calling from another state. "Yesterday one of the pastors left his wife and ran off with another woman." I was sorry; but not shocked or even surprised. Ten years ago I would have been shocked; five years ago I would have been surprised. Now I was sad. I have heard the same story too many times to be surprised ever again.

A veteran seminary professor was dismissed for immorality. After accepting a pastorate in another part of the country, his ordination was revoked because of further sexual sin.

When I spoke for a week at a Bible college, many students came for counseling. Among them were Pam, Barb, and Rachel. Pam said she went to her church's staff counselor for help in dealing with insecurities tied to childhood abuse by her father. This counselor was the first man Pam had ever been able to trust. Two months later he convinced her to have sex with him. Eighteen-year-old Barb is the daughter of a deacon at an evangelical church—who for years sexually abused Barb and her two younger sisters. Rachel confessed through a flood of tears that she came to Bible school to escape an ongoing affair with the senior pastor of her church.

Eighteen-year-old Toni, also a Bible college student, told me she committed immorality with her former youth pastor. The church never found this out, but it was not long before the pastor involved moved on to a new ministry. Toni's primary concern, however, did not relate to this former youth pastor but to her current affair with the church's *new* youth pastor (both men were married and had young children). Toni gave me permission to discuss her problem with the school's dean of women.

"What is going on with Christian leaders anymore?" asked this woman counselor. "Last year our music minister was dismissed for adultery—not only at our church but at several previous ones. But what really hurts," she went on, "is what happened to the head of the Bible department at my alma mater, a man I have known and respected for years. Six months ago the school had to fire him because he committed adultery. Since then, he divorced his wife and married the other woman!"

Barry was leader of an outstanding youth organization. He masterminded an outreach that over the years affected thousands for Christ. One day a heartbroken fellow pastor asked me that fateful question, "Have you heard about Barry?" He had been forced to resign because of immorality. Though he was repentant, a brilliant ministry was through. A tragedy—but not a rarity.

Most of these tragedies are kept as quiet as possible to save churches, Christian organizations, and individuals from embarrassment. Many others have made their way to the public eye, however. In past years these have included a leading Bible college president running off with a student, a pastor engaged in homosexual activities with young boys at his church, and an evangelist found murdered in the bed of his partner in adultery.

One of the most widely publicized cases was that of a nationally known crusader for Christian morality and president of a prominent Christian college. *Time* magazine revealed this man had been sexually involved with at least five students at his college, four of them men, over a period of three years. This Christian leader, who blamed his behavior on "genes and chromosomes," publicly denounced sexual immorality right up to the day he was exposed.

Leadership magazine printed a lengthy article entitled, "The War Within: An Anatomy of Lust." The author's name was withheld. We know only that he is a Christian leader who describes in detail his ten year slavery to lust, from which he was recently delivered. This is how he begins:

> I am writing this article anonymously because I am embarrassed. Embarrassed for my wife and children, yes, but embarrassed most for myself. I will tell of my personal battle with lust, and if I believed I was the only one who fought in that war, I would not waste emotional energy dredging up stained and painful memories. But I believe my experience is not uncommon, is perhaps even typical of pastors, writers, and conference speakers. No one talks about it. No one writes about it. But it's there, like an unacknowledged cancer that metastasizes best when no one goes for x-rays or feels for lumps.[10]

Though I would not call his experience typical, it is undoubtedly more common than any of us would like to believe.

Certainly, I have no wish to cast suspicion on Christian leaders or malign the reputation of the ministry I am part of. Many men and women in Christian ministry are shining examples of personal holiness. But a significant and growing number *are* succumbing to sexual immorality—tragically illustrating the need to devote unprecedented thought and effort to this issue.

Where Does This Leave Us?

One day recently, two of my three afternoon appointments began with confessions of adultery. The third involved the most deeply rooted and sordid history of homosexual behavior I have ever encountered. All three counselees were professing Christians—and in only one of them did I sense genuine repentance, though sin had wreaked havoc in each of their lives.

In a recent six day span, I faced the following counseling appointments: a forty-year-old man who slept with a woman he met at a home Bible study; a middle aged woman who left her husband to live with another man for two years; a young married man emotionally wrapped up with his secretary and contemplating divorcing his wife for her; a college student who had participated in a homosexual act with a man instrumental in his conversion; a Christian woman pursuing an affair with her church's deacon board chairman. Of the ten people involved in sin, only two were non-Christians.

For years I have asked myself a sobering question: For every believer in sexual sin who comes to me, how many more are there who go to others, and still more who go to no one at all? Obviously, my own level of awareness must be multiplied many times to gain a true perception of the moral condition of the evangelical church. I can only conclude that we are facing among Christians a moral epidemic of enormous and frightening proportions.

Make no mistake about it—the Christian church is riddled with immorality, among the young and the older, the single and the married, the laity and the leadership. No Christian is immune to sexual temptation. We do ourselves no favor to pretend that the same hormones and human weaknesses common to all people are somehow eradicated when we come to Christ. Enslaved by sexual sin in mind and body, plagued and haunted by its guilt, innumerable children of God are tragically incapacitated in their attempts to live for Christ. Nothing so hamstrings the believer's spiritual potency as sexual compromise—and never has the church in America been so compromised as now.

I know there is risk in putting such things in print. Yet I believe there is much more to be lost by keeping silent. We can no longer afford the luxury of naiveté in this critical area. It is, furthermore, impossible to overestimate the damage done to the cause of Christ by the sexual impurity of his people. The church's impact on a dark world is lost when believers attempt to straddle a spiritual no man's land, with one foot on the narrow path of Christ and the other on the broad highway of the world. The more muddled the line between world and church, the more bleak the future of both.

Just as certainly, however, this moral tragedy can be turned into spiritual triumph. The church's sexual purity could once again become her trademark—a reminder that church and world are not the same and that those weary of the world may find not only peace but purity in the church.

To this end this book has been written.

Chapter 1, Notes

1. *USA Today,* 13 December 1984, sec. B.

2. *USA Today,* 12 January 1984, sec. D.

3. John Leo, "In Search of Sexual Desire," *Time,* 4 April 1983, 80.

4. Carin Rubenstein, "The Modern Art of Courtly Love," *Psychology Today,* July 1983, 40.

5. Peter Marin, "A Revolution's Broken Promises," *Psychology Today,* July 1983, 51-57.

6. A. W. Tozer, *Born After Midnight* (Harrisburg, Penn.: Christian Publications, Inc., 1959), 36.

7. Ibid., 37.

8. John White, *Flirting with the World* (Wheaton, Ill.: Harold Shaw Publishers, 1982), 75, 81.

9. *The Oregonian,* 14 July 1984.

10. "The War Within: An Anatomy of Lust," *Leadership,* Fall 1982, 31.

Chapter 2

The Whos, Hows, and Whys of the Sexual Revolution

*I*n 1956, Harvard sociologist Pitirim Sorokin stated,

> This sex revolution is as important as the most dramatic political or economic upheaval. It is changing the lives of men and women more radically than any other revoluton of our time. . . .
>
> Any considerable change in marriage behavior, any increase in sexual promiscuity and illicit relations, is pregnant with momentous consequences. A sex revolution drastically affects the lives of millions, deeply disturbs the community, and decisively influences the future of society.[1]

Any movement this significant deserves our attention. In order to respond to the new world created by the sexual revolution, it is important to know its history—how and why it happened. These wholesale changes in our nation's sexual morality did not appear overnight. They are the cumulative product of significant people, ideas, forces, and events. If we understand them better, it may help us make our own impact for good on the course of moral history.

33

UNDERSTANDING THE REVOLUTION

Every revolution is against some established order. The American sexual revolution's assault was on the nation's order of sexual mores. These mores were firmly rooted in the Judeo-Christian ethic, itself founded on the teachings of the Bible.

As we will see in later chapters, the Bible affirms personal chastity, modesty, fidelity, and marriage as the only proper context for sexual intimacy. It unapologetically condemns premarital sex (fornication), extramarital sex (adultery), homosexual relations, incest, and all other sexual behavior outside of marriage. Furthermore, it condemns sexual lust (not desires but mental indulgences) and sees it as the root of all immoral behavior.

Before the sexual revolution, most Americans affirmed this biblical sexual ethic, with all its social and legal implications. Some of the same, of course, violated this ethic in private. But it is important to understand that the sexual revolution did not simply produce more infringements on the established moral standard. Rather, *it changed the standard itself*. Hence, as do all true revolutions, this one altered not only actions but attitudes, not simply behavior but belief. The sexual revolution was fundamentally a revolution not of the body but of the mind.

Sexual Negativism in the Church

Throughout much of church history a dark cloud hovered over sex. Church fathers like Chrysostom and Jerome spoke demeaningly of sex, even in marriage. Origen taught that sex was inherently wrong, Augustine that sex was part of the original sin of Genesis 3—despite the command to procreate in Genesis 1 and the one flesh marital relationship of Genesis 2.[2]

Such unbiblical perspectives led to equating celibacy with spirituality and advocating sexless marriage, in direct contradiction of the New Testament (1 Corinthians 7:3-5).

As a whole, Luther and the other reformers were milder in their disregard for sex, but negative nonetheless. Later the Puritans gained a reputation for sexual austerity, epitomized in the man who allegedly had his wife executed for smiling during intercourse.

Actually, the Puritans are victims of bad press—as a whole they made real strides toward a healthy view of sex within marriage. On one occasion, for instance, a man was disciplined by a Puritan church for refusing to have sex with his wife.[3] Many Puritans held to a positive view of sex in marriage, and, like the biblical writers, considered that view totally consistent with condemning sex outside marriage.

In contrast, the Victorian age was notoriously hypocritical. Sexual purity was outwardly elevated, yet married men were permitted to consort with prostitutes, partly to save their wives from the "indignity" of sex (how noble of them). As has often been the case in human history, where sex was demeaned sexual immorality was prevalent.

In her zeal to hold the line against immorality, the church miserably failed to embrace or project a positive view of sex. This failure contributed to the sexual pressure cooker that finally exploded in the form of the sexual revolution.

The church's antisexual posture was ultimately anti-human, since people are sexual beings. That posture not only set the stage for the sexual revolution but caused the church to be caught flat-footed when the revolution came. By the time the church's head cleared and it said, "Really, it's not sex we're against but the misuse of sex," no one was listening. Had the church all along taught a positive view of sex (see chapter 11), she could have taken the wind out of the sexual revolution's sails—and saved herself, and perhaps a good deal of society, from the great sex swindle of recent years.

The Birth of Secularism

The Renaissance, the transitional period between the Middle Ages and the modern era, was a time of great creativity and accomplishment in the arts and sciences. It marked the birth of humanism, of emphasis on human potential.

Later came the Enlightenment, an eighteenth century philosophic movement marked by individualism, scientific empiricism, the questioning of traditional doctrines and values, and the exaltation of human reason. Through the Enlightenment, humanism degenerated into secularism. God's moral laws (not least those pertaining to sex) were questioned, reinterpreted, and, increasingly, considered less relevant to modern man, who saw himself as coming of age and capable of making his own moral decisions.

Charles Darwin's *Origin of Species* (1859) was a historic landmark, not simply in biology but in philosophy and theology. The theory of evolution fit secularism like a glove. Man was already asserting his intellectual and moral independence from God. Evolution provided the missing link—a sense of physical independence from God. After all, if God was not man's physical Creator, how could he be his moral judge? Man was seen as the determiner of his own destiny, the architect of his own moral standards. No longer in need of a Creator, he was no longer in need of standards foisted upon him by a Creator.

While at first the masses resisted the nontheistic implications of evolution, the intellectual elite welcomed it. It was for them an answer to prayer.

INFLUENTIAL PEOPLE

Sigmund Freud

Sigmund Freud was to psychology what Darwin was to biology. Freud researched and counseled in Vienna at the end of the nineteenth century, in the sexually neurotic and hypocritical climate of Victorianism. There he witnessed sexual repression in the extreme.

It was in this loom of sexual repression that Freud wove his revolutionary ideas of human sexuality. Had he found instead a church that fostered in society a healthy view of sex in marriage, his findings would have been much different—and we probably wouldn't know his name.

Freud came to see sex as basic to all human needs, drives, and problems. He popularized new concepts and terms like "libido," "id," "ego," "super-ego," and "psychic energy." He fathered the famous Oedipal concept, which effectively placed the blame for incest on the child's desire to seduce the parent of the opposite sex. Freud was the first to legitimize sex both as a field of research and a topic of conversation.

Freud's pioneer research was influenced by his own sexual quirks. These included not only impotence, but incestuous and homosexual tendencies.[4] None of this minimizes Freud's unquestionable brilliance and immense contributions to human understanding. It simply points out—as does our knowledge of other sexual reformers—that it is difficult to separate one's sexual beliefs from his sexual experiences.

Freud's views often conflicted with Christian theology. He believed neither in God nor the after-life, and acknowledged his debt to Darwin in molding some of his most basic convictions. Freud's ideas tremendously influenced the directions of psychology, counseling, education, and even religion. It would be difficult to overestimate his role in the development of twentieth century Western thought.

Havelock Ellis

Havelock Ellis, also highly influenced by Darwin and once a disciple of Freud, carried considerable clout in the early stages of the sexual revolution. The seven volumes of his *Studies in the Psychology of Sex,* published between 1897 and 1928, were banned in England, and available in the United States only to the medical profession until 1935.

Why the furor over Ellis's writings? He was one of the first influential figures to publicly recommend premarital sex. Before the 1920s he defended the legitimacy of nonlegal unions, the same arrangements dubbed "living together" in the sixties. He also strongly opposed the existing legislation that made sexual relations with a girl under twenty-one illegal, arguing that if such an age was necessary, which he doubted, it should not exceed sixteen.

Havelock Ellis was the international hero of the contraceptive crusade. He was also a firm believer in eugenics, advocating voluntary sterilization of the genetically "inferior," and mandatory sterilization of the "feeble minded." His position was logically rooted in the Darwinian concept of man, especially the concepts of natural selection and the survival of the fittest. He was committed to the secularist doctrine of man's ability and, indeed, destiny to control himself and his environment in producing the highest form of humanity.

Ellis's research in homosexuality was done with John Addington Symonds, himself a homosexual. Most of the case studies were from the experiences of Symonds and his homosexual partners.[5] Others came from Havelock's own wife Edith's lesbian relationships, which he not only knew about but encouraged.[6] Not surprisingly, Ellis became convinced that homosexuality was neither a disease nor a crime, a position assumed by many today but almost unheard of before Ellis. Indeed, his famous work *Sexual Inversion* was more a piece of propaganda than serious research:

> Although cast in the form of a scientific treatise, the book was in essence an apology for homosexuality—a classic example of Ellis's lifelong effort to broaden the spectrum of acceptable sexual behavior. . . . all served to create an impression of homosexuality as an innocuous departure from the sexual norm, and one not without its advantages for society.[7]

Bertrand Russell

Perhaps no scholar ever wrote so prolifically in such diverse fields as Nobel prize winner Bertrand Russell. Able to tackle the realms of philosophy, science, mathematics, history, education, politics, religion, and ethics, he is widely regarded as the greatest intellectual of this century. Not the least of his lasting efforts was invested in reforming this nation's heritage of Judeo-Christian morality.

Russell was more active than Ellis in advocating trial marriage. He promoted "companionate marriage" in his *Marriage and Morals* (1929), maintaining that entering into marriage without sexual involvement was "just as absurd as it would be if a man intending to buy a house were not allowed to view it until he had completed the purchase." He also proposed, "No marriage should be legally binding until the wife's first pregnancy."[8]

Russell's personal life was as unconventional as his writings. In 1910, he left his wife for another woman. The years ahead brought three divorces and three more marriages, as well as several other affairs.

Margaret Sanger

In her own way, Margaret Sanger eclipsed both Ellis and Russell in her influence on the sexual mores of America. Though not the first advocate of family limitation, her untiring efforts justly earned her the title "the mother of birth control." She established the first birth control clinic in 1916 in Brooklyn, founded the American Birth Control League, organized the first World Population Conference in Geneva in 1922, and was the first president of the International Planned Parenthood Federation, founded in 1953. She served as Planned Parenthood's honorary chairman until her death in 1966. Wherever Planned Parenthood exercises its worldwide influence today, it bears the undying signature of Margaret Sanger.

Sanger tied the issue of contraceptives to the issue of women's rights. She was the predecessor of today's millions of Americans who see abortion as a woman's personal right, rooted in her equality and freedom of choice.

Sanger's *Pivot of Civilization* is a blueprint for changing the world through birth control and sterilization, both voluntary and involuntary. The book is a clear and direct application of Darwinian nontheistic evolutionary dogma.[9] Often portrayed today—particularly by Planned Parenthood—as the compassionate champion of the underprivileged, Sanger was really an elitist who labeled the masses "genetically inferior" and "human weeds."[10] "Funds that should be used to raise the standard of our civilization are diverted to the maintenance of those who should never have been born," Sanger complained. "More children from the fit, less from the unfit—that is the chief issue of birth control."[11] Like Ellis, Sanger saw eugenics—the genetic improvement and purification of the human race—as the ultimate purpose of birth control.

Sanger's personal life was consistent with her philosophy. Married three times (including an early "trial marriage"), she was involved in frequent adulterous relationships. Among her better-known lovers were H. G. Wells and . . . Havelock Ellis.

The Ellis-Russell-Sanger Connection

Havelock Ellis, Bertrand Russell, and Margaret Sanger shared in common a bitter disdain for the sexual values of the Christian faith. All three were prominent in what was then called the League for Sexual Reform. All three drew upon their gifts, skills, resources, and fame to promote a new sexual philosophy and lifestyle. Americans were gradually desensitized to their ideas which, in time, no longer seemed so radical and offensive. Eventually, they became agreeable, appealing, and widely accepted.

Ellis, Russell, and Sanger opened the floodgates for the speeches and writings of a whole new breed of intellectual and social reformers. By the 1930s these revolutionaries were defending not only premarital sex, living together, and temporal marriage contracts, but the legitimacy of prostitution, homosexuality, adultery, and abortion on demand.

It must be emphasized again that this sexual revolution was directly and knowingly aimed against the authority of God, the Bible, and the church. In reading Ellis, Russell, and Sanger, I am struck with their frequent, hostile, and bitter castigations of Christian faith and morality. Margaret Sanger said it clearly on the masthead of *The Woman Rebel:* "No gods, no masters."

Denouncing "all ethical systems which rest upon unquestioning obedience of higher authorities," she stated:

There has been a revolution in the world of morality of which we are now beginning to taste the first fruits. We are no longer living in a little closed and completed universe of which God's plan was revealed once and for all time to a little group of delegates. The center of our universe has shifted from Heaven to earth.[12]

Where the dogmatists read black, the world today is reading white. What they consider "morality" we consider moral imbecility.[13]

In her 1938 autobiography, Sanger penned words that could well have been the slogan of the sexual revolution that followed her: "Let God and man decree laws for themselves and not for me."[14]

THE UNDERMINING OF BIBLICAL MORALITY

As secularism spread, the biblical foundations for sexual morality were undermined. "Because the Bible says so" was no longer a good enough answer to the question, "Why shouldn't I have sex outside marriage?"

In the early twentieth century, most people outwardly conformed to the Judeo-Christian ethic. In reality, however, sexual morality was chiefly grounded not on the fear of God but on three other fears: (1) Fear of detection (discovery normally meant rejection and punishment); (2) fear of infection (venereal disease); and (3) fear of conception (unwanted pregnancy). As these moral policemen declined in power, so did the observance of biblical morality.

The 1920s saw increasing freedom, affluence, and, with the advent of cars, mobility. All this made the detection of immorality more preventable. Meanwhile, the gradual erosion of values made detection less traumatic even when it did occur.

Medical science was making great strides in combating venereal disease with antibiotics. Though V.D. was still a major health problem, the fear of infection was waning.

The greatest fear and deterrent to immorality, unwanted pregnancy, was addressed by birth control. The late nineteenth century brought the first reliable contraceptives, but it was not until the 1920s that they became increasingly available to the general public. Birth control had a positive and legitimate use: the family planning and sexual enjoyment of married couples. However, its most noticeable effect was vesting extramarital sex with unprecedented impunity. It was more than a notion of male supremacy that bred the famous double standard in which nice women were expected to be chaste while "nice" men consorted with immoral women. All along, the fear of pregnancy gave women a special incentive (unshared by men) to avoid premarital sex. Birth control changed all the rules.

Much of the women's rights movement was long overdue. Unfortunately, promiscuity became a proving ground for women's rights. The double standard was rightly deplored. But instead of attacking the double standard by crusading for male chastity, the women's movement encouraged female extramarital sex. The liberating result was that more women acted immorally (resulting, of course, in more available partners and therefore still higher immorality in men). Morally speaking, it was as if women achieved equality with men by jumping off a ten story building to join them on the pavement below.

The Moral Erosion of the Twenties

That birth control could usher in a new morality shows how weak the average citizen's moral foundation had already become. But we must remember that much of society was accepting Darwinian thought, including its implicit lack of accountability to any authority. Scholars in every field were working overtime attempting to disprove the Bible. Psychologists were relieving patients of their sexual repressions and inhibitions. Social activists were pushing for a new age, characterized by a new creed and a new lifestyle. Founded in 1920, the American Civil Liberties Union was already stripping legal standards of their

Christian implications. As society's controlling force, Judeo-Christian morality already had one foot in the grave. Birth control simply hastened its funeral.

The waters of biology, philosophy, psychology, education, medicine, and other disciplines converged into a unified torrent that pummeled the nation's moral dam. The result was the first great phase of the American sexual revolution—the "roaring twenties":

> In the 1920s, a radical change occurred almost overnight. The belief became a militant dogma in liberal circles that the opposite of repression—namely sex education, freedom of talking, feeling and expression—would have healthy effects and obviously constituted the only stand for the enlightened person. In an amazingly short period following World War I, we shifted from acting as though sex did not exist at all to being obsessed with it. [15]

With the war over, there was a sense of relief, relaxation, and celebration. The jazz age was born, bootleg liquor was plentiful, parties flourished, inhibitions dropped.

The economic struggle of the Great Depression, followed by the buildup to World War II, temporarily quieted the rebellious spirit of the roaring twenties. But not before they provided a preview of the coming sixties.

The Kinsey Reports

In 1948 Alfred Kinsey startled the country with his *Sexual Behavior and the Human Male*. He followed with *Sexual Behavior and the Human Female* in 1953. The reports were based on ten thousand personal interviews with American men and women—and went about as unnoticed as Pearl Harbor.

For the first time, people were able to look into the bedrooms of the rest of the nation. What they had always wondered about the sex lives of others, they were now told. And what they found was that sexual standards were far more liberal than they thought.

When sex was put in a goldfish bowl for all to gawk at, several significant things happened. People began to compare themselves with each other. Many concluded they were undersexed. After all, Kinsey said three quarters of the males questioned had premarital sex, half of those married had committed adultery, and a third had at least one homosexual experience since puberty. Half the women had experienced premarital intercourse, and a quarter of those married had committed adultery. The sheer weight of the numbers lessened immorality's stigma. "Everybody's doing it, or at least many people are, so why not me?"

> Kinsey's data were widely disseminated in the press, and for the first time, people in the United States were confronted with the wide gap between their sexual practices and their sexual mores. One probable effect of these studies was that many people became more free in their sexual behavior—or at least felt less guilty about it—secure in the knowledge that they were joining sizeable numbers of other citizens.[16]

Ironically, Kinsey's figures almost certainly exaggerated the moral looseness of the day. Most of those interviewed were college students, the most liberal section of the populace at probably the most liberal period in their lives. It also seems likely that those who volunteered for detailed interviews about their sex lives were the most sexually experienced. Whether accurate or not, the Kinsey reports were believed. Sexual experiences became fair game even for casual conversation. A lunch table discussion could now begin, "So what do you think of the Kinsey reports?"

Kinsey also opened the door for later researchers like William Masters and Virginia Johnson, who in the sixties and early seventies wrote *Human Sexual Response, Human Sexual Inadequacy,* and *The Pleasure Bond.* Masters and Johnson didn't just update Kinsey's poll—they observed and studied men and women in actual sexual experiences, using sophisticated electronic equipment to measure sexual stimulation and reactions. They even used an artificial "coition machine," simulating intercourse.

Between Kinsey's reports and the research of Masters and Johnson, people increasingly looked at sex as a thing, an entity that could be scrutinized, weighed, and measured. Sex was now in the hands of science, not ethics. Sex was classified, objectified, and depersonalized. Like a bacteria culture, it was put under the microscope and then on the display table.

More and more sex manuals were written stressing sex habits, idiosyncrasies, techniques, and positions—and ignoring the personal, moral, and spiritual dimensions of sex. If there was any mystery left in sex, which was increasingly doubtful, it seemed destined to soon be discovered, probably in a test tube. Then, no doubt, it would be patented, bottled, and distributed in supermarkets. In short, sex was stripped of its magic. It was no longer sacred.

Winds of Change in the 1950s

Moving back to the Kinsey era, it was 1952 that brought the first widely publicized sex change operation. Christina Jorgensen became a household name. Some shuddered, some applauded, some laughed—all who paused to think saw that medical science was bringing unprecedented implications to traditional morality.

The fifties also brought the influential voice of Margaret Mead. An anthropologist who studied preliterate societies like those in New Guinea, Mead lectured and wrote about the cultural conditioning of sexual behavior. America's traditional sexual mores were by no means universal. The noble savage had fewer taboos and seemed happier than we. Minds were open to new value systems, gleaned from the remote corners of the global village.

The fifties brought an increasing sense of nonaccountability to anyone but self. The "sacrifice for others" spirit of World

War II gave way, in the post-war prosperity, to selfishness and personal ambition. Many of the children raised in this climate (influenced by the liberal theories of Dr. Benjamin Spock, which he later recanted) would grow up to be takers, not givers, largely indifferent to their responsibilities and preoccupied with their rights.

The fifties beat movement preached alienation from the older generation, derisively called "squares." The "hip" beat-niks glorified personal freedom, enlightenment, and expression through heightened sensory awareness. This was induced by a blend of jazz music, poetry, sex, drugs, and gleanings from Zen Buddhism. The beat movement was ingrown, egocentric, and limited in influence. Still, its anti-establishment mentality, ex-perimentation with drugs and sex, and its own distinctive music were a foretaste of the sixties.

American youth were gaining freedom. More high school and college students had access to cars. Parking and necking were popular sports, performed to the background music of Fabian, Ricky Nelson, Buddy Holly, and Elvis Presley (the most potent youth sex symbol ever).

Drugs, Sex, and Rock 'N' Roll

By the sixties the generation gap was established, the seeds of rebellion sown. The youth revolution lacked only lead-ers, visible and charismatic leaders who could symbolize the odyssey of youth in search of a new moral philosophy and life-style.

In 1964 those leaders emerged—the Beatles. Their records sold millions overnight. The radios of a whole generation were tuned to their songs. Girls screamed and fainted at their con-certs, while parents shook their heads and wondered. Few sus-pected that this unlikely band from Liverpool would prove to be among the most effective propagandists of this century.

Within a few years the Beatles were the high priests of a youth kingdom built on drugs, sex, and rock. Their biographies and personal interviews attest to the free sex and frequent orgies that characterized their tours. Three of them married girlfriends already pregnant. They sang, "Why don't we do it in the road"—not about skateboarding. Later, leader John Lennon and future wife Yoko Ono appeared nude, front and back, on the album "Two Virgins." Not an apt title, since at the time the two were known bedpartners, and John was still married to another woman.

The Beatles were accompanied by groups like the Rolling Stones, dominated by lead singer Mick Jagger. His powerfully sensuous presence and sexually explicit actions on stage electrified the crowds. He sang, "I Can't Get No Satisfaction," and followed with a string of other hits that flouted sexual taboos, including "Let's Spend the Night Together."

While an already waning Christian morality went into eclipse, America's youth worshiped at the shrine of a new god, an indivisible trinity of drugs, sex, and rock. The winds of change that had blown since the twenties became a hurricane on the shoulders of the sixties' youth culture.

The sexual revolution was but one facet of a total revolution against established authority. Though the hippies spoke earnestly of love, sex was as much an act of rebellion as love—"See, we'll do what we want, and you can't stop us." In 1969 the famous rock festival Woodstock showed the other side of the free sex movement. Billed as a foretaste of utopia, for many it degenerated into a miserable orgy of filth, disease, drugs, and sexual perversion.

Ironically, though the hippie movement would pass, within a decade its radical sexual morality would infiltrate the mainstream of American society.

America's New Moral Climate

The sixties were days of change. The birth rate plunged, and the divorce rate soared. Nudist colonies popped up like lemonade stands in summer. Overage hippie Timothy Leary told *Playboy* that LSD was the key to female orgasm (a claim that failed to win him the Nobel prize). Most remarkable was the popularization of "sexual freedom" by society's influential elite—the intellectuals, professors, philosophers, psychologists, and writers.

By 1970 professors at Long Beach State were showing their classes actual films of heterosexual and homosexual intercourse. Planned Parenthood was invited to high schools all over the nation, showing sixteen-year-old sophomores how to obtain and use birth control devices. After the Supreme Court legalized abortion in 1973, school counselors acted as liaisons between teenage girls and abortion clinics.

None of this could have happened without one dominant force: the American media. As bees spread pollen, the nation's newspapers, magazines, books, movies, and television spread the changing values. They were the winged messengers and mouthpieces of the sexual revolution.

THE INFLUENCE OF THE MEDIA

Books

Novelists D. H. Lawrence, William Burroughs, Norman Mailer, and a host of others whose books were once censored, began to dominate the literary scene.

Writers such as Ian Fleming brought to America a new kind of hero—not the clean-cut, truth-telling, sexually unreproachable hero of yesteryear, but the dashing, daring, adventuresome James Bond type. Surrounded by action, violence, and gorgeous and seductive women, Bond made the jobs of daily breadwinning and fidelity to one woman seem incredibly bland.

In 1962 Helen Gurley Brown wrote *Sex and the Single Girl*, deliberately designed to shock and provoke (not to mention sell) with its no-blush instructions on how to carry on an affair. The clear message was "everybody's doing it and you can get in on it too." Virginity, it seemed, was no longer in vogue.

Magazines

Columnists introduced Hollywood morality into the living rooms of America, even those of families whose convictions prohibited attendance at movies. The phenomenally popular supermarket tabloids—*The National Enquirer* and its clones—capitalized on the nation's growing obsession with sex. Women's magazines, from glamour to romance, became the clearing house for the latest statistics on female orgasm, fantasies, and affairs.

As cagey as an alley cat and almost as moral, Hugh Hefner cashed in on the nation's moral deterioration with *Playboy*. From its inception in 1955, it came on bold and risqué, immersing itself in an illusion of intellectual respectability and journalistic integrity—not an easy task for a technically upgraded form of pornography. Soon *Playboy* was sold in local drugstores alongside candy, gum, and baseball cards. It became as much a part of America as Mom, apple pie, and the girl next door—who was no longer a subject to talk with but an object waiting and wanting to be seduced.

More than a magazine, *Playboy* was a reincarnation of the ancient Epicurean philosophy that elevated personal pleasure over scruples. Playboy window stickers and air fresheners flaunted the bunny, and a whole generation of young men came to believe that women had staples in their navels.

Once it depersonalized sex by shifting the fig leaf to the face, *Playboy* opened the floodgates to a glut of "easy money" soft-porn competitors who made Hefner look like St. Francis in their attempts to outdo each other's raunchiness—of which they repented all the way to the bank. The spread of hard core pornography took its own toll on the nation's moral fiber, and as we will see in a later chapter, is today a bigger problem than ever.

Motion Pictures

In the fifties and sixties, Hollywood taught American women the art of sexual teasing. Sex symbols such as Marilyn Monroe, Elizabeth Taylor, and Sophia Loren were their tutors. The door they opened to female sexploitation led to later films such as *I am Curious (Yellow)* and *Last Tango in Paris,* where actual intercourse and sexual perversions were shown on the screen.

The motion picture ratings system inspired a glut of "R" movies featuring nudity and sex scenes, yet not branded "X" to avoid the pornographic stigma. Meanwhile the industry that had shocked America with the word "damn" in *Gone With the Wind* soon made profanity and vulgarity chic—almost obligatory.

Television

Television extended the tentacles of the sexual revolution more than any other medium. The early television programs focused on all-American families, such as those in "Father Knows Best," "Ozzie and Harriet," and "Leave It to Beaver." But the sixties' extremely popular "All in the Family" majored in frank discussions not only of racism and bigotry but of every sexual subject from menopause to impotence to homosexuality. Even the incessant bathroom humor (including the toilet flushing in the background) was a way of saying, "we'll deal with anything on this show—there are no taboos to us." The nation watched each week to see which sacred cows would topple next.

In the sixties, "Peyton Place" brought sexual scandal into America's homes. "Laugh-In" legitimized the dirty joke. "Love American Style" showed how funny adultery could be. The entertainment programs and made-for-TV movies in the late sixties and early seventies paraded a sexual freedom only a few years behind Hollywood. Soon there were sexually exploitive situation comedies like "Soap" and "Three's Company," and "dramas" like "Charlie's Angels."

The success of these programs led to the next wave in the seventies and eighties—steamy evening soap operas such as "Dallas" and "Dynasty." Meanwhile, daytime soap operas, continuing their plunge into voyeurism and vicarious illicit romance, daily shaped the minds and morals of millions. And television's sexual boldness in advertising increased right along with its programming.

Television joined other media in paying homage to celebrities whose performances and personal lives consistently violated Christian morality. As the media assailed the underpinnings of marriage, the divorce rate soared and broken homes multiplied.

Where the Sexual Revolution Left America

The revolution enjoyed one swift victory after another. Filmed and printed erotica that would have shocked in 1965 elicited yawns in 1975. Within less than a decade, the sexual experiments of West Coast college students and hippies became the stuff of every day life for blue-collar workers in Des Moines and Texarkana. Perhaps never before had such a radical shift in mores occurred in so short a time.[17]

Given the deteriorating spiritual climate of America and the unprecedented potency of the media, the sexual revolution could only succeed. Time allowed a subtle erosion of values and a gradual desensitization to moral changes which, had they come all at once, would never have been tolerated.

In the process of research, it has been fascinating to read the literature of the early and mid 1900s. Some writers warned against the eventual widespread acceptance of fornication, adultery, homosexuality, and abortion on demand. They warned of a self-centered society where personal pleasure was elevated over the corporate good, where pornography and sex crimes flourished and the moral fabric of society was ripped at the seams. Their contemporaries, both secular and Christian, frequently accused them of overreacting. Yet time has proven that these lonely voices, buried in the avalanche of free thinking, were right.

Where was the church when all this was happening? What did it do to counter the country's moral decline? What is the church doing *today* to address the issues of sexual morality and the redemptive needs of sexual sinners? As we will see, the church's response to the sexual revolution left—and still leaves—much to be desired.

Chapter 2, Notes

1. Pitirim Sorokin, *The American Sex Revolution* (New York: Porter Sargent, 1956), 3-4, 7.

2. For a good historical summary of the church's perspective on sex, see Letha Scanzoni, *Why Wait?* (Grand Rapids: Baker Book House, 1975), 22-37; and Dwight Hervey Small, *Christian, Celebrate Your Sexuality* (Old Tappan, N.J.: Fleming H. Revell Co., 1974), 46-101.

3. Scanzoni, *Why Wait?* 35.

4. David Gelman, "Finding the Hidden Freud," *Newsweek*, 30 November 1981, 64-70.

5. Steven Marcus, "Devoted to Sex," *New York Times Book Review*, 22 June 1980, 29.

6. Madeline Gray, *Margaret Sanger* (New York: Richard Marek Publishers, 1979), 91.

7. Paul Robinson, *The Modernization of Sex* (New York: Harper and Row, 1976), 4.

8. Dan Gilbert, *The Conspiracy Against Chastity* (San Diego: The Danielle Publishers, 1939), 35.

9. Margaret Sanger, *Pivot of Civilization* (New York: Brentano's, 1922), 282.

10. Elasah Drogin, *Margaret Sanger: Father of Modern Society* (Coarsegold, Calif.: CUL Publications, 1979), 15.

11. Margaret Sanger, "Why Not Birth Control in America?" *Birth Control Review*, May 1919, 10-11.

12. Margaret Sanger, *The Civilizing Force of Birth Control*.

13. Margaret Sanger, *Sex in Civilization*, 532.

14. Quoted in Gilbert, *Conspiracy*, 15.

15. Rollo May, *Love and Will* (New York: W. W. Norton and Co., 1969), 38-39.

16. Joseph Julian and William Kornblum, *Social Problems* (Englewood Cliffs, N.J.: Prentice-Hall, 1983), 78.

17. George Leonard, "The End of Sex," *Esquire*, December 1982, 70.

Chapter 3

American Christianity's Response to the Revolution

*I*n its response to the sexual revolution, American Christianity was culpable in at least two areas: it failed to teach a positive and balanced view of sex, and it failed to respond to the revolution with outspoken conviction and courage.

The Christian world, somewhat leery of the secular voices but warm to its own, was led down the path of moral decay by some of its major denominations. Trusted clergymen persuaded significant numbers of lay Christians that Scripture must be updated, reapplied, taken with a grain of salt, or outright denied. Having compromised the teachings of Scripture in an attempt to win an audience, organized religion was left with few listeners and pitifully little to say.

In this tragic display of atrophied conviction and moral cowardice, many (though by no means all) segments of the church capitulated to the sexual revolution. We have already seen how the grassroots Christian community is riddled with the consequences. Nonetheless, organized Christianity has still not learned from its failures. In its sexual morality the church is still too often a tail wagged by the dog of the world.

THE CHURCH'S ROLE IN THE REVOLUTION

In 1963 eleven Quakers collaborated to produce *Towards a Quaker View of Sex.* The study justified premarital sex and adultery in certain circumstances and stated that homosexual relations were not sinful per se. The conclusions were particularly significant in that they came from a traditionally conservative religious group.

Mainline Protestant denominations followed with similar theological and moral statements, most of them hedging on or openly rejecting traditional Judeo-Christian sexual values. By 1972 Helen Colton was able to defend a blatantly anti-Christian morality in *Sex After the Sexual Revolution,* by quoting rabbis, Catholic priests, and Protestant theologians and ministers.[1]

In some ways, theological liberalism was the sexual revolution's strongest asset. Rather than a light of divine guidance, religion became a mirror of social preference. This is mystifying unless we understand that most of the seminaries that trained church leaders had years before—following society's move to secularism—surrendered their confidence in Scripture. Schools that once raised up apologists for a biblical ethic now produced, at their worst, some of the most effective mouthpieces for the sexual revolution, and at their best, a crop of intellectually astute and biblically illiterate moral milk-toasts.

Here was a strange thing: Christian religion, the revolution's most likely and capable opponent, joining her in an unholy alliance. Even Karl Menninger—named by his peers the greatest living psychiatrist—in *Whatever Became of Sin?* (1973), repeatedly bemoaned the failure of the clergy to courageously call sin, including sexual sin, by its proper name.[2]

Theology Redefines Morality

It was in the fifties and sixties that a new breed of theologians and moralists flexed their muscles in the church. Some propounded the "God is dead" theology (or nontheology). Many religionists had already concluded "God is distant."

Whether dead or distant, if God was out of the picture, so were the grounds for absolute morality. The church's attempted dethroning of God also dethroned moral absolutes and their corresponding—and increasingly unpopular—behavioral responsibilities.

Following the logic of philosophers like Alfred North Whitehead and liberal theologian Paul Tillich, Bishop John Robinson's *Honest to God* and *Christian Morals Today* saw the "New Morality" in harmony with the New Testament. Joseph Fletcher made the same defense in his widely read *Situation Ethics*. Many secular spokesmen advocated the same departure from biblical morality as Robinson and Fletcher. What made these men unique, though, was their appeal to the Christian religion itself as the basis for their philosophy. Fletcher made this bold claim of the "New Morality":

> Its roots lie securely, if not conventionally, in the classical tradition of Western Christian morals. It's an old posture with a new and contemporary look.[3]

In a lecture to Southern Baptist leaders (most of whom opposed his views), Fletcher made his position clear:

> I am prepared to argue in the utmost seriousness that Christian obligation calls for lies and adultery and fornication and theft and promise breaking and killing—sometimes, depending upon the situation. And that there is, therefore, negatively expressed, no normative principle of conduct which is universally and unexceptionally obliging, regardless of the relativities and circumstances.[4]

Fletcher went on to say, "each of the so-called Ten Commandments should be amended with the qualifier word 'ordinarily'—for example, the seventh commandment: 'Thou shalt not ordinarily commit adultery.'"

This position was, of course, readily welcomed by millions of religious Americans who would not ordinarily commit adultery, but found themselves in innumerable extraordinary situations which made it, according to Fletcher, acceptable—perhaps even a matter of Christian obligation.

The popularity of "Situation Ethics" (which became a synonym for the "New Morality") should come as no surprise, given the moral climate of the sixties. Many who wanted to taste the forbidden fruit of immorality were not prepared to directly reject the Christian faith. Now they were told they didn't have to. They could violate biblical standards and in the process still be good Christians.

Progressively outrageous claims began to arise within the church. In *Honest Sex,* Rustum and Della Roy said the typical American believed that the Bible commanded "premarital chastity" and included a "proscription of adultery." Not so, they said:

> Infinitely better scholars than we have established that one cannot find any literal or simple connection in the Bible claiming that the above . . . were God's law or will.[5]

Defending *Playboy* magazine from the criticisms of "some theologians" (and in the process winning them *Playboy's* endorsement on the book's cover), they claim:

> The death of the old morality has come about without much aid from the Church, but Christians can rejoice at its demise because it has made the way clear for a new approach.[6]

This same morally progressive attitude was reflected in a 1970 document of the United Presbyterian Church of the USA, which stated among other things:

> Increasingly, the expectation of premarital virginity is not being met either by men or women. This change is not necessarily to be regarded as a sign of the lowering of the moral standards of young people.[7]

Segments of the Roman Catholic Church have undergone the same moral erosion as liberal Protestantism. For instance, despite—or in reaction to—the Vatican's 1976 condemnation of all extramarital sexual relations, the following year a group of Catholic theologians produced a document defending "creative" sex outside marriage, supporting nonpromiscuous homosexual relationships, denying that bestiality was necessarily pathological, and declaring most pornography to be harmless to adults.[8]

How these religious moral positions differ even slightly from the prevailing secular ones is not apparent. Teaching that the law of God was written in pencil, liberal Christianity thrives on passing out erasers.

Where Is the Church Today?

In June of 1983 the Presbyterian Church (USA) governing body, representing 3.2 million members, voted to accept abortions "within a Christian ethical framework when serious genetic problems arise or when the resources are not adequate to care for a child appropriately."

This decision is significant not just because it allows abortions (so do innumerable groups, secular and religious), but because it does so with *explicit Christian authority.* It is not simply an honest rejection of biblical standards; it is a violation of scriptural principle, not to mention human decency, supposedly rooted in "a Christian ethical framework."

It is here that the church reaches its nadir—when it does not simply ignore Scripture in the face of the immoral but instead uses it, with all its authoritative clout, to *defend* the immoral. At this point the church becomes a more powerful ally of darkness than the world could ever be. It converts its saints to evil with the very law of God. The Protestant church in America need not worry about the secular immoralists on the outside; she is being slowly poisoned by the religious immoralists on the inside.

WHAT DOES THE FUTURE HOLD?

Harry Blamires's indictment is most obviously true in the realm of sexual morality:

> The Christian mind has succumbed to the secular drift with a degree of weakness and nervelessness unmatched in Christian history.[9]

Biblical Christianity is an intrinsically and intensely moral religion. Sexual morality is by no means the whole of morality, but it is an important part. The acceptance or endorsement of any immoral practice is ultimately an attack on the faith. More fundamentally, it is an attack on God himself, whose holy character is the basis of biblical morality.

Sexual immorality is a logical corollary to atheism, not Christianity. Its widespread presence and tolerance in the holy church of Christ is an essential contradiction of what the church is meant to be.

Two of the seven churches addressed in the book of Revelation are called to account for their tolerance of sexual sin, specifically for permitting some in their midst to promote immorality by their teachings (Revelation 2:14-16; 2:20-23). These kinds of false teachers are prominent in many denominations, seminaries, and churches today. To remove them now that they have become entrenched would be a monumental task . . . but an explicitly biblical one. Christ expected his churches to confront and oppose all immoral teaching in their midst. If they did not, he promised to remove his blessing from the church.

I am not simply pointing the finger at religious liberals. The proverbial camel has already stuck its nose into the tent of the evangelical church. If we become content with the presence of the camel's nose, then his head, neck, and forelegs are bound to follow. Left unchecked, the camel of sexual impurity could claim so large a part of the tent that Christian virtue may be unceremoniously pushed out the door. Should that day come—and we are fools if we think it impossible—the words of Jesus will not be, "Well done, thou good and faithful servant," but, "I will remove your lampstand."

Our primary challenge as Christians is not to raise the moral level of the non-Christian world. Our first duty is not to make the world better but to make the church better. One thing is certain—an unholy world will never be won to Christ by an unholy church.

Chapter 3, Notes

1. Helen Colton, *Sex after the Sexual Revolution* (New York: Association Press, 1972), 18-19.

2. Karl Menninger, *Whatever Became of Sin?* (New York: Bantam Books, 1978), 163, 224-25, 231, 236.

3. Joseph Fletcher, *Situation Ethics: The New Morality* (Philadelphia: Westminster Press, 1966), 13.

4. Joseph Fletcher, "Situation Ethics," (Nashville: Christian Life Commission, Southern Baptist Convention, n.d.).

5. Rustum and Della Roy, *Honest Sex* (New York: Signet, 1972), 68.

6. Ibid., 40-41, 192.

7. Ibid., 5.

8. Anthony Kosnik, ed., *Human Sexuality: New Directions in American Catholic Thought* (New York: Paulist Press, 1977).

9. Harry Blamires, *The Christian Mind* (Ann Arbor, Mich.: Servant Books, 1963), 3.

Chapter 4

The Prevailing Winds of America's Sexual Morality

I still believe in virginity and the "old-fashioned" wisdom of saving it for marriage—if possible. But I have changed some of my views on teen-age sexual behavior because this is a different world today than it was in 1955. A refusal to change my views in this extremely sensitive area, when changes of every conceivable kind are taking place, would bespeak a rigidity and a failure to face reality. It would be the mark of a mind that is not only closed, but nailed shut. [1]

Influential columnist Ann Landers represents millions of Americans who defended chastity in the fifties, weakened in the sixties and, tired of swimming upstream, surrendered to the new morality in the seventies.

What are the sexual behaviors and beliefs of Americans today?

Sex studies abound, and they confirm two important trends: (1) sexual morality in this country is still on the decline, and (2) the sexual morality of younger Americans is significantly lower than that of the older.[2] This is clearly demonstrated in the results of a recent Harris poll:

"It is all right for adults dating regularly to have sex."			"It is important for a woman to be a virgin when she marries."		
AGREE			AGREE		
age	men	women	age	men	women
65+	50%	28%	65+	51%	75%
50-64	60%	46%	50-64	51%	70%
30-49	70%	64%	30-49	24%	39%
18-29	80%	72%	18-29	24%	30%

Regardless of the statistics, every observant American must realize our sexual morality has undergone—and is still undergoing—a traumatic change.

The New Sexual Tyranny

Early in the sexual revolution, sex outside marriage was a nonconformist right. Later it became a conformist responsibility. Under the guise of sexual freedom, the revolution produced a new sexual tyranny:

Where the Victorian didn't want anyone to know that he or she had sexual feelings, we are ashamed if we do not. . . .

Sin used to mean giving in to one's sexual desires; it now means not having full sexual expression. . . . A woman used to be guilty if she went to bed with a man; now she feels vaguely guilty if after a certain number of dates she still refrains. . . .[3]

When Madelaine Harris's mother went to college, in the 1940s, there was a stigma attached to women who weren't virgins. When Madelaine went to college, there was a stigma attached to women who were. Equipped with pastel plastic packages of the

Pill, with their reassuring pictures of birds and flowers on the cover, Madelaine dutifully proceeded to lose her virginity.[4]

America's not-so-subtle contempt for chastity is evident in and cultivated by the media. Take, for instance, a movie for teenagers that hit the theaters in the summer of 1983: "The Last American Virgin." The advertisements made this threatening remark: "The Last American Virgin . . . See it or be it!" High school virginity—the moviemakers portray it a fate worse than death.

"Be honest with me," I said to a committed high school junior. "Is there *really* that much pressure to go to bed with guys?"

"Let's put it this way," she said. "Yesterday the girl whose locker is next to mine lost her temper at another girl in our class. She was so angry that she screamed at the girl 'You . . . you . . . you . . . *virgin!'* She tried to think of the worst name she could call her, and she came up with 'virgin.' Does that answer your question?" It did.

Our society's sexual standards once served as guides to righteousness and deterrents to evil. Now they serve as guides to evil and deterrents to righteousness.

To be well adjusted to the sexual mores of *this* society is to be sexually sick. A mental patient may be well adjusted to the routine of the lockup ward, but that does not make him healthy. Similarly, today's businessman carrying on an affair may have plenty of company—but his immorality is just as wrong and destructive as it's always been.

WHAT DIRECTION ARE WE HEADED?

Dr. Russell Lee, former director of the Palo Alto Medical Clinic, gives us this view of marriage and morals:

> Monogamous marriage is a bizarre and unnatural
> state. Marriage does violence to man's biologically

ingrained instinct for promiscuity, his strong drive for freedom from restraint, his need for new and changing experience.[5]

Humanist Manifesto II, penned in 1973, stated clearly the underpinnings of today's sexual morality:

> We find insufficient evidence for belief in the existence of a supernatural; it is either meaningless or irrelevant to the question of the survival and fulfillment of the human race. As nontheists, we begin with humans not God, nature not deity. . . .
>
> We affirm that moral values derive their source from human experience. Ethics is *autonomous* and situational, needing no theological or ideological sanction.
>
> In the area of sexuality, we believe that intolerant attitudes, often cultivated by orthodox religions and puritanical cultures, unduly repress sexual conduct. The right to birth control, abortion, and divorce should be recognized. While we do not approve of exploitive, denigrating forms of sexual expression, neither do we wish to prohibit, by law or social sanction, sexual behavior between consenting adults. The many varieties of sexual exploration should not in themselves be considered "evil."[6]

Sex without Morals

One of the most powerful voices of the sexual revolution has been prominent psychologist and prolific author Albert Ellis. Despite his habitual use of obscenities in his lectures—and that he has written for pornographic magazines and endorsed the rankest forms of erotica—Dr. Ellis remains a respected expert in sexual morality. He is probably quoted by more psychologists and educators than anyone in the field.

In his books and articles, Ellis often puts the word *perversion* in quotation marks, as if to suggest that there are no real sexual perversions, only perceived ones. His book *Sex Without Guilt* would be better titled *Sex Without Scruples*. In the spirit of the age, Ellis attempts to alleviate guilt by lowering morals.

Specifically, Ellis teaches that premarital sexual intimacy, or petting, is "absolutely harmless when it is carried to the point of mutual orgasm. The vast majority of males and females can easily come to climax through various types of petting; and there seems to be no good reason why, when they want to, they should not."[7]

Ellis's perspective on adultery is worth quoting at length because it captures the essence of the modern approach to sexual morality:

> Let us admit, at the outset, that many of the old grounds for opposing adultery are just as senseless, in today's world, as many similar grounds for combatting premarital sex affairs. For example:
>
> Intelligent and informed modern men and women do not consider adultery intrinsically wicked and sinful and therefore often commit it with little or no guilt or anxiety.
>
> They are well able, with use of up-to-date contraceptive techniques, to avoid the dangers of illegitimate pregnancy and abortions; and with the employment of prophylactic measures and the selection of appropriate partners, they can easily avoid venereal infection.
>
> They often need not worry about loss of reputation, since in many segments of modern society they are likely to gain rather than lose reputation by engaging in extramarital affairs.
>
> They need not commit adultery under sordid conditions, or on a non-loving basis, as they frequently can arrange to have highly amative and affectional, and sometimes exceptionally rewarding, affairs.
>
> They need not jeopardize their marriages, because

as the Kinsey research group has shown, adulterous affairs which are not known to one's mate can actually help enhance and preserve one's marriage rather than serve to sabotage and destroy it.

In view of these facts of modern life, it is most doubtful whether many of the old telling arguments against adultery still hold too much water. At the same time, several of the indubitable advantages of premarital sex relations, which we examined in the previous chapter, also hold true for adultery.

Thus, it may be said with little fear of scientific contradiction, that literally millions of men and women who engage in adulterous affairs thereby gain considerable adventure and experience, become more competent at sexual pursuits and practices, are able to partake of a high degree of varietism, and have substantial amounts of sexual and non-sexual fun that they otherwise would doubtlessly be denied. These, in a world that tends to be as dull and drab for the average man as our own, are no small advantages.[8]

The New Sex Educators

On the cutting edge of today's new treatment of sex is the Institute for Advanced Study of Human Sexuality and its sister group, The National Sex Forum (they operate out of the same San Francisco building and have overlapping staffs).

The Forum offers a fifteen hour introductory course, Human Sexuality 101, attended by more than sixty thousand people (many of them sex therapists and educators) between 1968 and 1982. The course, which is still going strong, is based on what is called "Sexual Attitude Restructuring." The process breaks down stereotypes and supposed misconceptions about traditionally immoral sexual behaviors.

Writer George Leonard, by no means a Christian, was impressed and disturbed by the effectiveness of the course's multimedia presentations. As you read his description, keep in mind that at least two of the leaders of this seminar are ordained ministers in mainline denominations:

> At one point, after what seemed like hundreds of filmed couplings over a period of several hours, there came a moment when the four images on the wall were of a gay male couple, a straight couple, a lesbian couple, and a bisexual group. The subjects were nude, and the camera angles in all four frames were such that no sexual organs were visible. I felt myself becoming disoriented. Was that a woman beneath that man . . . or another man? And that woman in the second frame from the right—was she kissing a man or a woman? I struggled to force the acts I was watching into their proper boxes. . . . Wasn't I *supposed* to make these discriminations? I searched for clues. There were none. I began to feel uncomfortable.
>
> Soon I realized that to avoid vertigo and nausea I would have to give up the attempt to discriminate and simply surrender to the experience. I didn't really have to know which was which. In all four cases, whoever and whatever was involved, the essential gestures, facial expressions, sounds, pelvic movements and rhythms were the same. Here were human beings responding to a common human urge, enjoying themselves, giving enjoyment to others. The differences, for which lives have been ruined, were now not only trivial but invisible.
>
> Sensory overload culminated on Saturday night in a multimedia event. . . . As we lounged on cushions in the darkness, the whole wall lit up with images of human beings and sometimes animals engaging in every conceivable sexual act, accompanied by wails, squeals, moans, shouts, and the first movement of

the Tchaikovsky violin concerto. . . . How did we react? There was shock, laughter, sporadic arousal, and, finally, boredom. By the end . . . nothing seemed shocking. The physical act of sexual joining seemed commonplace. I considered myself thoroughly desensitized.[9]

Wholesale moral desensitization—these sex educators' ultimate vision for us, our children, our churches, our communities, and our nation.

THE SEMANTICS OF SEXUAL SIN

An additional and significant factor in the moral desensitization process is the semantic manipulation engaged in by the proponents of the sexual revolution. A prime example is Nena and George O'Neill's *Open Marriage,* one of the most popular and influential books of the seventies and still selling well today. Favored with an endorsement by (who else?) Albert Ellis, the O'Neills share these insights with married couples:

> The idea of sexually exclusive monogamy and possession of another breeds deep-rooted dependencies, infantile and childish emotions, and insecurities. . . .
>
> In an open marriage, in which each partner is secure in his own identity and trusts in the other, new possibilities for additional relationships exist, and open (as opposed to limited) love can expand to include others. Fidelity does not have to be interpreted within the narrow context of closed marriage, in which you are suspected of possible infidelity every time you show an interest in someone of the opposite sex other than your mate. In open marriage, you can come to know, enjoy and share comradeship with others of the opposite sex besides your mate. These relationships enhance and augment the marital relationship of the open couple in turn.

These outside relationships may, of course, include sex. That is completely up to the partners involved. If partners in an open marriage do have outside sexual relationships, it is on the basis of their own internal relationships—that is, because they have experienced mature love, have real trust and are able to expand themselves, to love and enjoy others and to bring that love and pleasure back into their marriage, without jealousy.

We are not recommending outside sex, but we are not saying that it should be avoided, either. The choice is entirely up to you. . . . Outside sexual experiences when they are in the context of a meaningful relationship may be rewarding and beneficial to an open marriage. . . .

If outside companionships *are* to be more than casual ones, and might involve sex, then those relationships too should be approached with the same fidelity to mutual growth, and with the same measure of respect that you would show your partner in open marriage. You must be honest in your extramarital relationships as well. If you are not, the deception you practice outside your marriage will eventually seep back into the marriage itself.[10]

There you have it—"open," "loving," "mature," "meaningful," "rewarding," and "beneficial" adultery. Adultery that involves "fidelity," "mutual growth," "respect," and "honesty." Adultery has never been so wonderful; adulterers never so virtuous. And all in a book so widely received that a Christian psychologist recommended it to a Christian couple struggling in their marriage.

Language: A Molder of Morality
Language is both an expression of the mind and a molder of the mind. The calculated and subtle ways words are used can tremendously influence someone's receptivity to an idea—even

an idea which communicated in more traditional or straight-forward terms would be reprehensible.

Hitler was a master of semantic manipulation. He and his officers used terms such as *evacuation* and *emptying the ghetto* for the mass murders of Jews, and *treatment* for inhumane medical experiments. In his novel *1984,* George Orwell saw "doublespeak" as the future means of using words to control people—by covering the truth instead of conveying it.

Much doublespeak is euphemism. I saw some statistics that listed the rate of "Negative Patient Care Outcome." In other words, death. *Rapid oxidation* is the same as fire, but which sounds more threatening: "There is rapid oxidation in your home," or "Your house is on fire"?

While many euphemisms are harmless, others obscure moral issues. When a policeman accepts money under a certain condition it is called a bribe. In a similar situation, that money can come to a politician as a campaign contribution. Likewise, breaking and entering may be called an intelligence gathering operation.

In the realm of sexual morality, this kind of doublespeak or euphemism is common. Proabortionists often use terminology such as "the uterus was evacuated" or "the uterine cavity was emptied." "Termination of pregnancy" is a popular euphemism for abortion. This semantic manipulation is, in fact, frighteningly similar to that of Nazi Germany for it attempts (and often succeeds) to make more palatable the slaughter of the innocent.

When we use a word long enough, get used to it, it has profound effects on our perspective. Hence a word that sounds harmless and to which we've become accustomed makes us feel that the reality it describes is also harmless. *Smut* and *filth* say something *pornography* does not say. *Erotica* is much milder still. The same piece of literature once called pornographic is somehow more acceptable when labeled erotic.

Dirty novels and movies are no longer dirty. They are racy, intoxicating, engaging, delicious. Their audience is no longer deviants, perverts, or sex fiends, but adults. And not degenerate adults, but mature adults.

Consider the ubiquitous sign, "For mature adults only." Those who put quarters into peep show slots and gaze at a naked woman masturbating may indeed be adults, but by no stretch of the imagination can they be construed as "mature." In fact, their wistful gawking at these pitiful women is precisely the opposite of mature—it is childishly self-indulgent and demonstrates not an advanced but an impoverished sexuality.

"Due to mature subject matter, parental discretion is advised." What does "mature" mean here? Apparently, it must mean bloody axe killings, sadistic rapes, erotic seductions, and language that would make a lumberjack blush—since invariably that's what is in the program. A more honest warning would be, "Due to sadism, sexual exploitation, and gutter language, no responsible parent would let himself—let alone his children—watch this garbage." But don't hold your breath till it's used.

When psychologist Karl Menninger asked "Whatever became of sin?" in the book of that name, he was objecting to the desertion of terms that imply moral judgments or responsibility. The answer to his question, as he well knew, was simple—sin is alive and well, thriving everywhere. Only its names have been changed to protect the guilty.

"A Sin by Any Other Name . . ."

They used to be called *child molesters*. They are now called *pedophiles* or *child-lovers*. They have their own lobbying group and legal national organizations to promote their cause. Once called *whores* (and their clientele *whoremongers*), they became *prostitutes*, *hookers*, and *ladies of the night*.

Fifty years ago practicing homosexuals were called *sodomites*. The very term was morally repugnant. Then there was a wholesale adoption of the purely descriptive biological term *homosexual*. It did not have an inherent moral judgment the way *sodomite* did. Still, to most, the term *homosexual* elicited negative feelings.

In the sixties the term *gay* began to replace homosexual. Now it is the prevailing term; the process is complete. What is called in Scripture a sexual sin (I refer to the lifestyle, not the desire) undergoes a change not in contents but in label—from the highly negative *sodomite* to the more neutral *homosexual* to the upbeat and positive *gay*.

This adoption of new terminology for homosexuality (including many other innocuous terms such as *alternate lifestyle* and *minority sexual preference*) was gradual enough that we have come to accept it. We fail to appreciate how incredible it really is. If someone had gone into suspended animation twenty-five years ago and was revived today, he would be shocked to learn that most Americans use the term *gay* to describe practicing homosexuals.

The terminology affects our reactions to the thing itself. Many would cry out against sodomy, but who is the self-righteous killjoy who will speak against someone's "constitutional freedom to live a constructive and responsible gay lifestyle"?

I spoke recently with a homosexual who objected to my use of that term. "What would you prefer?" I asked.

"*Gay,* of course," he replied.

"That's interesting," I said. "I've talked with many practicing homosexuals who express a great deal of unhappiness, guilt, loneliness, and fear—fear of rejection, disease, physical abuse. If many homosexuals are this unfulfilled, how can you call them *gay*? You'd never call heterosexuals *happies,* would you? Yet a higher percentage are fulfilled than those you want me to call *gays*."

Adultery is another term slipping out of vogue. One now carries on an *affair,* a word that emphasizes the excitement of the new relationship rather than the destruction of the marriage. One's fellow criminal in adultery is now called a *partner, mistress* or, more commonly, a *lover.* It is interesting that such a relationship can be attributed to love when by its very nature it violates the most foundational love commitment a human being can make—marriage.

Open marriage has a nicer ring than *open adultery*, as Nena and George O'Neill were well aware. Yet there are those who are trying to strip even the term *adultery* of its negative connotations. Albert Ellis coined the phrase "healthy adultery."[11] Such a semantic game would once have been regarded as laughable or idiotic. *Healthy adultery?* One might just as well speak of healthy suicide, helpful robbery, benign slander, or constructive murder.

The words we use not only *reflect* our morals, but ultimately *affect* them. Like the vocabulary of "Newspeak," some of the old moral words are retained with new meanings. In Orwell's *1984* the word *freedom* was twisted in such a way as to be compatible with tyranny. No one would have tolerated the removal of freedom. But as long as the soothing word itself was retained, the thing itself could be removed.

In the realm of sexual ethics, look at what has happened to words such as *morality, faithfulness, love,* and *responsibility*. These words are not abandoned in the new sexual ethics—the attempt to do so might make us rebel. Instead, such words are redefined. Hence premarital sex (once called fornication) is incessantly called by Planned Parenthood "responsible," as long as birth control is used.

In *Open Marriage* the O'Neills use as a chapter division the caption "Fidelity Redefined."[12] It is unclear by what authority they fly in the face of the normal use of the English language. Linguistic integrity is one more virtue the sexual revolution has lacked.

THE UNDERLYING PHILOSOPHIES OF OUR TWISTED MORALITY

Several major tenets of secularism have fueled the sexual revolution and continue to push us toward sexual suicide. These philosophies constitute the wrong thinking that underlies most wrong action and must be consciously rejected if a biblical sexual ethic is to be reclaimed in the church, family, community, or nation.

Naturalism

Naturalism asserts that because something exists, it is therefore right. Certain sexual behaviors are defended on the basis that they are more common than we once thought. This is how the old immorality became the New Morality.

That many Americans suffer from fatigue, catch colds, smoke, overeat, drink before they drive, and have sex outside marriage proves nothing other than the obvious—they do. This should be no more comforting than knowing if I die of lung cancer, at least others will die with me. What *is* is not necessarily what ought to be.

Relativism

Imagine a man who, tired of a yardstick being thirty-six inches long, decides he wants to create a new yardstick fifteen inches long. He breaks it at the fifteen inch mark, boasts that a yard is no longer what it used to be, and appeals to others to accept his standard. That is the essence of relativism.

Of course, regardless of anyone's perception, a yard is still thirty-six inches. Likewise, God's sexual standards remain the same no matter who attempts to redefine or ignore them.

Hemingway captured the spirit of moral subjectivism that epitomizes our age when he said, "What is moral is what you feel good after and what is immoral is what you feel bad after."

We live in a country where obscenity is impossible to define (at least according to the courts). When it *is* defined, geography is the determining factor. What is obscene in a small midwestern town is perfectly acceptable on the streets of New York. The moral difference? Only the varying level of tolerance. Whatever is accepted is thereby acceptable.

Pluralism

This philosophical approach regards as mutually acceptable the beliefs and practices of different traditions, religions and points of view. The major problem with pluralism is that its application has become so one-sided. It is specifically the Christian's objection to certain beliefs and practices that is considered the unpardonable sin.

The Christian who speaks out against homosexuality, for instance, is certain to be labeled a bigot. The man who speaks out against the church, on the other hand, is a courageous spokesman exercising his constitutional rights.

Hedonism

Hedonism is the embodiment of the old Epicurean philosophy: "Eat, drink, and be merry, for tomorrow we die." The hedonist lives for himself. If you ask a young man sleeping with a different person after every party how he justifies his behavior, he will feel it is none of your business and probably tell you so. He might also try to defend his behavior. Likely, however, he will simply reply, "Who needs to justify anything? That's the way I want to live. It's my right."

In the sixties and seventies a popular slogan was "Do your own thing." It was by no means new. The days of the judges were some of Israel's darkest. The book of Judges ends with a horrible tale of rape, murder, and revenge. Violence and immorality were a plague on the nation, and the book's final verse tells why:

> "In those days Israel had no king [no moral authority]; everyone did as he saw fit" (Judges 21:25).

Chapter 4, Notes

1. Ann Landers, *High School Sex and How to Deal with It* (Field Enterprises, 1982), 1.

2. Perhaps the most thorough study since Kinsey was Vance Packard's *The Sexual Wilderness*, published in 1968. It was based on a survey of twenty-two hundred unmarried juniors and seniors at twenty-one American colleges and universities. The results reflected the already significant effects of the sexual revolution: 57 percent of the boys and 43 percent of the girls had experienced sexual intercourse.

The most significant conclusion of Packard's study was the greatly in-creased level of young females engaging in sex. Paralleling this was the fact that more college men were having sex; yet in contrast to 22 percent in Kinsey's 1948 study, only 4 percent in 1968 had ever had sex with prostitutes. The conclusion was obvious: men no longer had to buy sex outside marriage.

A 1980 study of 160,000 teens across the country was conducted by Myron Harris, professor of clinical psychiatry. Harris found that 46 percent of the girls and 70 percent of the boys were sexually active by age eighteen (Catherine Houck, "The Sexual Revolution: Did It Help or Hurt Marriage?" *Ladies Home Journal*, May 1982, 88). Similarly, *Newsweek* (1 September 1980, 48) reported that over 50 percent of girls fifteen to nineteen have had premarital sex. Studies at Johns Hopkins School of Hygiene and Public Health say over 63 percent of U.S. females have premarital intercourse by age nine-teen.

By 1971 adolescent nonmarried pregnancies were at 9 percent, by 1976 13 percent, and by 1979 16 percent (*Christianity Today*, 11 November 1983, 25). This despite the fact that contraceptives are commonly used by teens. It is also a tremendous embarrassment to Planned Parenthood, which has always held that if contraceptives were made available to adolescents, teen pregnancy would dramatically drop.

The Census Bureau reported that between 1970 and 1982 the number of unmarried couples living together in America tripled, to 1.86 million.

Major surveys indicated that in both 1937 and 1959, only 22 percent of the populace approved of premarital sex. Yet by 1973, more than three-fourths of the men and one-half the women approved (Joseph Julian and William Kornblum, *Social Problems* [Englewood Cliffs, N. J.: Prentice-Hall, 1983], 78).

In 1967 a survey done for CBS News found that 85 percent of the parents of college-age children still considered premarital sex wrong. The same pollsters found in 1979 that only 37 percent felt it was wrong—a decline of 48 percent in twelve years!

In 1984 *Glamour* magazine reported that 44 percent of its readers disap-proved of premarital sex, down from 51 percent only a year earlier. More sig-nificantly, though two-thirds of the women eighteen to twenty-four believe it is acceptable, less than one-third of those fifty-five or over approve (*USA Today*, 13 December 1983, sec. A).

A *Psychology Today* (July 1983, 44) poll of twelve thousand readers says one-half of married people in their forties have already committed adultery at least once. As the more liberal younger generation gets older, presumably, adultery will continue to increase.

Having cited these statistics, I would add this warning—many sex statistics are misleading. Always consider the source and the sample.

3. Rollo May, *Love and Will* (New York: W. W. Norton and Co., 1969), 39-40, 45.

4. Fran Schumer, "Is Sex Dead?" *New York*, 6 December 1982, 76.

5. Helen Colton, *Sex After the Sexual Revolution* (New York: Association Press, 1972), 145.

6. *Humanist Manifestos I and II* (Buffalo, N. Y.: Prometheus Books, 1979), 16-18.

7. Albert Ellis, *Sex Without Guilt* (New York: Lyle Stuart, 1966), 36.

8. Ibid., 54-55

9. George Leonard, *The End of Sex* (Los Angeles: J. P. Tarcher, Inc., 1983), 90-91.

10. Nena and George O'Neill, *Open Marriage* (New York: Avon Books, 1972), 237, 253-55.

11. Colton, *Sexual Revolution*, 150.

12. O'Neill, *Open Marriage*, 253.

PART 2

LIFE IN A TECHNOLOGICAL CORINTH

Chapter 5

Sex and the Media

S exual temptations are as old as civilization. Twentieth century America offers no new ones. The old temptations, however, come in sleeker, more colorful packages and are exported as never before to the privacy of the home through mail boxes and air waves.

Two thousand years ago the believers in Corinth faced sexual temptation whenever they walked the streets. But today we live in a technological Corinth. We don't have to go out on the streets. Through the wonders of technology, sexual temptation pursues us everywhere. Meanwhile, sin has been given a makeover that hides—but does not change—its ugly face. Thanks to the marvelous media, immorality appears more attractive than ever before.

"Seeing is believing"; "what you see is what you get." Not so with illusions. Through books, magazines, newspapers, television, movies, and music our senses are bombarded with a graphic and colorful picture of a vast and enticing sexual world, a world as unreal as it is attractive.

Marshall McLuhan was right when he said years ago,

All media work us over completely. They are so persuasive in their personal, political, economic, aesthetic, psychological, moral, ethical, and social consequences that they leave no part of us untouched, unaffected, unaltered.[1]

The Media and the Mind

All media touch the mind, stir it, move it, mold it—in every way affect it—even when the process is unconscious. Moreover, the cognitive is basic to the behavioral. We act out what we first think. Hence, whatever affects the mind will ultimately (though not always directly or immediately) affect behavior.

How we think is the reservoir we draw from when we choose how to act. The soundness of our behavior is dependent on the soundness of our thoughts. We *are* what we think—"As he thinks within himself, so he is" (Proverbs 23:7, NASB).

All behavior, speech as well as actions, begins with thoughts that are formed in the brain, using the raw materials sent there by the senses. What do the senses send to the brain? Their impressions of outward stimuli. Hence, the selection of what stimuli—what sights, sounds, smells, tastes, and touches—we will expose our senses to dramatically influences the way we eventually think and act.

Furthermore, the brain is not very selective; it records whatever the senses send its way. Like a photographic plate that accumulates light, so the brain accumulates images and impressions. Therefore, what we are today—and what we will be tomorrow—is largely the cumulative product of what we have stored in our brain. And what we have stored there is itself the result of our choices to be stimulated by certain input and not by others.

In the 1950s a respected British newscaster ran a tongue-in-cheek story about the "Annual Spaghetti Harvest." It included films of young women picking armfuls of long pasta hanging from trees, replete with comments about the dreaded "spaghetti weevil." Many Britishers genuinely believed the report, just as many Americans believed Orson Welles's 1938 radio broadcast of "War of the Worlds" and took to the streets to flee the invading Martians.

The point is two-edged: the media are by nature believable, and we are by nature gullible. We learn from birth to be empirical, to believe what we see. Though it is simple for the media to distort, exaggerate, and downright lie, it is not so simple for us to disbelieve them. If television can persuade people about the spaghetti harvest, can't it and other media persuade us to believe falsely about *anything*—whether politics, religion, ethics, or sex?

There is something a bit humorous (and harmless) about an intelligent Britisher going through life believing in the spaghetti weevil. But there is *nothing* funny about people believing that sexual sin is fulfilling, that the best sex is outside marriage, that extramarital sex is really okay, and that the joys of immorality outweigh its consequences. These are, plain and simple, lies. Not harmless jests, like the spaghetti weevil, but *lies*—destructive lies that ruin lives.

We can no longer afford the luxury of naiveté. The influences of the media on our beliefs about sexual morality must be reckoned with.

SEX AND ADVERTISING

No thinking man can consider the force and use of advertising in the modern world without being greatly disturbed.[2]

That most of us are not greatly disturbed about advertising illustrates the point—we're not thinking.

American businesses spend three billion dollars on advertising each year—for prime time television alone. Billions more are spent on daytime television, radio, magazines, newspapers, billboards, and innumerable other media. According to *TV Guide,* in 1981 the number of network commercials run each week was 4079, more than double the figure of 1967.

There is no free television, no inexpensive magazines. The price we pay is having to look at the commercials and advertisements, which are carefully designed to motivate us—often manipulate us—to spend our money on certain products. Whether the process is conscious or subconscious is immaterial. The fact is, advertising works.

What You're Really Buying

People buy products not for what they are but for what they are associated with. A man who buys a certain shirt with a certain insignia is buying more than a shirt—he is buying status. He smokes a certain cigarette to be a rugged individualist. He buys a certain beer because he likes to think of himself as an athlete and appreciates close male companionship. His wife buys beauty in the form of soap, his daughter buys male admirers in the form of blue jeans and shampoo. His son buys girlfriends by buying a car. We buy not just products but images.

Of course the images we buy often do not correspond to reality. Who does the beer commercials—alcoholics or athletes? And how often have you seen vomit, lost jobs, crippling car accidents, or broken families in a wine commercial? Look at the virile, healthy people in cigarette ads. How many cigarette ads show people in the oncology ward dying of lung cancer? About as many as show the disastrous side of sex outside marriage. Advertising never lets the truth get in the way of the persuasive goal.

Advertisers know their business better than we know ourselves. They play on our needs and our wants, the most powerful forces in our soul, and they know sex sells.

Sex: The Greatest Tool in Advertising

Why is sex such an effective seller? Because sex is such a powerful drive. It can be associated with a particular product and make that product more appealing. Sex sells everything from cars to toothpaste. When I say sex is an effective seller, I mean subtle, low-key, and playful sexiness. Sex sells best when we barely realize it's there.

From the beginning of the "oldest profession in the world," sex and money have been Siamese twins. In prostitution, sex is sold. In pornography, illusions about sex are sold. In advertising, sex is not sold but is itself the seller—the tool, the means of sales. It is first the attention getter, then the subtle but effective persuader.

The bottom line motive of big business is not the corruption of morals but the collection of money. If portraying chastity or premarital virginity and fidelity would sell a product more effectively, they would be used. The first, greatest, and only commandment of corporate advertising is "Sell."

The mind manipulators of Madison Avenue will stop using sex when sex stops selling . . . when you and I stop buying. And, given our sexual natures, drives, and vulnerabilities, that will probably never happen.

The Effects of Advertising's Sexploitation

What is the harm of using sex in advertising? Primarily, I see three negative effects:

1. The distortion of sexual realities.

Advertising creates a massive subliminal environment where men and women appear most frequently in fantasy relationships designed to enhance or optimize the mass audience's consuming orientation. We have, of course, made the illusionary media world the real or natural world, permitting the actual material environment to become quite pale, insipid, and ordinary by comparison.[3]

2. The cultivation and exploitation of human inadequacy.

Women are carefully trained by media to view themselves as inadequate. They are taught that other women—through the purchases of clothes, cosmetics, food, vocations, avocations, education, etc.—are more desirable and feminine than themselves. Her need to constantly reverify her sexual adequacy through the purchase of merchandise becomes an overwhelming preoccupation, profitable for the merchandisers, but potentially disastrous for the individual.[4]

3. The cultivation of self-centeredness and hedonism.

A commercial for an $8,000 automobile tells us "you need this car." We have already been taught to want it—now we are told we *need* it. Advertising cultivates not the pursuit of holiness but the pursuit of happiness—a happiness wrapped up in material objects and superficial short-term goals.

Meanwhile, we learn a "take what you want" philosophy that applies to sexual morality as well. I may want a car I cannot afford and which, therefore, would be wrong to buy. Or I may want an adulterous relationship which I know is wrong. But when I allow so powerful a force as the media to incessantly tug at my wants, they grow to such proportions that they *appear* to be needs. Finally I may succumb and buy the product (the car or the affair), in either case later facing the consequences of my foolishness (far worse for the affair than the car).

> Until something is done to reverse mass media sex miseducation, the church's positive witness will have much less impact. The biggest prostitution problem in our country does not come from the bordellos but from the advertising agencies in business suites where sex fantasies are linked to products in order to increase sales. Consumers share some of the responsibility for such prostitution.[5]

As its Creator, God takes personally this relentless assault upon and abuse of human sexuality. For, ultimately, the exploitation of sex is the exploitation of people, who are sexual beings made in God's image. As Christians, we must refuse to mindlessly submit to this perversion of sex. We must do all in our power to cultivate in ourselves and our families a distaste for and resistance to the exploitation of sex in advertising.

SEX AND THE PRINTED PAGE

"The pen is mightier than the sword." Since Gutenberg, the printing press has become mightier than a million swords. Throughout history the written word has molded minds and morality, and continues to do so today.

A visit to the bookstore is most enlightening. I counted thirty-four different books on sex in the new book rack in one Seattle store (this is a respected national chain, not a sleazy adult book store). The "Sex" department included 109 different books—not just books containing explicit sex (that's in the thousands), but books exclusively devoted to the subject of sex. They ranged from the "How To" manuals to sex lives of famous people, to illustrated histories and instruction manuals in gay and lesbian sex.

A recent bestseller explains the ins and outs of carrying on an affair with a married man. The bestselling *Happy Hooker* and its sequels are written by a former prostitute (she quit being a prostitute as soon as she made it rich telling people how great it was to be a prostitute). She has become a celebrity, appeared on innumerable talk shows, and, in short, proven to America's youth that an immoral and illegal lifestyle can be a ticket to fame and fortune.

Alex Comfort's bestselling *The Joy of Sex* has spawned *The Joy of Gay Sex* and *The Joy of Lesbian Sex*—to be found in almost every squeaky clean family mall book store. One store nearby carries the works of Rene Guyon, the patron saint of child molesters, who also defends masochism, incest, bestiality and says women should view a man exposing himself to them not as an insult but as "an act of homage." Also prominent are books of dirty jokes, most of them sexual.

The World of Romance Novels

Americans spend 450 million dollars a year on paperback romance novels. Harlequin alone printed 200 million romances in 1982. It currently releases sixty new titles each month.[6]

One romance writer, Janet Dailey, has written seventy-nine books that have sold ninety-five million copies in ninety-eight countries and nineteen languages. At least twenty million American teens and adults, mostly women, read these novels—many on a nonstop basis.

Never having read a romance novel, I picked up several to get a sampling. The promotional blurbs capture the essence of the books:

> One night long ago, Keele Petrakis had possessed D'Arcy Kincaid. Now his sensuous advances tell her he means to do so again. D'Arcy hopes to resist—but she needs his help to succeed in her career.

The publisher of one line of romance novels considers their stories superior to those of other publishers because they are "true-to-life novels about sophisticated women and their strong sensuous lovers. Novels that will set your *own* desires free. . . ."

Sophisticated? Questionable. True-to-life? Ludicrous. Free? Precisely the opposite.

At our local supermarket (not a bookstore, mind you), I counted 155 novels with explicitly sexual titles and jacket covers. Then I bumped into two separate racks of Harlequin romances, adding to my list another 120 titles that clearly reflect sexual themes.

Many readers—among them Christian women and girls—become addicted to romance novels for life, reading dozens and sometimes even hundreds a year. Many romance novels are geared to the interests of teenage girls. Judy Blume's novels—read by teens and preteens alike—are extremely popular, selling millions of copies and occupying a place in school libraries. If you have a teenage daughter, it's likely she reads Judy Blume. If she does and you haven't, you'd better and she'd better not. Blume's descriptions of premarital sex are frequent, vivid, and erotic—and clearly designed to reassure girls that sex outside of marriage can be wonderful.[7]

Pictureless Pornography

Though laden with sexual overtones, romance novels are not explicit enough for men. Consequently, some publishers specialize in a sort of pictureless pornography that pulls no punches.

Sorokin described the 1950s forerunners of the pulp novels that sell better than ever today:

> The sham literature of our age is designed for the commercial cultivation, propagation, and exploitation of the most degraded forms of behavior. It is pornography that appeals to the basest propensities of that "worst of the beast," as the demoralized human animal was named by Plato and Aristotle. The world of this popular literature is a sort of human zoo, inhabited by raped, mutilated, and murdered females, and by he-males outmatching in bestiality any caveman and outlusting the lustiest of animals; male and female alike are hardened in cynical contempt of human life and values. And what is especially symptomatic is that many of these human animals are made to seem to luxuriate in this way of life, just as, we must assume, the readers enjoy it. This cheap Dante's inferno of aphrodisiacs is painted in the most captivating colors. Instead of exhibiting its filth and rottenness, the pulp-sexualists daze the reader with the glamour of "smartness," "orgasmic" curves, "dynamic" lines, violent passions, and "freedom unlimited" to do anything one wants to do.[8]

By reading only the descriptions on the jacket covers, it is obvious that the books promote sexual perversions of every sort, including swapping, group sex, and incest. The insidious myth that women are asking to be raped, so common in pornography, is likewise prominent in these books:

> Carol knows how to give a man pleasure—her tantalizing body is a rare treasure. She is kidnapped and held for ransom—she doesn't mind, 'cause her abductors are well-built and handsome.

Of course, no one need go to the convenience store for all this literary poison, since even respectable magazines advertise erotic book clubs. Every year, Publisher's Central Bureau sends me and countless others a sale catalog offering innumerable titles like *The Joys of Sexual Fantasy* and *The World's Greatest Collection of Erotica,* some including nude photos of young girls. All this is sold alongside the great classics, religious works, and Walt Disney children's books.

Most disturbing of all, even the good (i.e., well written) literature is increasingly filled with sex scenes and profane language. Immorality seems almost as obligatory as characters, setting, and plot—even when it is totally unnecessary and out of place. If the glorification of immorality was limited to "the sex books," at least the distinction would be clear. Unfortunately, it is woven into the most popular and influential literature of our day.

Sex and the Magazines

While not pornographic, men's magazines such as *Esquire* and *True* depend on sex to sell. More alarming still are the detective and police magazines that graphically depict sexual crime, appealing to the reader not only as a voyeur but as a sadist.

Sports magazines are increasingly more explicit in their photographs. *Sports Illustrated*'s annual swimsuit issue is more sexually provocative every year and rivals the *Playboy* of the sixties. Unfortunately, the swimsuit issue also sells twice as many copies as any other issue, reinforcing the publisher's commitment to sexual exploitation and demonstrating that when it comes to sex, it is largely true that the public gets what the public wants.

Among the multitudes of magazines for women, one class in particular specializes in romance. These "confessional" magazines, by frequently employing the word "true" in their titles (e.g., *True Confessions, True Romance*), suggest that women are looking for reality, not just fantasy. The "true" is also incriminating; it tries to convince us that the unbelievable is believable. If the stories were more credible we wouldn't need to be continually reminded that they are really true.

Through these magazines women are led to drink at an unreal well in an unreal world. How tragic that the lives of many American women are so barren and lonely that they are driven to live vicariously through the atypical and sometimes bizarre (not to mention unbelievable) experiences of others. Sadder still that their views of reality are thereby warped, and they are drawn always further from the possibility of true personal fulfillment in a relationship.

Another class of women's magazines are the beauty or glamour mags, most of them pervaded with words and images of sex, sexiness, and seduction. *Cosmopolitan* is a glamour magazine that stands out because its editor, Helen Gurley Brown, played a prominent role in the sexual revolution (she wrote the bestselling *Sex and the Single Girl* in 1962).

An issue of *Cosmopolitan* is a full-blown sex education course, from the sex dominated ads (hundreds of them each issue), to the letters to the editor, to the articles, the cartoons, and the "Cosmo Counselor." In the single issue I read, I learned about orgasms, impotence, masturbation, and countless other sexual subjects, and walked away wondering what sexual rocks were possibly left to turn over in the year's other eleven issues.

The famous *Cosmo Report* of 1981 indicated that 68 percent of the readers had committed adultery, and 70 percent over the age of thirty-five had gone to bed with a man on their first date. After reading *Cosmopolitan*, I'm surprised they waited that long.

A look at the teen magazines shows they follow the pattern of female sexiness, superficiality, and sex-dominated advertising. It is particularly alarming that young female readers are pushed so early into "being sexy."

Millions of American minds are touched weekly through the supermarket tabloids. These are the newspapers with three-inch headlines that typically read, NUDE GHOSTS OF ELVIS AND JFK DESCEND FROM UFO AND GIVE PRINCESS DI MIRACULOUS HERB THAT CURES ARTHRITIS. Actual titles include "Hitler's Sex Life," "Sex Confessions of Daytime Superstuds," and "Love Secrets of Soaps Bitches." The lead caption of the latter article reads:

> Daytime TV's two superbitches are the secret envy
> of millions of American women because they get to
> go to bed with men who are not their husbands.[9]

The large number of Christian products and services advertised in these sensational tabloids indicates a significant readership of professing Christians. Out of 134 classifieds looking for love in one issue, thirteen specifically state they are born-again Christians; others would likely say the same. A typical one reads:

> Christian divorced lady, 34, considered very attractive, TV star type, long blond hair, seeks correspondence with honest, Christian male. Only Christians need reply. Photo please.

That professing believers, and no doubt a number of genuine ones, would regularly read material that majors in sensationalism, trivia, and shabby reporting is disturbing enough. That they would read material that glorifies the occult, astrology, materialism, and immorality is even more disturbing.

One step up (but only one) from these magazines are the extremely popular *People* and *Us*. A quick glance through each of them reveals, however, that if references to and pictures depicting sexual themes were removed, each could be printed as a pamphlet instead of a magazine.

Even family-oriented magazines and the newsweeklies seem compelled to publish sexually titillating articles and photographs. *Life* recently printed several blatant examples of sexual exploitation, including nude photos of Marilyn Monroe, a swimsuit issue that borders on pornography, and a perversely suggestive photo of a woman naked from the waist up, laying on top of and kissing a dog, with her tongue in his mouth. [10] Their inclusion reminds us that even respectable journalism has stooped to attracting our attention through sexual exploitation.

SEX AND TELEVISION

Promise me you'll read this section even if you have to miss your favorite TV show. The odds are against me. Surveys indicate that the average American watches more than twelve hundred hours of television a year; some considerably more. In the same year, he will spend a grand total of five hours reading books. [11]

More U.S. homes have television than indoor plumbing. Ninety-eight percent have one TV, over 55 percent have more. [12] Considering that forty years ago no one had any, the television has rapidly assumed a remarkable role in American life.

The average home's TV is on seven hours every day. [13] The average child two to five years old spends one-third of his waking hours watching television. A teenager has spent fifteen thousand hours watching TV by the time he graduates, three thousand more hours than the time spent in school. If the typical young American lives to be seventy, he will have spent ten full years—of twenty-four hour days—in front of the television.

No matter who says what about the effects of television on the mind and behavior, one thing is clear—it is impossible to spend that much time doing *anything* without being permanently affected by it.

The Minds and Morals Behind Television

Television is not just a seller of products to human minds, it is itself a product of human minds. *Public Opinion* reports that of 104 influential television writers, producers, and executives, 80 percent did not regard homosexual relations as wrong, 51 percent did not think adultery was wrong (only 17 percent felt strongly that it was wrong), and 97 percent favored a woman's right to have an abortion.

These statistics are far more liberal than that of the rest of American society. "According to television's creators, they are not in it just for the money. They also seek to move their audience toward their own vision of the good society."[14]

A team of Michigan State researchers studied television's soap operas and noted that in addition to continuous allusions to sex, the average soap includes two "intimate sexual acts" per hour. More significantly, however, it found that "94% of all daytime copulations, if rape and prostitution are included, occur between unmarrieds."[15] Obviously, this is a gross distortion of real life, where most sexual relations are between those married (to each other). But by sheer percentages it overwhelms viewers with the commonness and acceptability of fornication and adultery.

If television is to be believed, the wages of sin is not always death, you may or may not reap what you sow, God is nonexistent or irrelevant, problems are quickly and cheaply solved (always within thirty or sixty minutes), committed Christians are hypocrites and bigots, and only the ignorant, uptight, and unattractive confine their sexual activity to marriage.

Fifty million Americans go to church regularly. How many television characters go to church? How many pray, read the Bible, and live by biblical morality? Why don't they? Because the writers and producers don't. What they write and produce reflects their values, which are far afield not only of believers but of most of the country.

The moral gap between the media elite and the rest of society will not last long, of course. In time, most of us will think as they do now (just as we now think as they did fifteen years ago). Jesus said it this way: "everyone who is fully trained will be like his teacher" (Luke 6:40). For hours on end, Americans young and old sit at the feet of their media mentors.

Programming Content

Television offers an endless smorgasbord of brawls, chases, shootings, stabbings, rapes, and murders of every variety. Prime time is crime time. The average child will see on television twenty thousand acts of violence by the time he is eighteen. Given the glut of situation comedies, prime time soap operas, and made-for-television movies with sexually suggestive, often sexually explicit, dialogue and scenes, who knows how many acts of immorality he will see.

Says one producer, "Titillation always sells."[16]

TV's Statements on Homosexuality

Television has become without a doubt the most effective medium to desensitize the conscience of America to the homosexual lifestyle.

> Gay characters and situations in prime-time are becoming almost common place, and gay groups are happy about it.
>
> "We're very pleased," says Chris Uszler, chairperson of the Alliance for Gay Artists, "because they're getting away from treating gays and lesbians as an issue or a problem. There are more of what we call 'happens-to-be-gay' characters."[17]

The televised movie *Making Love* begins by building up what a wonderful person, doctor, and husband the main character is. Once we admire him enough, we watch him as he commits adultery in a homosexual relationship and leaves his wife for that lifestyle. His wife wants him back, but he refuses and she says, "It wasn't easy to do what he had to do. But I know that he had to." She remarries, he settles in with a man that he's been with for two years, and at the end of the movie they compare notes on their respective "marriages." "Are you happy, Zack?" she asks him. "Yeah, I really am," he says. She sums up the message of the movie saying, "I guess we both did okay."

Daytime Television

Promiscuous homosexuals, adulterers, and pornographers have always been around. Once, however, they went to prison. Now they go on the "Phil Donahue Show." The program's basic purpose seems to be to call on intelligent, articulate, and "well-adjusted" people to represent the violation of every scriptural principle that exists—or to call on traditional moralists and try to ridicule their position. The gradual result is that audiences become increasingly tolerant of what the Bible calls sin.

Daytime television is a world of its own. The soap operas maintain their steady stream of people getting in and out of bed with other people, while the game shows get their cheap laughs through sexually suggestive questions, quips, and comments.

Two Days of TV

Because I don't watch much television, I wanted to get a broad and accurate exposure to current programming. So I bought an issue of *TV Guide* and spent two vacation days flipping from channel to channel, watching many programs I had never seen (and, Lord willing, will never see again).

I saw several unmarried couples sleep together, discovered an X-rated bakery in New York and a gigolo convention in New Jersey, listened to a sex researcher on a popular talk show, and watched one movie in which everyone's clothes disintegrated and another of a brutal rape in a New England village. I saw the usual corruption and adultery on "Dynasty" and "Dallas," a leering game show host making sexual comments to a young woman, and X-rated story lines with B-rated acting on daytime soap operas.

On the brighter side, I watched a rerun of "Leave It to Beaver" which the *TV Guide* described as, "Wally buys a loud suit with lots of pockets." It was even less risqué than it sounded.

Sex on Cable and Pay TV

During my study of network television, I bought a programming guide that listed the other shows I could have watched in that same two day period if I subscribed to a cable service, HBO, and Showtime. The endless barrage of violent and immoral movies made the network fare seem almost tame by comparison.

Nationally, there are six pay-cable networks exclusively devoted to "soft" pornography. "In New York City, a late-night public-access series called 'Midnight Blue' presents topless dancers, sado-masochistic skits and visits to nudist colonies featuring full frontal exposure."[18] In 1981 Manhattan Cable TV featured "The Ugly George Hour of Truth, Sex and Violence." The entire program consisted of George, a former porno film star, cornering young women on city streets and asking them to step into a room and take off their clothes in front of the camera. When they complied, he videotaped them and showed the results on his program.

What direction is cable television headed? In the assessment of *Newsweek,*

> The plague of video exhibitionism threatens to sweep across the dial. As four new programs graphically illustrate, never have so many bared body and soul so willingly for the voyeur that lurks in all of us.[19]

Unfortunately, the sex craze on pay TV is a matter of supply and demand:

> When a separate network devoted to sexually oriented films has been offered through a cable-television system or as a late-night addition to subscription television service, the percentage of subscribers willing to pay the extra monthly charge regularly exceeds 50%, and has reached as high as 95%. . . .
>
> The number of cable subscribers is expected to nearly triple before 1990, while the number of video cassette recorders will increase five fold during the next four years. Producers and entrepreneurs are

scrambling to meet the anticipated demand for sexual entertainment adapted specifically for the home. Already, new cable networks with names like Escapade (now a joint venture with Playboy magazine) and Private Screening, along with stores that specialize in video cassettes, have begun to market erotic entertainment in much the same slick, sophisticated style that Hollywood has long used to merchandize its own set of fantasies.[20]

I still remember my introduction to movie channels some years ago. My wife and I stayed at a hotel that carried HBO. Since we both enjoy a good movie, we flipped it on to see what was playing. In the five seconds before we turned it off, we saw a woman, naked from the waist up, standing by a bed with a man on his knees pulling down her pants.

I find it interesting—and revealing—that many Christian families pay to have these movie channels in their homes. Admittedly some of the programming is good, and you don't have to watch the bad stuff. But I wouldn't buy subscriptions to ten raunchy men's magazines in order to get three or four good ones, would you? Maybe I wouldn't trust myself—or my children—to keep away from the bad ones. If I was morally strong at the moment I could throw away the bad magazines when they came in the mail, but I can't do that with a television. It just sits there, waiting to be turned on at any point of boredom, curiosity, or moral weakness. Maybe I can resist temptation this time, but the same dirty movie plays again tomorrow night, when the family's gone. . . .

I also don't like the idea of paying for something (even if I don't watch it) which so obviously violates the Word of God and dishonors his holy character.

Home Video

When friends recently brought over their video recorder, I went to a store to rent a movie. There were a dozen people there ahead of me, and no one to answer my questions. Seeing a huge black notebook and assuming it was a listing of their movies, I opened it up. It turned out to be a scrapbook of promotional clips from their X-rated movies—unadulterated pornography available to any child who could reach up to a three foot counter.

Home video goes beyond what is legal on cable TV. "Of all pre-recorded video cassettes sold, between 25% and 50% are X-rated, according to industry sources."[21]

However, the majority of rental movies played on home videos are not X-rated; they are major motion pictures that played in theaters anywhere from four months to years earlier. Video cassette players have provided the first direct link between Hollywood and the home.

SEX AND THE MOVIES

Laughter can be wonderful, but it is far more serious than we might think. What I laugh at makes a statement about my values. I don't laugh at that which violates deep-seated convictions. If something entertains me, it must in some sense be acceptable to me.

The media excels at prompting Americans to laugh at immorality—thereby gradually but effectively lowering our moral standards. And no medium has entertained us with immorality so effectively as the motion pictures.

Humorous Immorality

You don't have to look far to find examples of Hollywood's efforts to entertain us with the immoral. In *Young Frankenstein*, a woman is raped by Frankenstein's monster and ends up enjoying it, to the point of singing during intercourse. Anyone who laughs is laughing at rape. The film confirms the myth that many rapists hold—women want to be raped and enjoy it. *The Best Little Whorehouse in Texas*, a popular video also shown on network television, promotes the belief that prostitution need not be taken seriously; it can be acceptable, appealing, even funny.

Viewers may never see prostitution for what it really is—an ugly slave market of human exploitation and agony. *Airplane* and *Airplane II* draw humor out of a child molester leering at and talking suggestively to a little boy and in a girl having sex with a horse.

Significantly, each of these movies was rated PG, a comparatively mild rating with much less sex and violence than those rated R. Yet each utilizes sex—immoral sex—as a hook to win and keep its audience . . . and to educate that audience in another value system.

Movies for the Young

Teenagers are the largest audience of moviegoers in America.

> In the past few years, the movie industry has exploded with offerings aimed at young audiences. Recent statistics . . . show that one-fourth of moviegoers are between 16 and 20, and this age group goes to the movies at least once a month. Consequently, teens are the prime target for producers and film makers hungry for a hit.[22]

The two basic ingredients in many of the teen movies of recent years—violence and immorality—offer an irrefutable theology lesson in the depravity of man. That sex almost always plays a role in the frequent blood and gore movies is more than disturbing—it is pathological. The most common theme is that of a crazed murderer stalking a young girl. (It seems incredible for society to cry out against such horrible murders and at the same time be entertained by them.) The nonviolent sex movies are holding their own against the mad slashers. The most popular themes here are seduction (frequently in the form of "woman seduces boy") and losing one's virginity.

The next time your teenager says, "I'm going to a movie," you might want to ask, "Which one?"

THE EFFECTS OF TELEVISION AND MOVIES

Do television and motion pictures *really* affect our lives? Absolutely.

The proliferation of sex-saturated programs and movies has created a nation of voyeurs. And voyeurism is a sexual sickness whether done through binoculars, window shades, peepholes, or in living rooms and movie theaters. It is a symptom of sexual sickness and bondage, not sexual health and freedom.

Moreover, many motion pictures are targeted for the young—those whose sexual identities and values are still being shaped and who will determine the moral direction of our country.

Television affects our sleeping habits, our eating habits, and even our bathroom habits.[23] Passivity, consumption of alcohol, and obesity are all promoted by television. Think of those endless hours of gazing lifelessly with nothing to do but eat, drink, and watch commercials about eating and drinking.

In addition to these more obvious influences, television and the movies have introduced other serious negative effects into our national psyche.

1. Television and movies cultivate unhealthy cross-sexual relationships.

> After his thorough training to view women as sex objects, the media-oriented young American male finds it most difficult to relate or interact with women as human beings. . . .
>
> Every large American city has tens of thousands of working women—many highly talented, sensitive, and interesting women—who are unlikely to establish permanent mates because they physically do not fit into the current media-induced fantasy of what an attractive woman should look like.[24]

2. Television and movies promote inadequacy, insecurity, and superficiality.

Every time I meet a slender twenty-year-old girl who constantly exercises and starves herself yet feels she must lose fifteen pounds, I get angry at the media. The epidemic of anorexia nervosa is largely attributable to the "emaciated is beautiful" message American women (especially the young) are given from every program, movie, magazine, billboard, and store mannequin. Many, both male and female, are preoccupied with the superficial and trendy to the neglect of character and moral fiber.

3. Television and movies promote immorality and crime, both sexual and violent.

Some criminals have specifically stated that many of their ideas and techniques for crime came from television (often while they were watching in prison, prior to parole).

At least fifteen people committed suicide imitating a Russian roulette scene in *Deerhunter,* a popular movie shown on television. John Hinckley got his idea of stalking the president from the movie *Taxi Driver,* which he watched fifteen times. A nineteen-year-old boy watched the television movie *Lizzie Borden,* then killed his parents and sister and crippled his brother with an axe.

Violent rapes, murders, and crimes of every sort are common fare in the media. Is it any wonder that violent crimes increased so dramatically in the sixties, the very decade where television entrenched itself as the center of America's attention?

4. Television and movies desensitize viewers, especially children, to human dignity and needs and make them more callous to human suffering.

Even the news often focuses on grisly killings and sex slayings. But merely by watching prime time programs (even some cartoons), children are constantly bombarded with violence and immorality, putting tremendous adult pressures on them at far too young an age. What does it do to the psychosexual development of a prepubescent girl when she continually watches women seducing and propositioning men on television?

How many murders and seductions did your grandparents see as children? Probably a grand total of none. How about you? It depends on your age and whether or not you had a television when you were young. Now how many murders and seductions have your children seen? Hundreds—most of them thousands.

What is premarital sex to a teenager who has seen it on television ever since he was a preschooler? Upon finding he has fathered a child as a sixteen year old, why do his parents throw up their hands and cry, "God, where did we go wrong?" What is the big mystery? Through the media, he's been taught daily since childhood that sex outside of marriage is not only okay, but fun, exciting, perfectly normal, and generally free of consequences.

Do we really think that occasional moral sermons from parents or youth pastors can counteract the cumulative exposure of the thousands of hours of slick media tutorials that have discipled our children to believe the opposite? Why should we expect them to do anything but violate God's sexual standards when they have for so long seen it done in such grand and engaging style?

And while we're asking the tough questions, whose fault is it that the television we used as our child's babysitter turned out to be his kidnapper? You won't find it in the books, but television may be one of the most serious forms of child abuse in this country.

SUMMARY

Fellow Christians have often recommended a particular television program, assuring us "there's nothing offensive about it." Frequently we have followed their advice and turned on the program only to have to turn it off again within the first ten minutes. The content is often subtly and sometimes blatantly immoral.

Why didn't these sincere Christians see what appeared so obvious? Why didn't they see the glaring inconsistency of the

program with their biblical values? For the same reason *we*
would no longer see it if we chose to go on watching such programs. Desensitization of the conscience is as predictable as it
is potent. The more we expose ourselves to morally offensive
input the less offensive it becomes to us. Our moral sensitivities
are dulled. Eventually we are neither offended ourselves nor do
we understand why others are.

It is the height of ignorance to think that any person, young
or old, Christian or non-Christian, could read the literature and
watch the programs and movies described in this chapter and remain in any sense personally and morally unscathed.

A college freshman, born and raised in a strong Christian
family and active in our church youth group, told me of an
explicit sexual movie he had seen the night before. (This was
not a confession or admission, just a matter of fact that arose in
our conversation.)

"How did it affect you?" I asked.

He paused. "I don't know, actually. I didn't really think
about it. I don't think most people do."

And that is the tragedy. A mind is molded most completely
not when it thinks, but when it doesn't think. A Christian who
thinks would fare much better seeing such movies. But a Christian who thinks would never watch them in the first place.

Unthinkingly, without measuring, filtering, or processing,
we expose our minds to that which, were we thinking, would be
unthinkable. And each time—gradually, subtly, impercep-
tibly—we surrender just a little more mental and moral turf to
anti-Christian values. Our circle of holiness shrinks a smidgen
more, and the hard fought gains from spiritual disciplines, medi-
tation, and prayer dissipate until one day we wake up morally
bankrupt . . . or we do not wake up at all.

Chapter 5, Notes

1. Marshall McLuhan and Quentin Fiore, *The Medium Is the Message* (New York: Random House, 1967), 26.

2. Harry Blamires, *The Christian Mind* (Ann Arbor, Mich.: Servant Books, 1963), 28.

3. Wilson Bryan Key, *Media Sexploitation* (Englewood Cliffs, N. J.: Prentice-Hall, 1976), 20-21.

4. Ibid., 19.

5. Harry Hollis, "A Christian Model for Sexual Understanding and Behavior," in *The Secrets of Our Sexuality*, ed. Gary Collins (Waco, Tex.: Word Books, 1976), 81-82.

6. *USA Today,* 12 December 1984, sec. B.

7. For example, see Judy Blume, *Forever* (New York: Pocket Books, 1976), 33, 57, 86, 114, 149. 150, 220.

8. Pitirim Sorokin, *The American Sexual Revolution* (New York: Porter Sargent, 1956), 24-25.

9. *The National Examiner,* 31 May 1983, 1.

10. *Life,* October 1983, 126, 130.

11. H. J. Eysenack, *Sex, Violence and the Media* (San Francisco: Harper and Row, 1979), 49.

12. *USA Today,* 17 May 1984, sec. A.

13. *USA Today,* 17 April 1984, sec. D.

14. "TV Executives Differ Sharply from the Public on Moral Beliefs," *Christianity Today,* 8 April 1983, 56-57.

15. Rebekkah Bricker and Carolyn Dykhouse, "Do Skin and Sin on the Soaps Affect Viewers?" *People,* 14 June 1982, 76.

16. *USA Today,* 30 August 1984, sec. D

17. *TV Guide,* 28 April 1984, A-1.

18. Harry F. Waters, "Season of the Locust," *Newsweek,* 23 August 1982, 60.

19. Ibid.

20. Tony Schwartz, "The TV Pornography Boom," *The New York Times Magazine,* 13 September 1981, 45.

21. Ibid.

22. *USA Today,* 23 March 1984, sec. D.

23. City water systems dramatically drop their water pressure when toilets are flushed during prime time commercials (Gregg Lewis, *Telegarbage* [Nashville: Thomas Nelson Publishers, 1977], 24).

24. Key, *Media Sexploitation,* 18, 60.

Chapter 6

Sex and the Children

E very adverse sexual effect of the media is magnified among the young for two reasons. First, their minds, morals, and sexual identities are so moldable, much more than when they are older. Second, young people are exposed to the visual media (television and movies) more than any segment of society.

The unprecedented freedom, mobility, and affluence of today's young people, combined with high technology's saturation of their lives with the sex-preoccupied media, has foisted upon them a severe and unnatural degree of sexual pressure. Children are forced to deal with sexual feelings, drives, choices, and consequences long before they have become adults in any sense. On television, they view seductions, watch nightclub strippers, see prostitutes at work, and observe homosexual relationships *years* before last generation's youth even knew these things existed.

Made to face this adult world of turmoil and temptation, children learn to act like adults, talk like adults, and feel the intensity of adult pressures before they have learned adult methods of coping with them. Their lives are indelibly marked by a society that increasingly panders to, yet preys upon, its young.

THE PUBLIC SEX EDUCATION OF AMERICAN CHILDREN

American children spend a large portion of their waking hours in school. There they are tremendously influenced by the values, including the sexual values, of their peers. What other young people, especially their closest friends, think and say and do about sex matters to them and often sways them a great deal.

School is much more than a classroom. It is a learning community where as much is absorbed outside the classroom as in. Casual conversations, conflicts, rivalries, infatuations, rejections, locker room antics—all contribute to the learning process. The sexual attitudes, language, humor, and reported exploits of peers leave a profound impression on a child's mind.

This is not, of course, to underplay the importance of what is taught, both directly and indirectly, in the classroom. Like wet cement, the minds of children are—sometimes frighteningly— ready, willing, and eager to be shaped and, over time, solidified. What children are taught about sex from their authority-figure teachers will often be engraved on their minds.

I have examined hundreds of pages of sex education material from dozens of different school districts in several states. Some of it is good; some is unbelievably bad. The good material covers the biological aspects of human sexuality and stresses the importance of strong moral values that govern sex, leaving the specific teaching of those values to the home and church.

The bad material uses rank sexual slang and vulgar art work, labels as harmless virtually every form of immorality, and sometimes even suggests that students make their own decisions with advice from professionals, not their parents. Many have "values clarification" exercises that begin by saying, "There are no right or wrong answers." Some use surveys with questions like, "Have you ever had oral sex?" (asked of a class of fifteen year olds).

Most schools are somewhere between the good and bad extremes. Ultimately, the only way to know exactly what is being taught in *your* schools is to go and find out, a step I highly recommend.

Most sex education courses say a great deal about birth control but little about self-control. Planned Parenthood representatives are often brought into the classroom to peddle birth control alternatives and tell students how to obtain them without their parents' knowledge. In a nearby class of fifteen year olds (mixed boys and girls), a Planned Parenthood representative walked into the class with different colored condoms on each finger, waving them like puppets. Though teen pregnancy has risen dramatically since Planned Parenthood came on the scene, the organization continues its vain attempt to reduce pregnancies while effectively promoting premarital sex.[1] (Were Planned Parenthood in charge of traffic safety, it would no doubt teach children the art of dodging cars, rather than staying off the freeway in the first place.)

Since the 1930s, education has been on the forefront of changing values. The colleges that train our teachers today have generally accepted every plank of the sexual revolution's platform. If you need to see this for yourself, look through the textbooks used in the highly popular junior college and university "Human Sexuality" courses. They provide a crash course in the perspectives of contemporary secular education, perspectives passed on to future teachers and filtered through to future students.[2]

YOUTH SEX AND YOUTH MUSIC

More millionaires have emerged from the popular music industry in the past three decades than any other segment of the American economy. Music sells because it moves the soul.

Attempting to get up-to-date with today's youth music, I looked through some popular albums at the local variety store. Some of the songs were a bit disturbing: "Dirty Mind," "Love at First Feel," "Centerfold," and "Hell Ain't a Bad Place to Be," are just a sampling of what I encountered.

As I was flipping through these albums, a young man about twenty came up and greeted me. I knew him as a member of an evangelical church, and a counselor at a fine Christian youth camp.

"What are you doing?" he asked.

When I explained he said, "Yeah, some of this stuff is pretty bad. Have you ever heard the song "Sex"? It goes "I'm your mother, I'm your slut. . . ." He continued through the entire song (which didn't get any better).

"Can I ask you a straight question?" I responded. "Since you're a committed Christian, how can you justify listening to that kind of music?"

Reacting as if I'd just kicked his grandmother's leg brace, he said, "It's no big deal, really. Everybody listens to it. You don't have to believe it, you know. I don't even pay any attention to the words."

"That's interesting," I said, "since you just quoted a whole song to me word for word. You may not pay any attention to the words, but you sure remember them."

The conversation died an uncomfortable death, and we both went our ways, neither particularly convinced by the other.

Over the years, what attitudes, examples, and character have been modeled to the nation's youth by the Beatles, Rolling Stones, Elton John, David Bowie, Alice Cooper, Kiss, Sex Pistols, Cheap Trick, The Grateful Dead, Boy George, and countless others?

What does this music lead them to do? To worship God, serve others, be kind, sensitive, loving, and unselfish? Or to gratify sexual desire, be cruel, indifferent, and rebellious? What kind of relationships are promoted? Superficial relationships based on touch and sensual arousal, or meaningful relationships based on the interchange of truth and values?

Much of the popular youth music has brought us a new depth in heterosexual immorality, as well as a host of bisexual, homosexual, and deliberately effeminate and transvestite teen idols. And they are called "idols" for good reason. Many young people prostrate themselves before their music as really as the ancients did before their wooden gods—and will defend it with everything they have.

Cable's MTV is listened to almost nonstop by millions of American teenagers. It adds to the audio the often sensuous visual effects of a rock concert or fantasy. Rock video is a powerful medium, capable of leaving deep and lasting moral impressions.

Music is a medium that can just as surely awaken the spiritual impulses as the sexual, which is why the Bible elevates the role of music in worship. Music can move us to great heights or plummet us to great depths. Music can and does bring out the best and the worst within us. But young people and parents take heed: It will never leave us the same.

SEX ROLES AND OUR CHILDREN

The trend toward gender sameness is a sweeping one. Psychologist James Dobson says,

> I received a letter recently from a mother who was curious to learn why her local library had removed thousands of books from their shelves. Upon investigation she was shocked to discover that each volume depicting males and females in a traditional context was eliminated. If a mother was shown cooking dinner and a father was working in a factory, the book had to go. Obviously, no stone is left unturned in the campaign to change our ideas.[3]

It is interesting that the people who purge these kinds of books are usually the same ones who cry "censorship" when concerned parents seek to remove pornography from the libraries.

"Nonsexist childhood education" has become a field of its own. Censors scan school curriculum like vultures, pouncing upon male pronouns and replacing them with bland and awkward nonsexist language (any child who says "fireman" or "policeman" will surely grow to be antiwomen). Thinking most adults are hopelessly chauvinistic, nonsexist educators generally aim at the "blank slate" mind of children, who are supposed not to know any better.

Gender Blend

The world of fashion reflects the unisex movement. The hottest fashion craze of 1984 was "the androgynous look," described as "an epidemic of overscaled, mannish styles for women."[4]

Rock stars who model sexuality for a nation of young people are frequently gender blended. As I write, the two superstars of rock are Michael Jackson and Boy George. Michael Jackson capitalizes on the unisex look; Boy George looks like women used to except with more makeup. Grace Jones is a popular female star who appears part male, part female.

Walking through a store, my wife came across a popular poster of Michael Jackson. She asked our five-year-old daughter, "Do you think that's a boy or a girl?" Looking intently at the poster, she would begin to say "A boy" or "A girl," but stop when she saw some element of the picture that contradicted her answer. Confused and disturbed she finally said, "I just don't know. But I guess it would have to be a girl."

Gender distinctions are a source of identity and security for children. When idols deliberately appear effeminate and directly impersonate the opposite sex—and when even Christian parents do not see the danger of this (I have talked with many who don't)—it tells us how serious and pervasive the dilution of the sexes has become. In the name of sexual equality every God-created difference between men and women is being targeted for eradication. The issues have become hopelessly confused. Feminists seem determined to throw out true sexual differences along with unfair sexual discrimination. The result is a new generation of sexually confused and disoriented people.

So What's the Difference?

Look at the differences between men's and women's magazines. Those geared to women emphasize marriage, family, fashions, food, popular psychology, romance, and relational sex. Men's magazines focus on achievement—business achievement, sports achievement, and nonrelational sexual achievement. Why so different? Because men and women are so different.

Nor are such differences purely the product of culture and upbringing. Each of us is born with a sexual signature, an irrevocable stamp of maleness or femaleness. Surgeries and hormone injections can alter sexual appearances, but the chromosomes in every cell of the body still cry out either "male" or "female."

A great deal of research, most of it quite technical, has recently been done on the human brain. The most fascinating discovery is that not only towels come in "his" and "hers"—brains do too. Sex hormones significantly affect the brain's development. The biological differences between male and female sex hormones, in kind and degree, assure the different development of our brains.

The Psychology of Sex Differences is a massive scholarly work that tends to resist gender differences whenever possible. Still, the authors are compelled to acknowledge that "girls have greater verbal ability than boys," "boys excel in visual, spatial ability," "boys excel in mathematical ability," and "males are more aggressive."[5]

To those committed to gender sameness, these facts are disturbing, intimidating, and threatening. Indeed, they will go to great lengths to deny them. Seen from a biblical perspective, however, these facts of biology—and their consequent psychological and behavioral differences—are blessings from God. They make for a complete humanity in which men need women's differences and women need men's differences to develop the best home, church, and society.

Joyce Brothers, hardly a male chauvinist, says this in her book *What Every Woman Should Know About Men:*

> Men are different [than women]. In countless ways. But if they are, then so what? Men, it seems, have always been different. Does it really matter?
> It matters.

It matters very much. More than it ever has before.[6]

Does it really matter whether our children are being taught to affirm or deny gender differences? It matters. It matters very much. More than it ever has before.

SACRIFICING CHILDREN ON THE SEXUAL REVOLUTION'S ALTAR

Find a map of the United States and locate Montana, Wyoming, Colorado, North Dakota, South Dakota, Nebraska, Kansas, Minnesota, and Iowa. The combined population of these states was just over sixteen million in 1983. Now imagine a catastrophe that wiped out every living person in those nine states. Would it not be an unprecedented national tragedy? Tragedy, yes. Unprecedented, no.

Since the Supreme Court legalized abortion on demand in 1973, over one and a half million babies each year have been aborted. Between 1973 and 1983 at least sixteen million unborn human beings were killed.[7] This sixteen million represents more than ten times the combined casualities of every war in American history. Yet the war against the unborn goes on: four thousand plus babies killed in our country every day; a full one-third of all pregnancies ending in abortion; in some cities abortions outnumbering live births.[8] *This* is our greatest national tragedy.

Picture a hospital room where a surgical team is working hours on end to save the life of a premature twenty-six-week baby. The parents, grandparents, and hospital staff desperately hope and pray that the baby will live.

In the next room a virtually identical twenty-six-week-old baby, without complications, is being aborted—deliberately killed by a saline injection that burns off the skin and is absorbed into the lungs and digestive tract. It is an extremely painful process (yes, the fetus feels pain), requiring one to six hours to kill.

An alternative is prostaglandin abortion, which often results in the birth of a living, breathing, struggling baby that is then disposed of or allowed to die from neglect. All this so the mother's education, career, financial needs, living space and, sometimes, "consequence free" sex life need not be adversely affected.

The scientific evidence for life before birth is irrefutable.[9] Yet, choosing to believe what is most convenient to believe, prochoice advocates insist that the evidence is unclear and operate on an "If in doubt, feel free to abort" mentality. Had their parents done the same, many of them would not be alive to exercise their choice.

It is a tragic irony that some of those most adamant in the fight to save whales and baby seals from slaughter are the same who sport bumper stickers that say, "Abortion: A Woman's Right." Save the whales . . . kill the children.

It may seem strange to address abortion in a chapter on the sexual abuse of children. Yet the widespread practice of abortion is clearly a product of the sexual revolution and shares one other thing in common with child pornography, prostitution, incest, and molesting—irreparable damage is inflicted upon the weak and innocent by sexually and morally irresponsible adults.

A century ago no moral person could have conceived of this wholesale war being waged on the unborn; even less that it would be not only allowed but defended by respected national and church leaders. As our president and surgeon general pointed out in *Abortion and the Conscience of the Nation*,[10] America's moral decline is most evident in abortion's elevating of personal convenience over the lives of innocent children.

John Calvin gave this assessment hundreds of years ago:

> The fetus, though enclosed in the womb of its mother, is already a human being and it is a most monstrous crime to rob it of the life which it has not yet begun to enjoy. If it seems more horrible to kill a man in his own house than in a field, because a man's house is his place of most secure refuge, it ought

surely to be deemed more atrocious to destroy a fetus
in the womb before it has come to light.[11]

Twenty-five hundred years earlier, King David said this:

For you created my inmost being;
    you knit me together in my mother's womb.
I praise you because I am fearfully and wonderfully
        made;
    your works are wonderful,
    I know that full well.
My frame was not hidden from you
    when I was made in the secret place.
When I was woven together in the depths of the earth,
    your eyes saw my unformed body.
All the days ordained for me were written in your
        book
    before one of them came to be (Psalm 139:13-16).

SEXUAL ABUSE OF CHILDREN

Each year, at least one American child out of ten is sexually abused.[12] In a survey of twelve hundred college-age
females, 28 percent indicated they had sex with an adult before
age thirteen. Yet only 6 percent of the incidents were ever reported to authorities.[13]

There may be as many as 600,000 child prostitutes, who for the most part are not included in estimates of sexual abuse; neither are children who are
victims of pornographic exploitation. In a Chicago
police data profile of rape victims, nearly one out of
four rape victims treated in Chicago hospitals was a
child under fourteen. There seems little doubt that
the incidence of sexual abuse committed against children is vastly higher than anyone would like to believe, with a shocking possibility that the annual incidence could be in excess of one million.[14]

The magnitude of sexual child abuse can only be appreciated when we realize that each child molester is responsible for abusing an average of just over sixty-eight victims. Since the vast majority of molesters were abused themselves as children, with each victim they potentially spread the problem to many other children they will never touch themselves.[15] Because more often than not the offender is known to the child—and usually children do not volunteer the information out of fear or shame—many sexual offenses are easily perpetrated over long periods of time.

How does sexual abuse affect the child? Aside from the physical consequences, sexual abuse often significantly harms a child's self-image, ability to trust others, and capacity to carry on normal relationships. Among the sexually abused there is a high rate of running away, prostitution, drug abuse, theft and other crimes. Since sexual abuse contributes markedly to juvenile delinquency, it has many serious and long term effects on society. When these juvenile delinquents are older, they are usually those who perpetrate the most heinous and destructive crimes against society. And statistically, remember, it is they who will be the child molesters of the future.

CHILD PROSTITUTION AND CHILD PORNOGRAPHY

Few things are more heart wrenching than counseling child prostitutes. "Me and my friends all do it" one twelve-year-old boy told me. "You can turn one trick then play video games the rest of the day."

Estimates of the number of child prostitutes range from a hundred thousand to one million.[16] Every city has them on its streets—school-aged girls wearing thick makeup, shorts, and high heels; boys wearing tank tops and gym shorts, self-consciously waiting for customers (the youngest ones commanding the highest prices).

Most child prostitutes are runaways. And contrary to popular belief, 80 percent of runaways are from white, middle and upper class families.[17]

The child prostitution problem is inseparable from pornography. They are two sides of the same coin; each is used as an introduction to the other.

In 1977 *Time* shocked a blissfully ignorant public with a report on child pornography called "A Child's Garden of Perversity":

> *Lollitots Magazine* is one of the milder examples. It features pre-teen girls showing off their genitals in the gynecological style popularized by *Penthouse* and *Playboy*. Other periodicals, with names such as *Naughty Horny Imps, Children Love,* and *Child Discipline,* portray moppets in sex acts with adults or other kids. The films are even raunchier. An 8-mm. movie shows a 10-year-old girl and her 8-year-old brother in fellatio and intercourse. In another film, members of a bike gang break into a church during a first Communion service and rape six little girls. [18]

How extensive is the problem of child pornography in America? In 1976 one researcher found 260 separate child pornography magazines.[19] Many contain color photos of prepubescent boys and girls, often shown engaged in every conceivable sexual act—with other children, with adults, and even with animals. Incest is a popular theme, and some even show children in bondage, chains, and sometimes urinating and defecating (a source of sexual stimulation to some disturbed men). These magazines have extremely high profit margins, costing a few dollars to make and selling for anywhere from ten to twenty dollars.

As we will see in the following chapter, all pornography has significant effects on sexual attitudes and actions. Despite the fact that child pornography has been linked to child molesting in innumerable cases, Ira Glasser of the New York Civil Liberties Union, when questioned about "kiddie porn," stated (true to ACLU form), "Everything published ought to be absolutely protected by the First Amendment."[20]

Organized Child Molesting

Who are these people who buy a billion dollars of child pornography each year and trade pictures of naked children in sexual acts as children trade baseball cards? They are inappropriately called *pedophiles* ("lovers of children"), and men who seek sex with young boys are called *pederasts*.

Pederasts and pedophiles use candy, drugs, alcohol, and anything they can for bait. They make contacts in bus stations, school grounds, video arcades, fairs, and wherever children are. Child abusers publish manuals of child seduction and national guides like "Where the Young Ones Are."[21]

Thousands of child molesters have joined together in clubs with ties from coast to coast. Amazingly, some operate openly and are permitted to continue. In England, one such group is called PIE—Pedophile Information Exchange. They're openly demanding the legality of sex with children. They want the age of consent to be dropped to four years old. Active American groups include the Rene Guyon Society (their slogan is "Sex before eight or it's too late") and NAMBLA—the North American Man-Boy Love Association.

Our Own Culpability

While we heap scorn on those who exploit and destroy children, we must ask ourselves, *what has created the climate in which such perversity not only exists but grows?* How can that which is so reprehensible and repulsive still thrive? Again we must conclude the media are largely to blame—as are we for our tolerance.

One skit on "Saturday Night Live" featured a man on trial for child molesting. As he leered at a little girl in the courtroom, he described what he would like to do with her. At one point he ran across the courtroom trying to get at her. Incredibly, the live audience laughed hysterically.

A new depth in "respectable" child sexual exploitation was reached by *Harper's Bazaar* in its December 1983 issue. "Tiny Treasures" were little girls, apparently preschoolers, dressed and posed seductively. One photo was of a bare-chested girl holding a bottle of perfume. The caption read, "For seduction with just a hint of innocence."

We are outraged at sexual assaults on children; yet we tolerate media that feed both children and adults the idea of children's sexiness. We decry the seduction of the body; but tolerate and even endorse (through our purchases and admission fees) the seduction of the mind.

Why are we so surprised that incest and child molesting are dramatically increasing when we are unwilling to talk to store owners, television station managers, postal authorities, congressmen, and others who could make a difference? When we are unwilling even to shield our own families from the poisonous media perversions of this technological Corinth?

SUMMARY

The sexual revolution has brought death to children—physical death through abortion; moral death through sex role confusion, through the exaltation of immorality in the media and music, and through the amoral or immoral sex education of some schools; emotional and sometimes physical death through sexual abuse. Every revolution has its casualties. But none suffer more from America's sexual revolution than her children.

Chapter 6, Notes

1. Addie Jurs, " 'Planned Parenthood' Advocates Permissive Sex," *Christianity Today,* 3 September 1982, 16-21.

2. For example, Robert Crooks and Karla Baur, *Our Sexuality* (Menlo Park, Calif.: The Benjamin/Cummings Publishing Co., 1980).

3. James Dobson, *A New Look at Masculinity and Femininity,* (Arcadia, Calif.: Focus on the Family, n.d.).

4. *USA Today,* 23 April 1984, sec. D.

5. Eleanor Emmons MacCoby and Carol Magy Jacklin, *The Psychology of Sex Differences* (Stanford, Calif.: Stanford University Press, 1974), 351-52.

6. Joyce Brothers, *What Every Woman Should Know about Men* (New York: Simon and Schuster, 1981), 11-13.

7. *A.L.L. About Issues*, American Life Lobby, November 1983, 22.

8. *Crisis Pregnancy Center Volunteer Training Manual* (Washington, D.C.: Christian Action Council, 1984), 12.

9. Landrum Shettles and David Rorvik, *Rites of Life* (Grand Rapids, Mich.: Zondervan Publishing House, 1983).

10. Ronald Reagan, *Abortion and the Conscience of the Nation* (Nashville, Tenn.: Thomas Nelson Publishers, 1984).

11. *Crisis Pregnancy Center*, 7.

12. Eloise Salholz, "Beware of Child Molesters," *Newsweek*, 9 August 1982, 45.

13. *Basic Facts about Sexual Child Abuse* (Chicago: National Committee for Prevention of Child Abuse, 1982).

14. Ibid.

15. Salholz, "Child Molesters," 35.

16. *USA Today*, 23 April 1984, sec. A.

17. Shirley O'Brien, *Child Pornography* (Dubuque, Iowa: Kendall/Hunt Publishing Co., 1983), 22.

18. "A Child's Garden of Perversity," *Time*, 4 April 1977, 56.

19. O'Brien, *Child Pornography*, 20.

20. Ibid.

21. Ibid., 37.

Chapter 7

Pornography and Other Sex Crimes

*C*hild pornography is only a small part of America's thriving pornography industry. Sales of pornographic products exceed seven billion dollars each year—as much as the motion picture and record industries combined. At least half that money is skimmed off by organized crime.[1] In fact, two grand juries determined that organized crime controls a full 90 percent of the hard-core porn traffic in the United States.

Two to three million Americans view pornographic movies each week. Fifty percent of the profits in the videotape industry comes from pornographic movies. Mail order pornography is a multi-million dollar business. Over eight hundred adult theaters and fifteen thousand adult book stores exclusively show and sell pornography in America. Tens of thousands of variety, grocery, convenience, and book stores sell "soft porn." Together, *Playboy* and *Hustler* have a readership of ten million people—more than that of *Time* and *Newsweek* combined. Six of the ten most profitable newsstand monthlies are "men's magazines."[2]

In the early fifties stores carried no soft pornography. In the sixties *Playboy* established a firm position "behind the counter." In the seventies *Penthouse* took its place beside

Playboy. Now, at three local convenience stores in my rural area, the average is twelve behind the counter magazines.

What Is Pornography?

Pornography may be defined as any visual, written, or recorded stimulus designed to cultivate or heighten a person's desire toward immoral sexual behavior. Not every mention of immorality is pornographic. The Bible often talks about immorality but always with the purpose of deterring the reader from it, *not* attracting him to it.

Pornography is increasingly characterized by extreme sexual violence. Sadomasochism—with its whippings, chains, bondage, stabbings, and rapes—is common fare in hard porn magazines. Why the violence? Lonely and disturbed men consume pornography like salt water, gorging themselves to the point of sickness and despair. Always craving more, they require new depths of depravity to stimulate them, depths so violent and grotesque I dare not record them. The pornographic world is a world of nightmares that defies belief.

In 1975 New York police became aware of eight "snuff" films in which actresses engaged in sexual acts with several men. In the course of the film the women, to their horror, would suddenly be attacked, tortured, stabbed to death, and sometimes dismembered, all in front of the camera. Viewers paid up to $200 to see these "authentic" films.[3]

Knowing the Christian faith is their greatest potential enemy, pornographers often attack it. The November 1982 *Playboy,* for instance, carried an article that mocked Christ's virgin birth, rewriting it in modern terms as a cheap sexual seduction of God by Mary, in league with her husband, because they wanted a baby of high intelligence. *Hustler* and *Screw* magazine have gone even further, displaying a naked woman on the cross and depicting not only Christian leaders but Jesus Christ himself in sexual perversions.

Defending the Indefensible

Given pornography's true nature, it is incredible that it is sometimes called a "victimless crime." Nothing could be further from the truth. The subjects photographed are one kind of victim, those they portray another, and the viewer—sucked ever more deeply into the black hole of lust—yet another. Those against whom the pornography addict acts out his aggressions are the ultimate victims, as are their families and society as a whole. Whether obvious or subtle, pornography *thrives* on victims.

Despite all this, numerous books, articles, and commission reports have gone to great lengths to defend pornography. Most often, it is defended by the First Amendment: "Congress shall make no law . . . abridging the freedom of speech, or of the press. . . ." Who knows how many millions of dollars the American Civil Liberties Union has poured into their relentless efforts to hide pornography behind the Constitution.

Recently postal authorities exercised their legal responsibility to hand over to the FBI the names of people importing large amounts of illegal child pornography from Scandinavia. The ACLU was outraged. After all, the rights of these citizens were being violated! Yet these self-proclaimed freedom defenders seem not at all outraged at the exploited, raped, and murdered children whose civil liberties, human dignity, and lives are robbed by the very people they defend. As a result of the ACLU's efforts, freedom rings . . . the cash registers of organized crime.

That free speech and press are not absolute is demonstrated by the old observation: "No one has a right to [falsely] shout 'Fire' in a crowded theater." Likewise, no one has the right to print or speak lies about others or to plagiarize their work. The First Amendment is not and has never been an unqualified license to say or print whatever anyone wants. It was intended to protect a free and decent society, not to make the unprincipled wealthy as they prey upon the weak.

"Expert witnesses" (professionals flown in by—who else?—the ACLU) often testify at obscenity trials that pornography isn't really obscene or that obscenity is a constitutional right. They top off their argument with the kind of quantum-leap logic that goes like this: "If we let them ban *Teen Slut* today, they'll be burning the Mona Lisa tomorrow." A similar line of thinking is that if drunk drivers are given suspended licenses, the next thing we know they'll take away all our cars.

Pornographers and their defenders often make their cases by finding a token passage or picture that is "socially redeeming." Similarly, restaurant owners threatened with closure by a health inspector might attempt to justify their right to serve food by pointing to an edible carrot amongst the spoiled, moldy, and disease-ridden offerings of their salad bar.

Another favorite defense of pornography is the idea that sexual activity is a reality, and there is no justification for censoring anything real. Measured by Christian morality, however, what is real and what is right are often galaxies apart. But the truth is that what pornography conveys is *not* real. Pornography doesn't tell the truth; it lies about sex. Pornography portrays human bodies with proportions that are not the norm. It depicts sex in freakish, bizarre, and grotesque manners. It states or implies that women are asking to be raped and that children are seductive. Pornography lies in a thousand ways. Pornography is real; what it portrays is not.

Pornography is trash precisely because it treats people as trash. It is antiwomen, antichildren, antihuman, and anti-God, in whose image its victims are made.

The pornography industry thrives because greedy people want the money of lustful people and ignorant or indifferent people do nothing to stop it.

Theories about Pornography's Effects

The greatest blow to antipornography efforts in modern history was the Presidential Commission on Obscenity and Pornography created in January 1968. After two years and two million dollars, the commission concluded that there was no cause-effect relationship between pornography and violence. Pornography was declared essentially harmless.[4]

The results of this study were decried by several members of the Commission itself, notably Charles Keating, who founded "Citizens for Decency through Law," an antipornography group.

The president and U.S. Senate also rejected the findings of the report. The Commission not only failed to use common sense but ignored much of the evidence. This should have come as no surprise since most of the Commission members were solidly anticensorship. Incredibly, those responsible chose as chairman of the Commission an active leader of the ACLU, an action akin to asking an executive of the American Tobacco Growers to chair a commission to determine whether smoking can harm your health.

There are many different theories about the effects of pornography. One is simply that there *are* no effects. This position displays gross ignorance of the human mind, the persuasive power of visualization, the relation of the cognitive to the behavioral, and the inherent power of the sex drives.

Another theory is that viewing pornography is a catharsis —a harmless outlet that actually reduces aggressive and violent behavior. Presumably thought up by a research team sponsored by organized crime, this theory is preposterous. It not only goes against all the scientific data, but flies in the face of experience as well.

Similar to the concept of catharsis is the boredom theory— the idea that the more pornography is available, the more commonplace and boring it becomes, and therefore, the less it will be craved. This is a dangerous half-truth. Scientific tests do show that prolonged exposure to pornography lessens sexual stimulation. Boredom *does* set in, often after there has been a sexual release. But temporary boredom or release does not change the important fact that the pornography addict *always* comes back for more. A chocolate addict, given a ten-pound

Hershey bar, may devour it, get sick, and not want chocolate for a day or two, but he will come back more hooked than ever, wanting and needing more.

Increased exposure does not lead to indifference but to desensitization, which produces a craving for more potent and destructive stimulation. It is true of drugs and alcohol, and just as true of pornography. It is this ongoing cycle of addiction and desensitization and further addiction and desensitization that demands new depths in sexual perversions. The old turn ons don't work anymore. No wonder that in 1970 the typical cover of a pornographic magazine was of a woman posing alone. By 1983 a survey of seventeen hundred pornographic magazines showed that nine out of ten covers depicted scenes of bondage and domination. The deeper someone gets into pornography, the deeper his tastes and demands for the worst of perversions.

The Truth about Pornography's Effects

The no-effect, catharsis, and boredom theories are wrong. The only view that fits reality is that pornography has significant effects on sexual attitudes, perceptions, drives, morals, behavior, and interpersonal (especially cross-sexual) relationships.

In 1972 London University professor H. J. Eysenck declared:

> It cannot any longer be argued with any degree of conviction that pornography, or the portrayal of violence, has no effect on the behavior of the people who see these things on the screen, or read about them in books or magazines. . . . Both behavior and emotional reactions are affected and the effects are not transitory.[6]

In 1978 Eysenck coauthored *Sex, Violence and the Media*, a scientific collection of data, carefully accumulated and evaluated. He concluded that without a doubt pornography measurably increases one's tolerance of and inclination toward acts of violence, including rape.[7]

Victor Cline reached the same conclusion in an excellent collection of articles on pornography in *Where Do You Draw the Line?*[8] Cline's research affirms that pornography is addicting, desensitizing, and escalating, and that it pushes its users to act out what they see. Similarly, Edward Donnerstein of the University of Wisconsin and Neil Malamuth of UCLA say their research "has shown conclusively that viewing violence—especially sexual assault—has notably spurred male viewers to violent acts toward women."[9]

Police vice squads report that more than three-fourths of child molesters admit they have imitated sexual behavior they have seen in pornography. In the state of Michigan, of thirty-eight thousand reported sexual assault cases in the years 1956-1979, 41 percent involved the use of pornography "just prior to or during the crime."[10] I have in front of me eight newspaper clippings about sexual crimes which specifically mention the criminal's addiction to pornography. Neil Gallagher cites many case histories of hideous crimes, including rape, sodomy, sex torture, and murder, directly linked to viewing pornography.[11]

A Christian View of Pornography?

I am concerned that some Christians leaders are underestimating the seriousness of viewing pornography. A Netherlands pastor states:

> Surely the Christian will be moved more by the human sadness that helps create the pornography market than by his own distaste for the product. There is also the possibility that pornography will lose its appeal once it is on the free and open market for a time. *It is no sin to look at pornography;* but only sadness and frustration can keep people looking at it for long [italics mine].[12]

"Distaste for the product" implies a matter of personal preference—as if the issue was not clear-cut. More troubling is the suggestion that unrestrained distribution of pornography may help the problem. Narcotics are easier than ever to obtain and the result is a bigger problem, not smaller.

Most striking, however, is the categorical statement that looking at pornography is not a sin. Is it *never* a sin? Doesn't pornography stimulate to lust? Didn't Jesus say lust was sin? Isn't it sinful to choose to be stimulated to lust?

Note the logic in this quote from an American evangelical seminary professor:

> Is the person who gets excited by sexually stimulating photographs lusting? The answer must be that it all depends. An adolescent paging through a *Playboy* magazine may be doing more than satisfying his curiosity; but he's not necessarily lusting after those faceless figures of centerfold land. The husband who is distracted, tired, depressed and in general out of tune with his own sexuality, may feel the need of a sexual stimulus that his wife, unfortunately, does not provide. If he sneaks a look at some touched-up picture of an undressed woman, he may, in fact, be merely receiving the stimulus he needs to make love to his wife. Now it may be sad that some men or women need this kind of stimulus; their spouses may have reason to put more life into their own sexual style. But in this real world of pressures and distractions, any person who insists on being the only sexual stimulus in the world for his/her spouse is courting disillusionment.[13]

What this author sees as sad is certainly that, but isn't it also sin? And isn't there a message here that indulging in a little pornography on the side won't *really* hurt anything? That maybe it can even *help* by rekindling attraction to one's spouse?

I have seen men who once, then repeatedly "sneak a look" at pornography and are drawn toward adultery. Often they lose their sexual attraction to the one woman God has given them to enjoy sex with. I have also seen the low self-esteem of real women who have lost their husbands to the fantasy nymphs of

Playboy and Hollywood; who see themselves compared to abnormal female physiques with which they cannot compete. As their husband's sex partner, they feel second-rate and inferior, and their own enjoyment of sex is nil. Dehumanized, degraded, and demoralized, they too are victims of the victimless crime.

The world supplies us with plenty of ammunition to rationalize lust and defend pornography. We don't need any more from the church.

The Pornography-Prostitution-Rape Link

Pornography is related to two other crimes: prostitution and rape. I speak of "crimes" in a moral not a legal sense. Much pornography is legal, even some prostitution is legal, and most abortion is legal. Yet morally, they are all crimes.

Prostitution is the selling of one's body for use in sexual activities. It is a major problem in most cities and is often tied to organized crime, drug abuse, pornography, and illegal activities of every sort.

Prostitutes are both female and male. Most of the women are young, and almost all the males are boys. The customers of both are invariably men. Winked at by society and all too often glorified by the media, prostitution is given a sugar-coated appearance that belies the horrible human exploitation at its base.

The crime of rape occurs with frightening regularity. In 1977, the Department of Justice reported 154,000 cases of rape. The FBI estimated unreported rape cases were at least ten times that number.[14]

It is often stressed that rape is a crime of violence not sex. I don't believe this is entirely true. Though certainly a crime of violence, we should not underestimate the role of sex in the question of how and why the rapist has come to hate and seek vengeance upon women. Often it is a result of prolonged exposure to women as inhuman sex objects—as teases deserving or wanting to be raped.

The marked increase of rape is directly linked, I believe, to the dehumanization of women fostered not only by the fantasies of pornography but by those of the respected media. We have no reason to believe that rape will decrease as long as minds are exposed to sexual myths about women and children and as long as the legal system treats rape as less than a most serious offense. Rape should result, minimally, in long imprisonment without parole. Release should be made only when there is significant evidence that the criminal will not repeat the crime.

So many rapists are released because of insufficient evidence (their word against the woman's), and so many are paroled even if they are convicted, that many women fear revenge if they turn them in. Add to this the personal humiliation rape victims are dragged through (sometimes) by the police and (often) by defense attorneys and the media, and it is no wonder that nine out of ten rapes are never reported.

Rape victims experience wide ranges of personal trauma, including fear, guilt, insecurity, loss of self-respect, and loss of trust, as well as physical symptoms such as headaches, stomach pain, and insomnia (pregnancies by rape sometimes though rarely occur). An excellent book for rape victims and those ministering to them is *Raped,* by Deborah Roberts.[15]

There are countries in which rape is virtually nonexistent. Ours, however, has fostered a sex-saturated climate in which sexual distortions flourish and, therefore, rape thrives. Only by making fundamental changes in our sexual mores will we be able to help American women and children again be safe on their streets and in their homes.

Chapter 7, Notes

1. Randy Frame, "Pornography: Once More into the Trenches," *Christianity Today,* 4 March 1983, 73.

2. *Pornography Fact Sheet* (New York: Women Against Pornography, n.d.).

3. Neil Gallagher, *The Porno Plague* (Minneapolis, Minn.: Bethany House Publishers, 1981), 14-15.

4. *Presidential Commission Report on Obscenity and Pornography* (New York: Bantam, 1970).

5. Gallagher, *Porno Plague*, 173.

6. Quoted in John H. Court, *Pornography: A Christian Critique* (Downers Grove, Ill.: InterVarsity Press, 1980), 78.

7. H. J. Eysenck and D. K. B. Nias, *Sex, Violence and the Media* (New York: St. Marin's Press, 1978).

8. Victor B. Cline, "Comments and Conclusions," in *Where Do You Draw the Line?* ed. Victor B. Cline (Provo, Utah: Brigham Young University Press, 1974), 343-58.

9. *The National Decency Reporter,* May-June 1983, 3.

10. Harry Genet, "Why People Don't Fight Porn," *Christianity Today,* 1 January 1982, 52.

11. Gallagher, *Porno Plague,* 19-25.

12. J. Rinzema, *The Sexual Revolution* (Grand Rapids, Mich.: Wm. B. Eerdmans Publishing Co., 1974), 104.

13. Lewis B. Smedes, *Sex for Christians* (Grand Rapids, Mich.: Wm. B. Eerdmans Publishing Co., 1976), 211-12.

14. *Pornography Fact Sheet*.

15. Deborah Roberts, *Raped* (Grand Rapids, Mich.: Zondervan Publishing House, 1981).

Chapter 8

The Homosexual Movement

*T*he New York Gay Ball in 1965; the police raid on the Stonewall Inn in Greenwich Village in 1969; Gay Pride Week in 1970, where twenty thousand marched in New York City alone—each has been cited as the birth of the homosexual movement.

This movement is no longer poor or unorganized. Its leaders are highly motivated, tactically trained, and heavily financed. They are skilled in communication, education, politics and, often, religion. They are singlemindedly dedicated to one task: making the homosexual lifestyle an integrated and accepted part of American culture.

In a matter of a few decades the homosexual movement has measurably transformed the nation's perception of homosexuality, homosexual behavior, and the homosexual subculture. It has made great strides toward disassociating homosexual behavior from sin, degradation, and disease and identifying it as a legitimate alternative lifestyle.

Twenty years ago no one could have predicted the success of this propaganda effort. If the average citizen of the midsixties were suddenly transported to 1985, he would be shocked to see the level of openness, prominence, and general acceptability achieved by the homosexual movement.

The homosexual movement has come out of the closet; now it is blending into the woodwork. No aspect of American society remains untouched. Those once hostile to it now tolerate it; those once tolerant of it now embrace it. Most of us, Christians included, have gradually acclimated to the commonness of homosexual behavior. We have been and are being desensitized to its unnaturalness and sinfulness. If the next twenty years proceed like the last, homosexuality will be taken for granted by most Americans.

THE HOMOSEXUAL MOVEMENT'S BELIEFS, GOALS, AND CHARACTERISTICS

When I speak of those in the homosexual movement, I mean socially active and politically outspoken homosexuals. I do *not* mean all who have at some time committed homosexual acts, and certainly not those millions who struggle with homosexual temptation. Just as there are nonhomosexuals who defend the cause and are therefore part of the movement, there are innumerable homosexuals who abstain from the lifestyle and still others who do not flaunt or defend their lifestyle but seek to escape it.

To begin to understand the homosexual movement necessitates an awareness of some basic doctrines that govern homosexual attitudes and behavior. Here are some of the major beliefs of the homosexual movement:

1. Homosexuality is an inborn nature—not an illness, not a choice, and not subject to change by an act of the will, psychological therapy, or religious experience.
2. Homosexuality is as natural as heterosexuality, it just happens to occur less frequently. It is not an undesirable condition except for its social

stigma, which is the result of misguided or hateful homophobics.

3. Homosexuals constitute as legitimate a minority as blacks or Chicanos. Homosexual rights are just as valid as women's rights.

4. Homosexuals have made essential contributions to the development of Western culture. (Homosexual literature is often filled with references to famous homosexual artists, musicians, poets, and statesmen.)

5. Homosexuals should openly acknowledge their condition—"come out of the closet"—and live their desired lifestyle. They should be proud, not ashamed, to pursue homosexual relationships.

6. Those homosexuals who embrace the Christian faith (a significant number) argue that God created them as they are, accepts them as they are, and endorses a lifestyle in keeping with the nature he has given them.

Those who have read gay literature know the leaders of the movement mean business. They will make every sacrifice necessary to promote homosexuality as an acceptable and even desirable lifestyle.

The extent of this single-minded commitment to a positive gay image was forcefully illustrated by a homosexual spokesman who decried the "unfair discrimination" of a request, initiated to prevent the possible transfer of AIDS, that promiscuous homosexual males not donate blood. This homosexual leader's entire concern was for the gay image—not the lives of thousands of innocent people who might contract the deadly disease through a contaminated national blood supply.

Goals

The specific goals of the homosexual movement are in keeping with its beliefs, as evidenced by the results of a National

Gay Task Force survey of its members. That survey revealed the following priorities: the right of admitted homosexuals to be public school teachers; the right of homosexuals to adopt children; the passage of the equal rights amendment; the passage of prohomosexual legislation; the removal of antigay policies in government agencies; utilization of the court system to advance the goals of the homosexual movement; and the utilization of the media to promote a positive image of homosexuals.[1]

Characteristics

The gay community is characterized, among other things, by rampant sexually transmitted diseases (STD). According to *The Washington Post,* a survey of four thousand homosexual males indicated well over half had contracted at least one STD.[2] In San Francisco the venereal disease rate is almost twenty-two times the national average.[3] The state of California alone spends twenty million dollars a year to treat homosexual STDs.

The disease problem stems from two elements in the male homosexual subculture. First, the unnatural means of sexual relations result in the exchange of disease-carrying bodily fluids. Second, many homosexual men are extremely promiscuous. The *Village Voice* estimates the number of partners in the life of a male homosexual at more than sixteen hundred. When some New York gay leaders encouraged greater selectivity in sexual relations to avoid AIDS, the Toronto gay newspaper *Body Politic* accused them of "seeking to rip apart the very promiscuous fabric that knits the gay-male community together."[4]

The gay community thrives on the regular contact of its members, largely through the thousands of gay bars across the country. These are, so to speak, the parishes where practicing homosexuals congregate and fellowship—and where those with homosexual temptations visit and are first initiated, then absorbed, into the subculture.

In gay baths men meet and copulate with total strangers and often have sex with multiple partners. Government official Dan Bradley described his first visit to a gay bath: "I must have had sex with ten different guys that first night. I was like a kid in a candy store."[5] The baths allow sexual relations in front of others or in private cubicles, often without even the exchange of names. Some bath houses or "gay health clubs" have rooms for group sex and pornographic movies.

Gay leather shops sell spiked collars, whips, and pain-inflicting devices designed to heighten sexual pleasure. Sadism and masochism parlors amount to sexual torture chambers that defy description. Sometimes they employ medical personnel to treat wounds and apply stitches to damaged genitalia.

Many who avoid the gay bars and baths buy sexual favors regularly. In 1976 one researcher estimated there were more than 300,000 boy prostitutes in the United States. In 1978 the business of homosexual prostitution grossed about two billion dollars.[6]

The homosexual movement maintains an extensive communications network. It has its pornographic magazines such as *BlueBoy* (estimated readership 800,000). But more importantly, it has its weekly or monthly newspapers that are widely circulated in the gay community. Typical of these is a Portland paper, *The Cascade Voice,* a large forty-eight page tabloid issued every three weeks. It is full of sexually graphic advertisements, including seminude and sadomasochistic pictures, female impersonators, and classified ads requesting sex partners. It lists dozens of Portland homosexual gatherings and events coming up in the next week alone—and seventy-five in the next three weeks.

A New York organization, "Man to Man," matches homosexuals via computer and promises fourteen new contacts per month. Police have found catalogs of between fifty thousand and a hundred thousand men and boys advertising or seeking homosexual favors. "Gay Guides" describe complex codes consisting of the colors and positioning of handkerchiefs on the hip for use in gay bars, where one can indicate the type of sex he wants, choosing from a dozen or more different options. The *Queen's Vernacular* is a lexicon of over twelve thousand words that explains the distinctive language of the gay subculture.

In his monumental work, *The Homosexual Network,* Father Enrique Rueda makes this telling observation:

It would be accurate to describe the homosexual sub-culture as a complex web of interlocking organizations and institutions which, while resocializing its members, provides them with political, social, psychological (and at times even economic) support. Once a person becomes involved in this sub-culture, he has little or no reason to leave it; immersion in the sub-culture may become total. Some of the elements of the sub-culture even facilitate the relief from sexual needs which undoubtedly assail every homosexual. Strange as it may appear, becoming a full-fledged member of the homosexual sub-culture entails centering one's life on one's sexual peculiarities. It constitutes an ever-stronger bonding of the homosexual to others like himself, objectively decreasing the individual's freedom even as it provides him with a sense of liberation. From a traditional point of view, this is no liberation at all, but rather enslavement to an all-consuming passion. In short, "gay liberation" is not merely the acquisition of social and political privileges as a "legitimate minority," but a freeing of the homosexual to seek the complete satisfaction of his sexual appetites without the restrictions which children, family responsibility, and the tenets of the Judeo-Christian ethic impose on heterosexuals. In this way, the homosexual sub-culture is solidly anchored in the psychological needs of its members which, in turn, it heightens. The more deeply the homosexual participates in "his" sub-culture, the stronger is his condition. Conversely, the deeper the homosexuality, the stronger the sub-culture in which he subsists.[7]

Increasing Respectability and Acceptance of the Homosexual Movement

I have spoken with homosexuals who are embarrassed by the seamy side of the movement seen in the bars, baths, and inner-city activities. They are concerned with more than sexual relations and seek to promote more socially respectable and professional forms. Distinctively homosexual businesses are increasingly common. There are not only gay restaurants but gay dental practices, gay insurance agencies, and at least one gay savings and loan. A homosexual newspaper advertises Realty Referrals, a "free nationwide service which puts you in touch with an agent who appreciates your lifestyle and knows the local gay community where you are about to buy or sell."

Gay student organizations that were once nonexistent and then underground are now almost as accepted as speech clubs and ski teams. Often they are involved in the school newspapers and use them for prohomosexual propaganda.

Homosexual organizations abound among many professions, including psychologists, public health workers, counselors, lawyers, and educators. And virtually every city of any size has organizations such as Boston's Gay and Lesbian Advocates and Defenders, and Houston's Gay Political Caucus. Sometimes the names of these organizations only hint at their true identity, such as Bachelor Lawyers of Washington. Other times there is no hint at all. The Portland Town Council is a powerful homosexual political organization that mobilizes the gay voting bloc and sways nongays in the process.

Even nonhomosexual organizations such as the American Library Association, which finances its own Gay Task Force, have helped further the movement's aims. In 1973 the board of the American Psychiatric Association, under pressure from the National Gay Task Force, changed its official position by declaring that homosexuality was not an illness. Many of the twenty-five thousand member psychiatrists were outraged and called for a mail referendum on the issue. The National Gay Task Force engineered a massive mail campaign lobbying for support of the board's decision. Signed by three prominent psychiatrists, the letter failed to mention it was engineered and distributed by a homosexual organization. The board's decision narrowly passed. As a result, the official position of the psychiatric community is that homosexuality is no longer an illness.

Given this backdrop, it should come as no surprise that the media, educators, government agencies, legislative bodies, and the courts are increasingly portraying homosexuality in a more favorable light. This shift in attitude toward homosexuality has been so pervasive that many educated people look with disdain upon those who still object to the homosexual lifestyle. Tragically, the most potent endorsement of the homosexual movement has come from the organized church.

HOMOSEXUALITY AND THE CHRISTIAN FAITH

In the literature of forty years ago it is difficult to find any serious defenses of homosexuality by professing Christians. One of the first, and certainly the most significant, was Derrick Sherwin Bailey's *Homosexuality and the Western Christian Tradition,* published in 1955. An Anglican, Bailey opened the door to rethinking a matter of ethics that had always stood on the surest ground among Christians. Prior to his study, the defense of homosexual behavior was restricted only to those who clearly rejected biblical authority.[8]

Only sixteen years after Bailey's work, a United Methodist church in San Francisco married two homosexual men, to the applause and cheers of five hundred others. Ten years later, the First United Methodist Church of Boulder, Colorado, kept Rev. Julian Rush as minister of youth and education despite his publicly acknowledged homosexuality and his active role in Denver's Gay and Lesbian Community Center. Later two admitted homosexuals were ordained to the Methodist ministry, though in 1984 the denomination voted to prohibit such actions in the future.

In 1976 the New York City Presbytery asked the denomination for guidance on whether to ordain an avowed homosexual under its jurisdiction. A nineteen member task force studied the issue. Fourteen of the nineteen saw no overriding moral principle to prevent such an action and recommended that decisions be made by the local presbyteries and sessions.

Writing in *Christian Century* in 1982, Mary V. Borhek says she once "believed that homosexuality was an abomination to God." Since learning her son was gay, she says, "I have done a 180 degree reversal." She has written a book on her theological enlightenment and transferred her membership to a church favorable to homosexuality. She goes on to suggest it is "heretical" (note the religious term) to resist affiliation with those churches that advocate homosexual practices.[9]

A well-known church in Portland recently took out a large ad in the Sunday paper. Prominent was the figure of a dove, symbolizing the presence and power of the Holy Spirit. As a ministry to the surrounding community, the church was featuring a concert of sacred music—performed by the Gay Men's Chorus.

The Homosexual Movement's Greatest Ally

How the Christian religion deals with homosexuality is of paramount importance to the homosexual movement for, despite our "post-Christian era," the Christian religion remains a powerful force in America.

Religion and morality have always been two sides of the same coin. Nothing affects attitudes, behavior, and tolerance levels like religious beliefs. Therefore, if any cause is to find acceptance it *must* win over the churches. This is especially true of any cause that apparently violates traditional church doctrines. Undoubtedly, the church is the last barrier between the homosexual movement and general social acceptability.

> There is no question that the main stumbling block in the theoretical and practical acceptance of homosexuality by American society has been traditional religion. This has been perfectly understood by the

leadership of the homosexual movement. For many years systematic efforts to utilize religion in support of homosexuality have been implemented not only by the founding of religious organizations which cater almost exclusively to homosexuals while purporting to justify their sexual propensities and activities, but also by the establishment of organizations within other religious institutions for the purpose of using them for the promotion of the homosexual ideology.[10]

How the church portrays the homosexual lifestyle will determine the beliefs of many, whether or not that portrayal is in harmony with Scripture. Consequently, the prohomosexual movement has infiltrated all but the most conservative and traditional U.S. denominations. Indeed, many homosexual leaders are themselves seminary trained, and many clergyman have adopted the dual roles of leaders in the church *and* the homosexual movement.

Millions of Protestant and Catholic church-goers have no idea that a portion of their Sunday morning offerings goes to homosexual organizations, including some within their own denomination. Neither do they realize that the facilities their donations buy and maintain are used by homosexual organizations to raise funds for their causes.[11]

The sad truth is that large segments of the church have become pawns in the hands of the homosexual movement. In doing so, they have poured on the ground the healing elixir that could meet the needs of homosexuals in search of cleansing, peace, and fulfillment.

Evangelical Gays

It would be easy to conclude only liberal churches endorse the homosexual lifestyle. On the contrary, the largest homosexual denomination in the country is the "evangelical" Universal Fellowship of Metropolitan Community Churches (UFMCC).

The first Metropolitan Community Church was founded in Los Angeles in 1966 by Rev. Troy Perry, formerly an ordained Pentecostal minister and author of *The Lord Is My Shepherd and He Knows I'm Gay.* In six years Metropolitan boasted more than thirty-nine chartered congregations and forty-three missions and study groups, with a combined membership exceeding seventeen thousand. In ten years it grew to sixty-seven thousand, in well over a hundred locations across the world.

When I contacted a Metropolitan church, I found warmth and an apparently Christ-centered mentality. Their doctrinal statement was solidly evangelical. They believe in the deity of Christ, the virgin birth, the resurrection, and salvation by grace. They promote evangelistic outreach. They perform evangelical weddings but with one twist—most couples married are of the same sex.

Gay Theology

Gay theology is an attempt to biblically defend the homosexual lifestyle. It is infecting major segments of the church. Among the common teachings of gay theology—many of them rooted in D. S. Bailey's classic study—are the following:

1. The sin of Sodom was inhospitality, not homosexuality (specifically contradicting Jude 7).
2. The Old Testament prohibitions against homosexuality are in the same class with prohibitions against eating rabbits and oysters and picking up sticks on the Sabbath; in other words, they are no longer relevant.
3. Prohibitions against homosexuality were applied only to priests, and even then for matters of ritual and symbolic purity.
4. Homosexuality was prohibited because of Israel's obsession with population growth.
5. Jesus never condemned homosexuality.
6. David and Jonathan, the apostle Paul, and Jesus himself may have been homosexuals.

The Homosexual Is My Neighbor,
But Is the Bible My Authority?

Unfortunately some evangelical Christians—characterized by admirable compassion but careless Bible study—have themselves propagated and legitimized aspects of gay theology.

In *Is The Homosexual My Neighbor?* Letha Scanzoni and Virginia Ramey Mollenkott state, "the time now seems ripe to take an altogether new approach to homosexuality."[12] Their approach is new to evangelicalism but is almost indistinguishable from the trends in both the secular world and liberal Protestantism. The only difference appears to be that Scripture is used to defend what once seemed indefensible: homosexual behavior.

Rightly pointing out how ugly and destructive homophobia can be, Scanzoni and Mollenkott try to atone for the church's mistreatment of homosexuals by telling them they really don't have a problem. The authors retell Norman Pittenger's story of two men in a faithful homosexual relationship who "found great joy in sexually celebrating their love on Saturday night and then kneeling side by side the next morning to take Holy Communion together." Pittenger said what these men did was "both beautiful and right," and the context seems clearly to suggest that Scanzoni and Mollenkott agree.[13]

The same authors see homosexual contact as "not at all 'unnatural' if we are going to use practices in the animal world as our criteria." They attempt to prove their point by citing recent research about lesbian seagulls.[14] Scanzoni and Mollenkott go on not only to defend but actually encourage the role of homosexual teachers in our schools.[15]

The reader is left with the impression that any Christian who does not either reject or reinterpret the clear biblical proscription of homosexual behavior is a homophobic who does not love, care for, or understand homosexuals. This despite the fact that many prominent need-meeting outreaches to homosexuals (e.g., Love in Action and Outposts) are staffed primarily by "ex-gays" who themselves wholeheartedly affirm Scripture's condemnation of homosexual behavior. Instead of writing books defending or Christianizing the homosexual movement, these ministries are reaching out in love to bring the power and purity of Christ to homosexuals tired of sin and seeking new life and hope. (What Scripture says about homosexuality and how the church can help the homosexual will be discussed later in this book.)

CONCLUSION

When Christians claim that God did not create homosexuality, that he rejects and judges homosexual behavior, militant homosexuals become angry. When they claim that God forgives and cleanses homosexuality, they are offended ("Who needs forgiveness?"). But when Christians claim that the power of God can help homosexuals break out of their lifestyle, they are outraged. For if God can empower men and women to live in sexual purity, then the homosexual movement is stripped of its most basic tenet: that homosexuality is not a choice and that restraining homosexual drives and abstaining from homosexual behavior is either unnatural or impossible.

That Christians should incur the wrath of the homosexual movement for such a position is understandable. That they should incur the wrath of fellow Christians is tragic.

I am well aware some genuine believers struggle with homosexual desires. I have counseled many of them. Numbers of them are in churches where they need to be reached out to in love and helped to cultivate sexually pure lives. But it does them no good—and much harm—to tell them they have no problem, or they are unchangeable, or that God accepts homosexual behavior, promiscuous or otherwise, whether inside "marriage" or not. They need to hear from us not baptized echos of the world's voice but the ancient yet timeless voice of Scripture. We must give them God's Word not man's, grain not straw (Jeremiah 23:28).

Through its masterful use of the power of both politics and religion, the homosexual movement has succeeded in radically affecting the sexual morality of millions of Americans . . . altering, perhaps forever, our most fundamental sexual perceptions and passing on to future generations an entirely different view of human sexuality.

Chapter 8, Notes
_____

1. Enrique T. Rueda, *The Homosexual Network* (Old Greenwich, Conn.: The Devin Adair Co., 1982), 214.

2. *The Washington Post,* 1 September 1981, sec. A.

3. Rueda, *Homosexual Network,* 53.

4. B. D. Colen, "Is There Death After Sex?" *Rolling Stone,* 3 February 1983, 18.

5. Taylor Branch, "Closets of Power," *Harper's,* October 1982, 39.

6. Rueda, *Homosexual Network,* 186.

7. Ibid., 46.

8. Derrick Sherwin Bailey, *Homosexuality and the Western Christian Tradition* (London: Longemans, Green and Co., 1955).

9. Mary V. Borhek, "Can the NCC Accept a Gay Denomination?" *Christian Century,* 14 April 1982, 461.

10. Rueda, *Homosexual Network,* 243.

11. The first Conference of the Pederast NAMBLA (the North American Man/Boy Association) was held in a Boston church in 1978. Speakers included an Episcopalian pastor, a Catholic priest, and a Unitarian minister.

The United Church of Christ, American Lutheran Church, and many others have lended support to homosexual clergy, congregations, and supported same sex marriages.

Homosexual organizations exist in many Christian denominations. Among them are the American Baptist Gay Caucus, the Friends Committee for Gay Concerns, the Presbyterian Gay Caucus, the United Church of Christ Gay Caucus, and the United Methodist Gay Caucus. There are innumerable independent groups like the Chicago Gay Seminarians and Clergy, and the publishers of the *Gay Theological Journal.* Many other groups have titles that do not reflect their homosexual identity, such as Lutherans Concerned and Evangelicals Concerned.

The Catholic prohomosexual chapters are called Dignity and the Episcopalian, Integrity. Dignity has at least ninety U.S. chapters and Integrity at least forty (Rueda, *Homosexual Network,* 588-97). A recent Dignity convention in Seattle attracted six hundred Catholic homosexuals and lesbians, and they were welcomed via videotape by the archbishop, who was away visiting Rome at the time.

12. Letha Scanzoni and Virginia Ramey Mollenkott, *Is the Homosexual My Neighbor?* (San Francisco: Harper and Row, 1978), 116.

13. Ibid., 62-63.

14. Ibid., 65.

15. Ibid., 102-3.

Chapter 9

Sexual Morality and the Future of America

*E*ven a casual reading of the previous chapters should make clear that America's moral decline is bringing severe consequences. No society can rise above its treatment of sex.

Nothing is free, least of all sex, which is bound to our deepest sources of energy, identity, and emotion. Sex can be cheapened, of course, but then, inevitably, it becomes extremely costly to society as a whole. For sex is the life force—a cohesive impulse—of a people, and their very character will be deeply affected by how sexuality is managed, sublimated, expressed, denied, and propagated. When sex is devalued, propagandized, and deformed, as at present, the quality of our lives declines and our social fabric deteriorates.[1]

Righteousness exalts a nation,
   but sin is a disgrace to any people.
                    (Proverbs 14:34)

Our coinage reminds us there was a time when America, for the most part, could say "In God We Trust." That time is no longer. Not only do we live in what Francis Schaeffer called a post-Christian era, but an often anti-Christian one. After the U.S. Supreme Court bowed to the secularist movement by legalizing abortion on demand in 1973, *Christianity Today* offered this sobering reflection:

> Christians should accustom themselves to the thought that the American state no longer supports, in any meaningful sense, the laws of God, and prepare themselves spiritually for the prospect that it may one day formally repudiate them and turn against those who seek to live by them.[2]

There is a subtle irony about a society that prohibits the distribution of Bibles in school classrooms but allows them in jail cells. We want divine principles to reform our criminals but not corrupt our young.

When God is rejected or, even worse, ignored, ultimate authority is gone and moral chaos reigns—though by virtue of habit the society may for some time still appear civilized. With God recalled from his divine office by a secular society, man has been left in charge. It isn't working. Like those whose "god is their stomach" (Philippians 3:19), the modern American lives by appetite and desire, not wisdom and righteousness. The old structures of discipline and dedication (erected when biblical values prevailed) still stand enough to prevent total social collapse. But for how long?

Symptoms of a God-Forsaking Nation

Larry Crabb uses the following chart to display the progression of spiritual and moral deterioration in an individual.[3] It also applies to any society composed of many such individuals. The chart is essentially a visualization of Romans 1:18-32.

STAGE A	STAGE B	STAGE C
Basic human needs can be met only by God ↓	Without God the highest needs which can be met ↓	Inevitable long-term consequences of a life without God ↓
Significance ⟶	Power ⟶	Violence
Security ⟶	Pleasure ⟶	Immorality

As the chart indicates, if human beings do not meet their needs for significance and security in God, they pursue other alternatives. Power is a substitute for significance, pleasure a counterfeit for security. Since these do not ultimately meet human needs (only God can), in desperation power is abused (hence violence) and pleasure is enthroned (hence immorality).

Both violence and immorality characterized Israel in the days of the judges (Judges 19-21). The merger of violence and immorality in a society surfaces in violent sexual crimes such as rape, child molesting, and sex slayings—and, in our case, in the glorification of such crime through the media.

A most significant aspect of this social deterioration is the staggering increase in family violence. More murders are committed by a family member of the victim than anyone else. Wife beating and child abuse have risen to alarming rates. Adultery and incest have decimated countless homes. Innumerable families are shattered by violence and immorality.

The family is the glue of society; peace and purity the glue of the family. God is the giver of peace and purity; the church their facilitator and enforcer. But immorality's stranglehold on both family and church has prevented them from reversing society's downward spiral. The result is weakening moral fiber on every hand—a scattered family, an anemic church, a dying society.

Who Are Our Heroes?

Much can be determined about a nation's ideals and future welfare by the character of its models. Who are the most admired people in America? Spiritual leaders, civil leaders, altruistic social reformers? Hardly.

The heroes and idols of America are actors and actresses, jet-setters and yacht owners, entertainers and rock stars. With a glass of wine or a joint in one hand and somebody else's mate in the other, they prance, jiggle, curse, and swindle their way into the hearts of Americans. Our homage to such celebrities tells us as much about us—and our probable destiny—as it does them.

Meanwhile many of our leaders, men and women once respected, have disillusioned us. They have proven themselves as morally bankrupt as we, and often worse. One congressman stands before his colleagues and says his sexual relations with a young boy page are part of his private life and "nobody else's business." A year later he runs for reelection. Another congressman boasts to his constituents that he is dating a girl whose picture was on the cover of *Playboy*.[4]

When government officials patronize prostitutes, cheat on their wives, and do political obeisance to the demands of homosexual, feminist, and other antifamily movements, they reinforce the stereotype of the corrupt politician, leaving Americans skeptical of other leaders who may be true models of morality and integrity. (The same is true in the church—whose leaders are condemned as hypocrites because of the moral weakness of their colleagues.)

Morality Is Morality

Sexual morality cannot be isolated from the whole gamut of ethics. Will a man who cheats on his wife hesitate to cheat on his time clock? Will a woman who breaks her sacred vow to her husband refrain from breaking a promise to her customers?

Consider how many people cheat on their taxes, thereby robbing their neighbors. *Time* states that in a sample of four hundred nurses, nine out of ten failed to report all their income—the *average* owed $3,500 in back taxes. In the last decade, the difference between taxes owed and taxes paid has risen from 29 million to over 100 billion dollars.[5]

West Point and other elite schools have suffered major scandals over students cheating on homework and tests. Countless phony diploma mills and degree factories constitute a multi-million dollar business in America, pandering to deceit, oversized egos, and a society that winks at both.

At a workshop I attended on teen prostitution, one agency employee asked the leader, a government funded researcher, "How can we get more federal funds for our project?" The leader's unflinching response, in front of a hundred of us, was: "You just lie—give big impressive numbers on your reports and you'll get your grants and funds." The same leader earlier made a major point about professional ethics in counseling teen prostitutes.

It is this kind of dishonesty, among respectable people, that can ruin a democracy and free enterprise system. Such ethical erosion poses an alarming threat to our whole way of life.

A Self-Centered and Self-Serving Citizenry

The preoccupation with personal rights rather than personal responsibilities is taking an incalculable toll on this nation. Sociologist Amitai Etzioni calls it the "hollowing of America," the new "ego-centered mentality" rooted in individualism and the psychology of self.

The deification of one's right to happiness (meaning "the right to do whatever I want") quickly steps over the line of other people's right to happiness. When I heard a rapist and murderer say recently, "I'm glad I did it," I thought of Hemingway's maxim: "What is moral is what you feel good after."

This "me first" mentality has led not only to violent crime but sexual promiscuity, drug abuse, alcoholism, embezzlement, shoplifting, vandalism, juvenile delinquency of every sort, and, perhaps most tragically, abortion on demand and its corollary, infanticide of the deformed and "unfit."

Harvard sociology professor Pitirim Sorokin wrote almost thirty years ago:

No law-abiding and morally strong society is possible when a large number of its members are selfish nihilists preoccupied with pleasure. For inevitably such men and women come into conflict with one another, and are led to chronic violation of moral and legal imperatives and to endless transgression of the vital interests of each other. There results a progressive undermining of the existing legal and moral order, and a perennial war among members of the collectivity seeking a maximum share of material possessions and gratifications. In this struggle the established code of the society is repeatedly broken; standards of conduct are increasingly trespassed, and ultimately they lose their authority and control over individual behavior. The society drifts closer and closer to a state of moral anarchy in which everyone regards himself as law giver and judge entitled to juggle all moral and legal standards as he pleases.

With moral stamina thus weakened, the society loses its inner solidarity and the civic virtues necessary for its well being. Its internal peace is increasingly broken by disturbances and revolts, its security chronically punctured by brutal forces of criminality.

The sex-obsessed society unhesitatingly breaks both divine and human law, blows to smithereens all values. Like a tornado, it leaves in its path a legion of corpses, a multitude of wrecked lives, an untold amount of suffering, and an ugly debris of broken standards. It destroys the real freedom of normal love; and in lieu of enriching and ennobling the sexual passion, it reduces it to mere copulation.

The destructive consequences of sexual anarchy extend over all the main values, and go deep into the vitals, of the society. Its obsession leads, first of all, to the degradation of both man and society. All the mental, moral, cultural, and social characteristics of homo sapiens become the handmaids of the sexual master. From their very youth, the members of such a society are habituated to look at the opposite sex as a mere instrument for pleasure. To these individuals, talk of human dignity, religious and moral commandments, and rules of decency is just bosh.

Similarly, the society degrades the values of womanhood and manhood, of motherhood and fatherhood, of childhood and venerable age, of marriage and family, and even of love itself. These concepts are made to seem ugly and ignoble, they are dragged into the muddy water of the social sewer, mixed with its filth and ground into the sexual muck. It is no wonder, then, that in such a society no child, no adult, is secure. And it is no surprise that the urban centers prove to be more dangerous than the wildest jungles.[6]

It is symptomatic of American moral decline that many of the worst offenses are defended on the basis of the Constitution and civil liberties, though the Constitution and its Amendments were never intended to grant freedom of perversion and exploitation. The misuse of the Constitution may well result in the eventual destruction of the country the Constitution was written to protect.

Tax money is funneled to proabortion, homosexual, and feminist groups. Criminals go in and out the revolving doors of America's prisons. The courts show leniency to known murderers, rapists, child molesters, and pornographers while they defend the slaughter of the unborn and the imprisonment of fathers who insist their children be taught biblical and moral principles in a church school uncontrolled by the state. In short, we are becoming masters at acquitting the guilty and condemning the innocent (Proverbs 17:15).

Learning from Other Nations

The sexual revolutions of other modern nations should serve as a warning to us. Premarital sex is much higher in

Sweden and Denmark than in our own country, and pornography is rampant. In Zurich, Switzerland, prostitution is now legal. In one district the prostitutes are free to solicit from 8 P.M. to 3 A.M. But a coalition has petitioned to begin their work shift at 5 P.M. in order to catch the commuter crowd right after work and to give them more time with their children in the evening.[7]

Sorokin wrote of Russia's "sexual liberation" under Lenin and the fascinating results:

> One could marry and divorce as many times as desired. Husband or wife could obtain a divorce without the other being notified. It was not even necessary that "marriages" be registered. Bigamy and even polygamy were permissible under the new provisions. Abortion was facilitated at state institutions. Premarital relations were praised, and extramarital relations were considered normal. . . .
>
> Within a few years, hordes of wild, homeless children became a real menace to the Soviet Union itself. Millions of lives, especially young girls, were wrecked; divorces skyrocketed, as also did abortions. The hatreds and conflicts among polygamous and polyandrous mates rapidly mounted,—and so did psychoneuroses. Work in the nationalized factories slackened.
>
> The total results were so appalling that the government was forced to reverse its policy. The propaganda of "the glass of water" theory [that satisfying sex drives was no different than satisfying thirst] was declared to be counter-revolutionary, and its place was taken by official glorification of premarital chastity and of the sanctity of marriage. . . .
>
> Considering that the whole cycle occurred under a single regime, the experiment is highly informative. It clearly shows the destructive consequences of unlimited sex freedom, especially in regard to creative growth. In the period from 1918 to 1926, when that

freedom was fostered, the Soviet government was preoccupied with destructive work, and the imprisoned Russian nation was unable to achieve much in the task of positive reorganization or creative cultural growth.

After 1930, when the task of curbing sex freedom was essentially accomplished, the destructive activities of the government began to subside, and its constructive work gained momentum. Increasingly fruitful were the efforts toward industrialization and economic growth, the building of the armed forces, the rapid development of schools, hospitals, and research institutes, the fostering of the physical and even the social sciences, and of the humanities. There followed a renaissance of the fine arts and literature, a notable decrease of the previous persecution of religion, and a restoration and glorification of the great national values of Russia, which had in the preceding period been vilified by the Communist regime.[8]

The twentieth century is not the first to see society riddled with immorality. The ancient Greeks elevated loose women, homosexual relations, and pedophilia. The Romans gradually surrendered the strong families and morals that once made them great, replacing them with laxity and weakness. The often-made comparisons between the final years of Rome and modern day America are striking—self-indulgence, political corruption, adultery, homosexuality, sexual orgies, live sex acts in the theater, brutal sports in the arena, and a creeping family deterioration and moral laziness that led to self-destruction.

When the ruling group and the society as a whole relax their code [of sexual morality], within three generations there is usually a cultural decline, as was the case in the later stages of the Babylonian, the Persian, the Macedonian, the Mongol, the Greek, and the Roman civilizations. . . . We find that among civilized societies those which have remained strict in their sexual codes for the longest period have reached the highest levels.[9]

Historian Arnold Toynbee likewise concluded that a society's creative energy is tied to the control of sexual drives. Sexual self-control is linked directly to national strength and accomplishment; lack of self-control with national weakness and deterioration. Toynbee's research indicated that of history's twenty-one greatest civilizations, nineteen perished from internal moral corruption, not external enemies.

After ten years of relentless research of more than eighty civilizations, J. D. Unwin concluded, "Any human society is free to choose either to display great energy or to enjoy sexual freedom: the evidence is that it cannot do both for more than one generation."[10] C. S. Lewis came to a similar conclusion in his essay "We Have No 'Right to Happiness'":

> Though the "right to happiness" is chiefly claimed for the sexual impulse, it seems to me impossible that the matter should stay there. The fatal principle, once allowed in that department, must sooner or later seep through our whole lives. We thus advance toward a state of society in which not only each man but every impulse in each man claims *carte blanche*. And then, though our technological skill may help us survive a little longer, our civilization will have died at heart, and will—one dare not even add "unfortunately"—be swept away.[11]

Unless there is spiritual repentance and a massive reversal of moral values in this country—unless Christians take the role outlined in our final three chapters—Ruth Graham is right: "If God doesn't judge America, He'll owe Sodom and Gomorrah an apology."

We should not forget that in Sodom's sexual revolution, God fired the last round.

Chapter 9, Notes

1. George Gilder, *Sexual Suicide* (New York: The New York Times Book Co., 1973), 1.

2. "Abortion and the Court," *Christianity Today,* 16 February 1973, 33.

3. Lawrence J. Crabb, Jr., *Effective Biblical Counseling* (Grand Rapids, Mich.: Zondervan Publishing House, 1977), 72.

4. *USA Today,* 1 September 1983, sec. A.

5. Otto Friedrich, "Cheating by the Millions," *Time,* 28 March 1983, 26-33.

6. Pitirim Sorokin, *The American Sexual Revolution* (New York: Porter Sargent, 1956), 88-89.

7. *USA Today,* 7 February 1983.

8. Sorokin, *Sexual Revolution,* 114-15.

9. Ibid., 111.

10. J. D. Unwin, quoted by Arnold Lunn and Garth Lean, *The New Morality* (London: Blanford Press, 1964), 25.

11. C. S. Lewis, *God in the Dock* (Grand Rapids, Mich.: Wm. B. Eerdmans Publishing Co., 1970), 322.

Chapter 10

Backlash to the Great Sex Swindle

*L*enina shook her head. "Somehow," she mused, "I haven't been feeling very keen on promiscuity lately. There are times when one doesn't. Haven't you found that too, Fanny?"

Fanny nodded her sympathy and understanding. "But one's got to make the effort," she said sententiously, "one's got to play the game. After all, every one belongs to every one else."

"Yes, every one belongs to every one else," Lenina repeated slowly and, sighing, was silent for a moment: then, taking Fanny's hand, gave it a little squeeze. "You're quite right, Fanny. As usual, I'll make the effort."

This dialogue from Aldous Huxley's *Brave New World* illustrates what happens to sex when it is ripped from the protective moorings of marriage. It becomes bland, boring, empty, and meaningless. It leaves one wondering what it was that used to seem so great about sex. And that is precisely what has happened in our own brave new world.

Many people are now beginning to question the joys of "sex." A September 1980 *Cosmopolitan* magazine survey of more than 106,000 women showed that a revolution had indeed taken place in sexual behavior as well as in attitude. But a majority of the women surveyed indicated their disillusionment and disappointment with "the emotional fruit the sexual revolution has borne." According to the *Cosmopolitan* report, "So many readers wrote negatively about the sexual revolution, expressing longings for vanished intimacy, and the now elusive joys of romance and commitment, that we've begun to sense that there might be a sexual counterrevolution underway in America."[1]

Discovering the Hidden Costs of Free Sex

In 1969 psychotherapist Rollo May wrote *Love and Will*, called by the *New York Times* "the most important book of the year." Right as the sexual revolution was rising to a pitch, May stated:

> By anesthetizing feeling in order to perform better, by employing sex as a tool to prove prowess and identity, by using sensuality to hide sensitivity, we have emasculated sex and left it vapid and empty. The banalization of sex is well-aided and abetted by our mass communication. For the plethora of books on sex and love which flood the market have one thing in common—they oversimplify love and sex, treating the topic like a combination of learning to play tennis and buying life insurance. In this process, we have robbed sex of its power.[2]

George Leonard, once a strong proponent of the sexual revolution, would have taken issue with May in 1969. By 1982, however, he had changed his tune:

As for "sex" it has become something you "have." You have a car, you have dinner, you have a swim, you have the chickenpox . . . and you have sex. . . .

Casual recreational sex is hardly a feast—not even a good, hearty sandwich. It is a diet of fast foods served in plastic containers. . . . Indiscriminate, obligatory "getting-it-on" is losing its charm. The best-kept secret of the sexual revolution is at last coming out of the closet; what people want most of all (though sometimes they can hardly bear to say it) is a return to the personal in all things—especially in erotic love.[3]

Author of *The End of Sex* and a frequent talk-show guest, Leonard coined the expression "high monogamy"—his term for the radical idea of the lifelong commitment of two partners to "erotic exclusivity," sex only with each other. (Sounds suspiciously like marriage, doesn't it?)

Writing in *New York* magazine, Fran Schumer quotes a veteran of the sexual revolution:

"It doesn't surprise anyone when you say 'Good night' these days," she says. "People aren't interested in sex. They'd rather have someone they can see than someone they don't want to face the next day because they went to bed with them prematurely."

This is not the kind of frank admission anyone could have made ten years ago, when the sexual revolution was just hitting its stride. That movement appears to have moved ahead in its life cycle. People are saying "No" more and sleeping around less. The one-night stand has lost a measure of allure: in its stead are relationships. Words like "commitment" and "responsibility" command new respect, as do "intimacy" and "love." Its stormy adolescence behind it, a movement spawned in reaction to 50's taboos is now heading placidly to middle age. . . .

Indeed, a generation that skipped the hand-holding stage of adolescence is rediscovering dating. There's romance instead of lust, courtship in place of seduction. Pushed into the closet by the revolution, virginity has pushed its way back out.[4]

Some social gauges reflect this backlash to the sexual revolution. In 1982, for the first time in twenty years, the divorce rate dropped and an unprecedented 2.5 million couples married.[5] A recent Harris Poll indicates that three-fourths of Americans feel "society stresses the importance of sex too much," and despite behavior of some to the contrary, a full 96 percent believe it is important for both men and women to be faithful to their spouse.[6]

Why this rash of sexual conservativism? Boredom may be part of it. But many people are not just bored; they are hurt. They view the revolution with a jaundiced eye. They see it as a Trojan horse that promised treasure while it bootlegged in disaster. They're victims of a great sex rip-off—and they're beginning to resent it.

Where Are They When You Need Them?

"Where are the pied pipers of promiscuity when you need them?" people are beginning to ask. Who are these sultans of sex and gurus of sleaze who sell us the movies, television shows, magazines, and products that titillate and seduce us but leave us empty? Why have we listened to men whose consciences are governed only by their bank accounts?

Where is Planned Parenthood when a sixteen-year-old girl they convinced to get an abortion (without telling her parents) commits suicide because she couldn't handle the guilt? Where is the judicial system and parole board when your eight-year-old son is forced into sodomy by a repeat offender they let out of prison? Where is the ACLU when your sister is tortured and raped by a pornography addict glutted with the sadomasochistic mind-poison they've defended with the First Amendment?

Where are the gender-diluting feminists and gay activists when your family is ripped apart by the pain of one member's submersion into the homosexual subculture? Where are the romance novelists when a girl has given herself sexually only to men she's loved, but all of them are gone, and she is left lonely and bitter? Where is the television scriptwriter, magazine editor, or novelist when your wife is finally convinced the grass is greener elsewhere and leaves you for another man?

While the media glorify affairs, many find out the hard way they've been lied to. In a recent survey of women, 40 percent indicated they had extramarital affairs, three-fourths of those because they were emotionally unsatisfied with their husbands. However, less than half the women who had affairs said they even enjoyed extramarital sex—not to mention the devastating consequences.[7]

Some women are finally waking up to the infuriating truth: rather than benefiting from it (as they've been incessantly told), they are in fact the revolution's victims. Though the sexual revolution told women their sexual nature was like men's—that they could enjoy sex without commitment—millions have found out the hard way that this is simply a lie.

Why Women Are the Revolution's Greatest Victims

The issue of gender differences is aptly addressed by anthropologist Donald Symons in *The Evolution of Human Sexuality*. He believes the acid test of the extent of male-female sexual differences is found in homosexual relationships—where men and women are not forced to compromise with the opposite sex.

> There is a substantial male homosexual market for pornography and no lesbian market whatsoever. This suggests that the tendency to be sexually aroused by "objectified" visual stimuli is simply a male tendency, not an expression of contempt for women.
>
> The tremendous importance of physical attractiveness and youth in determining sexual desirability

among both homosexual and heterosexual men implies that these criteria are relatively innate in men.

Knowledge of a potential partner's character—even via a brief conversation—can sometimes diminish a male's sexual interest by interfering with his fantasies. A female's sexual interest usually requires knowledge of the partner's character and prior involvement. Among men, sex sometimes results in intimacy; among women, intimacy sometimes results in sex.

Lesbians form lasting, intimate, paired relationships far more frequently than male homosexuals do. The tendency to desire and enjoy sexual variety appears to be a male proclivity, manifested by homosexual men to an unprecedented degree only because their behavior is not constrained by the necessity of compromising with women.

That homosexual men behave in many ways like heterosexual men, only more so, and lesbians behave in many ways like heterosexual women, only more so, indicates that some aspects of human sexuality are not so plastic after all.[8]

The sexual revolution's bread and butter has been the fallacy that women can enjoy promiscuity as readily as men—that gender equality in fact *demands* that they do so. A 1984 *NBC Reports* interviewed many women sucked into the promiscuity of the seventies but tired of sex games in the eighties. They admit now they haven't enjoyed their liberated lives. What they really want is to be married and have a family.

C. S. Lewis, in the last piece he wrote for publication, said:

> A society in which conjugal infidelity is tolerated must always be in the long run a society adverse to women. Women, whatever a few male songs and satires may say to the contrary, are more naturally

monogamous than men; it is a biological necessity. Where promiscuity prevails, they will therefore always be more often the victims than the culprits.[9]

Traditionally, men married women, among other reasons, because commitment was the horse that pulled the cart of sexual intimacy. But the sexual revolution put the cart before the horse. Not only women but all of society now suffers, for man is at his best when made faithful and responsible in a marriage and family setting.

Promiscuity rips at the seams of a civilized society. It has been tried and found wanting, but countless millions suffer because it has been tried and millions more continue to try it and make their discoveries the hard way. The reader who hasn't yet gone the route of sexual experimentation could save himself and his family a lot of grief by learning the lesson from others. Sexual immorality is a dead end street. Fortunately, some are beginning to realize this, and marital fidelity is winning back some lost ground.

Diseases of Promiscuity—Nature Strikes Back

Sexually transmitted diseases (STDs), formerly called venereal diseases, are one of God-created nature's ways of reminding us that we aren't built to be promiscuous. Gonorrhea is still at epidemic proportions, and some of its strains are increasingly resistant to antibiotics. Syphilis still rears its ugly head, as do venereal warts and about twenty other lesser known diseases of promiscuity.

In the seventies the illusion was that STDs were going the way of smallpox—until 1982, when the media attention on genital herpes took the country by storm. It is estimated that over twenty million Americans have this form of herpes, with 200,000 to 500,000 new cases annually. This represents over a thousand percent increase between 1965 and 1981.

Called "the new scarlet letter," herpes had a profound effect on sexual behavior:

Among its more subliminal effects, herpes has re-
turned to sex its former shadings of corruption and
sin. The virus has come to symbolize massive guilt;
it's viewed as the mark of an angry God punishing
people for the sins of the sexual revolution. The irony
is that it's just those who pioneered the revolution
who are most likely afflicted with the disease. . . .[10]

A thirty-six-year-old bachelor fearful of the disease stated,
"Herpes did for me what no therapist was ever able to do . . . it
forces me to get to know someone before I go to bed with her."[11]

Shortly after the first wave of the herpes scare, the terrify-
ing disease AIDS (Acquired Immune Deficiency Syndrome)
emerged in the homosexual community. Originally labeled "the
gay plague," AIDS has spread beyond homosexuals, infecting
intravenous drug users, hemophiliacs (dependent upon donated
blood), and for unknown reasons certain Haitians. The disease
has spread from infected parties to some women and children.

Nearly three-fourths of AIDS victims are still male homosexuals. Usually they are highly promiscuous, often having
over five hundred and sometimes over a thousand sex partners.
Estimates of eventual fatality rates for AIDS victims range from
50 to 100 percent. Those who are still surviving cannot live normal lives. If they elect to continue sexual relations (as many do)
they are bound to infect others.

A Return to Biblical Morality?
Unquestionably, the advent of herpes and AIDS has
spawned an ad hoc sexual conservativism.

If the revolution was winding down anyway,
herpes and acquired immune deficiency syndrome
(AIDS) have stopped it dead in its tracks. Overnight,
herpes has sobered a generation that oral contraceptives freed from second thoughts, and AIDS has
traumatized the gay community. What other misgiv-
ings the revolution may have turned up, none has pro-

vided so obvious a symbol as these to demand its final days.[12]

The dread of disease, however, is a far cry from the only true and lasting moral reform, one based on firm moral foundations.

We should be grateful for *any* swing away from promiscuity but not necessarily impressed by it—any more than we would be impressed with the moral reform of a burglar who curtails his unethical behavior for fear of burglar alarms and homeowners with guns. Herpes and AIDS have brought temporary fear, not lasting repentance and transformation. Once a cure for these and other diseases is effected, the door to "safe" promiscuity will open again, and those whose moral reformation is based merely on self-preservation will be the first to barge through.

Is the Sexual Revolution Over?

In April 1984 *Time* magazine's cover declared: "Sex in the '80s: The Revolution Is Over." *Is* the revolution really over? In one sense, yes, it is over. If that's the good news, though, here's the bad—the wrong side won.

No revolution is over until someone has won. If the sexual revolution was against the traditional Judeo-Christian morality based on Scripture, and that revolution is over, then biblical morality lost.

> What we are witnessing—a new freedom in discussing sex, and promoting it, and experimenting with it—is not the Sexual Revolution, but the follow-up action that implements the Revolution. The Revolution is over in the sense that there is now no possibility that we shall return to the state of affairs that existed in the past. From now on, we shall slowly adjust our attitudes and behavior to the new concept which seems certain in time to gain almost universal acceptance.[13]

Sexual morality without biblical absolutes is a house without a foundation, a ship destined to sink. Sexual reform without a return to the authority of Scripture is ultimately as fruitless as rearranging the furniture on the Titanic (though it might improve the quality of life on the Titanic in the meantime).

The real question is not "Has the sexual revolution left us?" but *"Where* has it left us?"

> The new conservativism is no victory for puritans. No sexual counter-revolution is underway. The sexual revolution has not been rebuffed, merely absorbed into the culture. [14]

Apart from a widespread national return to God, never again will the followers of Christ be able to take their sexual cues from this society. We must fend for ourselves, forge out our own biblical ethic, and enforce it where we can. In the process we must open wide our doors and invite in those weary pilgrims made open to the Christian faith because they have tasted the bitter waters of the world's sorry alternative.

Chapter 10, Notes
----

1. George Leonard, "The End of Sex," *Esquire,* December 1982, 74.

2. Rollo May, *Love and Will* (New York: W. W. Norton and Co., 1969), 63.

3. Leonard, "End of Sex," 74, 78.

4. Fran Schumer, "Is Sex Dead?" *New York,* 6 December 1982, 69.

5. John Leo, "The Revolution Is Over," *Time,* 9 April 1984, 75.

6. *USA Today,* 19 April 1983, sec. D.

7. *USA Today,* 5 July 1983, sec. D.

8. Donald Symons, "He Versus She," *Science Digest,* December 1983, 86.

9. C. S. Lewis, "We Have No 'Right to Happiness,'" *God in the Dock* (Grand Rapids, Mich.: Wm. B. Eerdmans Publishing Co., 1970), 321.

10. Schumer, "Is Sex Dead?" 91.

11. Ibid., 88.

12. Schumer, "Is Sex Dead?" 69-70.

13. David Mace, *The Christian Response to the Sexual Revolution,* (Nashville: Abingdon Press, 1970), 68.

14. Leo, "Revolution," 83.

PART 3

GOD HAS SOMETHING TO SAY

Chapter 11

Sex: God's Gift to Humanity

*I*n a 1984 cover story in the science magazine *Discover*, the question was asked, "Why sex?"

> Sex is an inefficient, risky way for an organism to reproduce itself. . . . Sex, the scientists say, requires an inordinate amount of time and energy. . . . Because sex diminishes a parent's genetic tie to its offspring, it contradicts a basic biological tenet: that the main goal of an organism is to transmit as many of its genes as possible to the next generation. In fact, sex dictates that a parent can pass on only half its genes to each of its progeny.
>
> Asexual reproduction (without sex) seems a likelier choice for nature to make. It is faster and more efficient, and it allows a creature both to replicate itself without the bother of mating, and to procure offspring that carry all of its genes. If by some fluke sex happens to arise in a species, theoretically it should not take hold; the sexual creatures should soon be supplanted by the original asexual stock.

Says George Williams, a population biologist of the State University of New York at Stony Brook, "At first glance, and second, and third, it appears that sex shouldn't have evolved." Indeed, the persistence of sex is one of the fundamental mysteries in evolutionary biology today. [1]

After further exploring what they call "the paradox of sex" and "the riddle of sex," the authors come to this fascinating conclusion:

Are biologists any closer to an answer than they were fifty years ago? Perhaps not. Says John Maynard Smith of the University of Sussex, in England, one of the leading students of the mystery, "One is left with the feeling that some essential feature of the situation is being overlooked." [2]

The scientist's feeling is justified. There *is* an essential feature of the situation being overlooked. His colleague was right also—sex shouldn't have evolved. In fact, it didn't. It was created by the greatest "overlooked essential feature" in the universe.

In the Beginning Was Sex

God is the architect, engineer, and builder of sex. It is a carefully planned facet of our humanity, created for our good and his glory. Anyone who questions whether sex is good questions whether God is good. The rightness and legitimacy of sex stand or fall with the morally pure character of the One who created it.

To put sex in perspective, we must begin at the beginning—creation. Having fashioned man and woman with their distinctive sexual natures, "God blessed them and said to them, 'Be fruitful and increase in number; fill the earth and subdue it'" (Genesis 1:28).

The divine command to reproduce required the sexual merger of man and woman. This was one command they were happy to obey (unlike our scientists, they did not consider mating a bother). Sex was part and parcel of Eden's paradise.

God confers his stamp of approval on each facet of his creation. All that he had made was devoid of blemish or flaw; all of creation was declared good (Genesis 1:10, 12, 18, 25). Yet, following the creation of man, God says there is something "not good" (Genesis 2:18). What was not good was that Adam was alone.

But Adam was not just lonely—God's solution was not to create other men for companionship. Only a woman could fill the void. Following the creation of Eve, "God saw all that he had made, and it was very good." What was included in that which was very good? Maleness. Femaleness. Sexuality. Sex.

"It was good," "it was good," "it was good," "it was good," "it was not good," "it was very good." Creation was incomplete until the debut of the second sex. God never intended a unisex humanity.

Eve was like Adam, yet unlike him. Same humanity, different gender. Man and woman were equal but not the same. Their oneness was not a uniformity stemming from sameness but a unity transcending differentness.

This marvelous integration was culminated in their sexual union: "For this reason a man will leave his father and mother and be united to his wife, and they will become one flesh" (Genesis 2:24). Man and woman consummate marriage through God-ordained sexual union. This means not just the blending of bodies but also the merging of minds, the assimilating of souls.

Genesis 2, the last account of a world without sin, ends gloriously with two sexual beings, unclothed and unashamed, free to enjoy sex. God looks on their nakedness and their sexual union with the smile of complete approval.

Sex Is Someone You Are

God designed the sexual union to be a truly intimate experience. This is demonstrated by the primary word for sexual intercourse used in the Old Testament, the Hebrew word *yadah*, "to know." "Now Adam knew Eve his wife, and she conceived and bore Cain" (Genesis 4:1, RSV).

Yadah speaks of an intimacy wherein two parties see each other as they truly are. The concept is not of some distant, objective, or academic acquaintance but a personal, intimate, and experiential knowledge of another. *Yadah* is the same word that is used of a believer's relationship with his God (e.g. Daniel 11:32). To know one's marriage partner in the act of sex is analogous to developing intimacy with God.

Our word *intercourse* suggests this. Sexual intercourse is an interpersonal *communicative* experience with one to whom we are exclusively and unconditionally committed. There is nothing even remotely casual or impersonal about sex.

Many, perhaps most, pagan religions incorporated sexual relations into their worship of false deities because of the metaphysical dimension of the sex act. Somehow, sexual intercourse was thought to forge a link between the pagan worshipers and the personages that inhabited the spiritual world. A Chinese proverb says, "Sexual intercourse is the human counterpart of the cosmic process."

Writers have compared sex to the opening of a door and a peek into heaven, where the soul temporarily leaves the body. Certainly the Christian worshiper who enjoys the God-intended role of sex in his marriage can regard his experience as a spiritual one. Regardless of our denominational backgrounds, should we not see something sacramental about marriage? And if marriage, also sex, the bond of marriage. In its rightful place, sexual expression transcends the boundaries of the physical and propels its participants into the realm of the spiritual.

We must distinguish between sexuality and sexual activity. My sexuality exists independently of what I do. It is a matter of identity, not behavior. God is the author of all sexuality and the personal creator of my sexuality. Sexuality exists independently of marriage or the sex act. Jesus was a sexual being, though he did not marry or engage in sex. To be human is to be sexual. The two are inseparably linked. Sex is not just something you do. Sex is someone you are.

George Gilder points out our loss in reducing sex to a physical act:

> The words no longer evoke an image of a broad pageant of relations and differences between the sexes, embracing every aspect of our lives. Instead "sex" and "sexuality" are assumed to refer chiefly to copulation, as if our sexual lives were restricted to the male limits—as if the experiences of maternity were not paramount sexual events. In fact, however, our whole lives are sexual. Sexual energy animates most of our activities and connects every individual to a family and a community. Sexuality is best examined not in terms of sexology, physiology, or psychology, but as a study encompassing all the ulterior life of our society.[3]

Sexuality is not confined to the sex drive, though it certainly embraces it. Freud was right when he insisted that the sex drive is a powerful force that affects the entire personality. Channeled properly, it is a boon to human creativity and the advancement of culture.

As an extension of our sexuality, sexual thoughts and actions are more than just something we think or do. They are something we are, and someone we are becoming. Having sex with someone is so much more than sharing a bed. It is sharing a life, surrendering one's inner self to another. Within God's intended context it is beautiful. Outside, it is not.

No matter how flippantly we treat sex, it will never be flippant with us. There is nothing casual about sex, nothing simple or isolated about the act of sex. A direct link exists between sex and the human soul. Whenever a person has sex, he lays his life on the line.

The Reason for Sex

Since early church history there have been those who believe the only purpose for sex is to prevent the cessation of humanity (no sex, no people). These people assume, I suppose,

that a Christian couple with four children has had sexual intercourse twice as often as a couple with two. It is this kind of antisexual attitude that drove society to sexual repression and set the
stage for the sexual revolution.

The argument that sex is only for procreation is as unimagi-
native as it is old. Couldn't an all-knowing Creator devise some
other means considerably more simple, dependable, and refined
that would serve the solitary purpose of procreation? If he
wanted to, he could have married couples set out a crib on the
back porch whenever they wanted another child (sort of a tooth
fairy approach to family planning). But to the delight of some
and the chagrin of others, God has made procreation only one
function of that multi-dimensional experience called sex.

Of course, procreation *is* a major purpose of sex. But when
we consider that the vast majority of times a couple has sex will
not result in conception, we must realize there is much more to
sex than procreation.

We should not feel compelled to choose between sex as a
means of procreation and sex as a means of pleasure, as if the
two are mutually exclusive. Both are intended by God, as is the
expression and cultivation of spiritual and emotional oneness in
marriage. To reduce sex to nothing more than a means to the end
of childbearing is to miss the point of the marital oneness implicit in the one-flesh relationship.

The body is to be an instrument of the spirit, and the uniting of bodies is in its essence the uniting of spirits (1 Corinthians 6:15-17). Note that the immediate context of Genesis
2:24, where the sexual union is first specifically mentioned,
says nothing about bearing children. In that passage the exclusive concern is the present act of marriage, not the future potential of parenting.

As surely as God is the creator of sex and sex drives, he is
the designer of the physical and psychological pleasures woven
into sex. It was not Satan who made sex pleasurable to push us
toward sin, but God who make it pleasurable to pull us toward
fulfillment.

If you doubt this, consider the fact that one part of the female anatomy, the clitoris, serves *no other function* than to give women a sensation of pleasure in sex. Obviously, God made sex to be enjoyed.

Solomon on Sex

If the Genesis account and the created nature of sex are not enough to convince us that it is a pure and beautiful gift from God, the clear statements of Proverbs and the Song of Solomon should end all debate. Note the clear, albeit poetic, expressions of sexual intimacy and fidelity in the following passage from Proverbs:

> Drink water from your own cistern,
>   running water from your own well.
> Should your springs overflow in the streets,
>   your streams of water in the public squares?
> Let them be yours alone,
>   never to be shared with strangers.
> May your fountain be blessed,
>   and may you rejoice in the wife of your youth.
> A loving doe, a graceful deer—
>   may her breasts satisfy you always,
>   may you ever be captivated by her love.
> Why be captivated, my son, by an adulteress?
>   Why embrace the bosom of another man's wife?
>   (Proverbs 5:15-20)

God wants sex to be enjoyed so much in marriage that there will be no compulsion to have sex outside of marriage. This passage, as well as others, demonstrates that a positive (yes, erotic) sex life in a marriage is one of the greatest guards against sexual impurity. Note that Solomon does not deal only with intercourse but with love play ("May her breasts satisfy you always"), showing again that pleasure is a legitimate part of sex.

Should Proverbs' message of sexual pleasure in marriage fall on deaf ears, the Song of Solomon thunders the same message at a decibel level too high to ignore. The Song of Solomon takes us into a beautiful dialogue between two newly-weds. Young Solomon's message to Shulamith, his bride, in-cludes such erotic exclamations as these:

> Your breasts are like two fawns,
>   like twin fawns of a gazelle
>   that browse among the lilies (4:5).

> How delightful is your love, my sister, my bride!
>   How much more pleasing is your love than wine,
>   and the fragrance of your perfume than any spice!
>   (4:10).

> Your graceful legs are like jewels,
>   the work of a craftsman's hands.

>   . . . .

> How beautiful you are and how pleasing,
>   O love, with your delights!
> Your stature is like that of the palm,
>   and your breasts like clusters of fruit.
> I said, "I will climb the palm tree;
>   I will take hold of its fruit."
> May your breasts be like the clusters of the vine,
>   the fragrance of your breath like apples,
>   and your mouth like the best wine (7:1, 6-9).

Even to the English reader, the sexual tone of these expressions is unmistakable. But to the Hebrew, who readily understood many of the poetic metaphors lost on us, the Song was throughout an unashamedly erotic expression of marital love.

In 7:1-9 the husband describes his wife's naked body in great detail. Rather than being ashamed or embarrassed by this, she is pleased and responds, "I belong to my lover, and his desire is for me" (7:10). In the following verses she invites him to come away and spend the night, then go early in the morning to the vineyard, and promises, "there I will give you my love" (vv.

11-12). Obviously, this God-fearing wife is just as interested in sex as her husband.

For too long the Song of Solomon has been avoided, ignored, or allegorized into oblivion. While many commentaries are helpful in unlocking the meaning of its poetic expression, I recommend Joseph Dillow's *Solomon on Sex*.[4] It helps catch the flavor of this beautiful book of Scripture, and also includes practical advice for enriching sex in marriage.

Jesus and Paul on Sex

The New Testament consistently maintains the same exalted view of sexual union in marriage that is established in the Old. Jesus endorsed married love not only implicitly by his attendance and assistance at the wedding at Cana (John 2) but explicitly in Matthew 19:4-6:

> "Haven't you read," he replied, "that at the beginning the Creator 'made them male and female,' and said, 'For this reason a man will leave his father and mother and be united to his wife, and the two will become one flesh'? So they are no longer two, but one. Therefore what God has joined together, let man not separate."

In Ephesians 5:25-33 the apostle Paul makes a direct comparison between a husband's love for his wife and Christ's love for his bride, the church. Christ is the model of personal sacrificial giving of self for the highest good of the beloved. In verses 31-32 Paul illustrates the intimate union of Christ and his bride with the marital sexual union of man and wife. What a tribute to marriage and marital sex to be chosen for such a comparison!

It is also interesting that Christ gives himself for his bride in a way that makes her "holy," "radiant," "without stain and blameless" (vv. 25-27). Husbands are commanded to do the very same for their wives (v. 28). The husband is responsible to cultivate and maintain his wife's purity sexually and in every way. To enjoy a sexual relationship with her is to express his love and further engender hers.

In 1 Corinthians Paul affirms sexual intercourse as basic to maintaining the sexual purity of a marriage. Sexual intercourse is not just conceded, permitted, or expected in a marriage. It is explicitly *commanded:*

> The husband should fulfill his marital duty to his wife, and likewise the wife to her husband. The wife's body does not belong to her alone but also to her husband. In the same way, the husband's body does not belong to him alone but also to his wife. Do not deprive each other except by mutual consent and for a time, so that you may devote yourselves to prayer. Then come together again so that Satan will not tempt you because of your lack of self control (1 Corinthians 7:3-5).

Many couples are glad to obey, but for others this is a major problem. We must realize that carnality surfaces not only in sexual promiscuity but in the selfishness that sexually denies one's marriage partner. It is not enough for us to say that sex is a marital privilege. It *is* that, but it is also a sacred responsibility. When carried out consistently, it serves to protect the moral fiber of the marriage relationship.

Resisting the Antibodies

If Scripture is so clear on the matter, why have Christians tended to be so negative toward sex? The problem actually began early in church history, when theology was strongly influenced by Greek philosophy.

The Hebrews were holistic in their perceptions of life. God made the body, God made sex, God made marriage, of which sex was a part. Marriage was good, sex was good. Very simple—and very accurate.

Greek thought, on the contrary, was characterized by a dualism in which the spiritual world was good, and the physical world was bad. Plato, for example, called the body a "prison" that held captive the soul.

In the early centuries A.D. there were two schools of Greek thought: Stoicism and Epicureanism. The Stoics treated their bodies harshly, denying themselves even the most simple pleasures. Spirituality, to them, consisted of depriving themselves of all comfort and pleasure. In contrast, the Epicureans readily indulged their bodies, gratifying every appetite. While very different in behavior, the Stoics and Epicureans shared a common disregard for the body. The Stoics demeaned it, so refused to satisfy it. The Epicureans demeaned it, so felt free to abuse it in the pursuit of pleasure.

Early Christians who tended toward legalism adopted Stoic philosophy and lifestyles. Believers elevating personal liberty gravitated toward Epicurean ideals and behavior. Christians on both extemes tended to view the body as vulgar and base.

C. S. Lewis speaks of Christians to whom the body was "'a sack of dung', food for worms, filthy, shameful, a source of nothing but temptation to bad men and humiliation to good ones."[5] Origen carried this philosophy to the extreme by castrating himself in a vain attempt to solve the problem of lust.

Sometimes the apostle Paul is accused, even by Christians, of fostering this tragic disdain for the human body. The notion that Paul's view was "sex is of the flesh" betrays a common but serious misunderstanding of Pauline theology.[6] Certainly, Paul maintained consistently that sexual *immorality* is of the flesh. But what is the flesh? In Paul's writings, the flesh is not synonymous with the body. Rather, the flesh is the sin principle, the depraved force that influences a man toward sin, prompting him to misuse the members of his body to disobey God. While Paul speaks of the flesh as the Christian's enemy, he speaks of the body as the temple of the Holy Spirit (1 Corinthians 6:19). If the shekinah glory of God dwells within our bodies, surely they are not inherently sinful!

When the Christians of Corinth were indulging in the excesses of gluttony and immorality, Paul reminded them their bodies were "for the Lord, and the Lord for the body" (1 Corinthians

6:13). Furthermore, the bodies they were abusing would be raised up and inhabited for all eternity (6:14). Indeed, Paul devotes all of chapter 15 of the same book to the resurrection of the body, a concept held in disdain by the Greeks, who wanted only to rid themselves of their bodily prison.

Paul sees consecration as the submitting of the body to do the will of God (Romans 12:1-2). He is careful to discipline his body (1 Corinthians 9:27), but never to degrade it. He says the body is the temple of the Holy Spirit, and that the Christian can glorify God with his body (1 Corinthians 6:19-20). He even compares the holy church of God to a human body, with Christ represented by the head (1 Corinthians 12:14-27). Properly understood, Paul was not anti-body!

"Your hands made me and formed me," the psalmist says to his Lord (119:73). David expressed to God, "You knit me together in my mother's womb. I praise you because I am fearfully and wonderfully made" (Psalm 139:13-14). The body, including its sex organs and sex drives, is something to thank God for, not be ashamed of.

Christ's incarnation is permanent proof that the body is not sinful. The human body is compatible with deity—God was not too good to inhabit a body! Jesus' body never made him sinful. Heaven will be inhabited by redeemed bodies, both Christ's and ours.

If our bodies are good and sex is not sinful, why must we cover our bodies from each other? Because human hearts *are* sinful. Clothes lessen the visual stimuli that prompt fallen beings to treat others as sex objects and to lust after sex outside its God-intended context. Within marriage, God's ideal is still that of paradise where there was no shame in beholding each other's nakedness (Genesis 2:25).

A New Perspective

There you have it. The body was not put together by a pervert. Sex was not invented in a dark alley behind a porno shop. It was made in heaven—where purity reigns. As Christians, we must look at sex through the eyes of God.

The church needs to scrape off the barnacles of un-biblical tradition and unscientific superstition so that a wholesome view of sex can appear. We cannot afford any longer the excess baggage of negativism. The harm that this heresy has done is immeasurable because it has robbed men and women of the ability to appreciate and enjoy sex as God intended.[7]

Despite the bad press given it by misguided believers, sex is God's gift to humanity. In marriage, let us celebrate sex. May husband and wife never be ashamed to enjoy together what God was not ashamed to create.

Chapter 11, Notes

1. Gina Maranto and Shannon Brownlee, "Why Sex?" *Discover,* February 1984, 24.

2. Ibid., 28.

3. George Gilder, *Sexual Suicide* (New York: New York Times Book Co., 1973), 1-2.

4. Joseph C. Dillow, *Solomon on Sex* (Nashville: Thomas Nelson Publishers , 1977).

5. C. S. Lewis, *The Four Loves* (New York: Harcourt Brace Jovanovich, 1960), 142-43.

6. Ray E. Short, *Sex, Love or Infatuation* (Minneapolis: Augsburg Publishing House, 1978), 93.

7. Harry Hollis, "A Christian Model for Sexual Understanding and Behavior," in *Secrets of Our Sexuality,* ed. Gary Collins, (Waco, Tex.: Word Books, 1976), 82.

Chapter 12

When Sex Becomes Sin

*"H*ow can anything so good be so bad?" If sex is as good as we portrayed it in the previous chapter, why is it that many sexual acts are condemned in Scripture? The answer is that like most good things, sex was created to exist within prescribed boundaries. As long as it stays within those boundaries, it is good. The moment it moves outside them, it becomes bad.

Take water and fire as examples. Water is a great gift of God. Without it we would die. Yet when water is out of control, when it violates its proper boundaries, it can wreak terrible destruction—as anyone knows who has seen a flood or a tidal wave. Fire is likewise a great gift of God, but when out of control it can destroy a house, decimate a forest, and inflict painful and horrible death.

The best gifts of God are powerful, and when out of control that power becomes ruinous. So it is with sex. Sex outside marriage is so bad precisely because sex inside marriage is so good.

God's Will Is not Lost

Many of us spend great energy, time, and money trying to "find God's will" (with the implication that it's somehow lost or obscure). But there's no mystery about God's will in most matters of sexual behavior:

> It is God's will that you should be holy; that you should avoid sexual immorality; that each of you should learn to control his own body in a way that is holy and honorable, not in passionate lust like the heathen, who do not know God; and that in this matter no one should wrong his brother or take advantage of him. The Lord will punish men for all such sins, as we have already told you and warned you. For God did not call us to be impure, but to live a holy life. Therefore, he who rejects this instruction does not reject man but God, who gives you his Holy Spirit (1 Thessalonians 4:3-8).

The apostle Paul considers our personal holiness inseparable from our sexual behavior. There is no holiness where there is immorality. Like oil and water, the two do not mix. If we violate God's sexual standards, no matter what else we do or don't do, we simply cannot be in God's will. We need to pray for power to accomplish his will in sexual matters but not to find out what that will is. Scripture makes it clear.

The Moral Climate of Biblical Times

The biblical standards of sexual morality stood in stark contrast to the accepted social norms of most of the ancient cultures. The people of Israel were surrounded by heathen nations characterized not only by pagan worship but the grossest forms of immorality. Canaanite religions featured the worship of phallic fertility gods and multi-breasted goddesses, and their rituals often included lewd dances followed by sexual intercourse and full-scale orgies. Prostitutes, both male and female, were a central part of the temple worship.

While the societies in the New Testament era were generally more civilized than the Canaanites, their sexual mores were just as bad. The Greek writings of Plato, Lucian, and many others elevated homosexuality. Immorality was a way of life in Greek cities like ancient Corinth, where a thousand prostitutes, priestesses of Aphrodite, walked the streets and gave their fees to the temple priests. In time, the city's name was coined in a verb form (*corinthiazomai*) that actually meant to have intercourse with a prostitute.

The Christians in New Testament Corinth lived in a new city built a hundred years after ancient Corinth was destroyed. Nevertheless, the same spirit of immorality prevailed, still rooted in the mingling of pagan religion and immorality (1 Corinthians 6:15-20). No wonder the Corinthian Christians, raised in this environment, had such struggles with sexual temptation.

Taking their cue from the rampant immorality of the Greek culture they assimilated, Roman emperors set a national example of notorious immorality. The emperor Caligula lived in incest with his sister, as did Nero with his own mother. Nero also married a young man. Julius Caesar was likewise a known homosexual, and the emperor Hadrian was extremely promiscuous with men and women alike.

Promiscuity was the norm, fidelity was a foreign concept. But the fledgling Christian faith did not surrender to the secular drift, insisting that those who named the name of Christ live in sexual purity: "Chastity was the one completely new virtue which Christianity introduced into the pagan world."[1] It was a distinction so basic, so fundamental, that the absence of purity would nullify the credibility of the gospel. No wonder it is repeatedly stressed in the New Testament epistles.

> But among you there must not be even a hint of sexual immorality, or of any kind of impurity, or of greed, because these are improper for God's holy people. Nor should there be obscenity, foolish talk or coarse joking, which are out of place, but rather thanksgiving. For of this you can be sure: No immoral, impure or greedy person—such a man is an idolater—has any inheritance in the kingdom of

Christ and of God. Let no one deceive you with empty words, for because of such things God's wrath comes on those who are disobedient. Therefore do not be partners with them (Ephesians 5:3-7).

Other passages specifically state that those living in sexual immorality will not inherit the kingdom of God (1 Corinthians 6:9-10; Revelation 22:14-15). Certainly, these verses are hard to reconcile with the grim reality of sexual sin among Christians. Even if we do not know what to make of them, however, they demonstrate how much God hates sexual sin. They also show the basic incompatibility of the new life in Christ and the life of immorality. Simply put, Scripture leaves no place for sexual impurity in the Christian life, Christian family, or Christian church.

How Scripture Treats Sexual Sin

The heart of God's law is expressed in the Ten Commandments (Exodus 20:1-17; Deuteronomy 5:1-21). We must remember that these were not arbitrary laws, nor were they given only to make a better society (though that was their effect). These commandments are rooted in the very nature of God. They are a transcript of his character. They reveal God's holiness and bring that holiness to bear on the realities of daily life and relationships. And they were written on *stone,* not erasable bond.

One of God's ten fundamental laws prohibited sexual involvements outside one's own marriage: "You shall not commit adultery" (Exodus 20:14). Remember this stood in stark contrast to the nations that surrounded Israel where immorality was an accepted—even celebrated—way of life.

This commandment, however, does not complete the decalogue's instruction on sexual purity. The tenth commandment forbids the longing to possess what is not rightly yours and includes this warning: "You shall not covet your neighbor's wife" (Exodus 20:17).

Adultery is tangible. But coveting is something internal, something that could exist for a lifetime without resulting in criminal behavior. Yet God shows he is concerned not only about a person's actions but also his thoughts. Extramarital sex is condemned in the seventh commandment; lust is condemned in the tenth. Lust, as we will see in the following chapter, is not only the fountainhead of all sexual sin but is itself sexual sin in its most basic form.

Other Old Testament passages likewise speak of the seriousness of sexual sins. Leviticus 18 prohibits numerous sexual perversions, from incest to homosexual relations to bestiality (18:6,22-23). Deuteronomy 22 and 23 deal with a wide variety of sexual sins and their appropriate punishments. Under Old Testament law, sexual sins were crimes not just against God but against individuals *and* society as a whole—and most were punishable by *death*.

Capital punishment for sexual sins in Israel should teach us two things. First, incidentally but importantly, it defuses the persistent claim that capital punishment is not a deterrent to evil. The explicitly stated purpose for such punishment was to "purge the evil from among you" (Deuteronomy 22:21, 22, 24). Obviously, there is *some* deterrence—an executed offender doesn't repeat his crime.

Furthermore, "when the sentence for a crime is not quickly carried out, the hearts of the people are filled with schemes to do wrong" (Ecclesiastes 8:11). Whenever sin is stripped of its consequences, it becomes less forbidding, more appealing. Immorality, like any sin, propagates itself among a community of people, and if left unchecked will become rampant. This is as true in the New Testament church as it was in Old Testament Israel, as Paul warns the Corinthians:

> It is actually reported that there is sexual immorality among you, and of a kind that does not occur even among pagans: A man has his father's wife. And you are proud! Shouldn't you rather have been filled with

grief and have put out of your fellowship the man
who did this? Even though I am not physically present, I am with you in spirit. And I have already
passed judgment on the one who did this, just as if I
were present. When you are assembled in the name
of our Lord Jesus and I am with you in spirit, and the
power of our Lord Jesus is present, hand this man
over to Satan, so that the sinful nature may be destroyed and his spirit saved on the day of the Lord.

Your boasting is not good. Don't you know that a
little yeast works through the whole batch of dough?
Get rid of the old yeast that you may be a new batch
without yeast. . . .

You must not associate with anyone who calls himself a brother but is sexually immoral or greedy, an
idolater or a slanderer, a drunkard or a swindler. With
such a man do not even eat.

"Expel the wicked man from among you" (1 Corinthians 5:1-7, 11, 13).

Perhaps the most important truth we can glean from the
severe penalty for sexual sin (in both testaments) is how serious
and repugnant it is in the eyes of God. I am not advocating capital punishment for sexual sins today. Paul's prescription for the
unrepentant is weighty enough—excommunication from the
protective spiritual community was symbolic of death and could
only be reversed by sincere confession and repentance.

Despite the fact that capital punishment is no longer
sanctioned for sexual sins, we must resist the prevalent notion
that the Old Testament death penalty for immorality was a product of that era's barbarism. In reality, that severe penalty did not
originate from man's bloodthirsty nature but God's holy character. It was an unequivocal portrait of his intolerance of sexual
sin. Thousands of years have passed, dispensations and laws
have come and gone, but the holy character of God that de-
manded such severe consequences for sexual sin remains un-
changed.

While it is popular to claim, "All sin is alike to God," Paul makes it clear there is something different about sexual sin:

> All other sins a man commits are outside his body, but he who sins sexually sins against his own body. Do you not know that your body is a temple of the Holy Spirit, who is in you, whom you have received from God? You are not your own; you were bought at a price. Therefore honor God with your body (1 Corinthians 6:18-20).

Sexual sin is in no sense unforgivable, and Scripture never calls it the worst of sins (it is not, for instance, one of the "seven deadly sins" of Proverbs 6:16-19, as are pride and causing dissension among brothers). Nevertheless, Scripture so powerfully and consistently condemns sexual sin in every form that we are mistaken if we do not view it with a special hatred, fear, and sobriety.

A Closer Look at Scripture's View of Immorality

Scripture uses many terms for sexual immorality. Some of these are close synonyms, and many have overlapping meanings. To summarize, under Old Testament law there were four readily identifiable major categories of sexual sin:

1. *Fornication:* any sexual relations outside of marriage, including those between two unmarried people.
2. *Adultery:* sexual relations with someone other than one's spouse or with the spouse of another.
3. *Homosexuality:* sexual relations between two people of the same gender—males with males or females with females.
4. *Bestiality:* sexual relations with an animal.

Other sexual crimes are specifically addressed but fall under one or more of these categories. Rape and incest, for instance, are particularly despicable brands of fornication that might also be adultery or homosexuality, depending on who is involved.

Still other sexual sins are dealt with not in precept but in principle. When Ham looked upon the nakedness of his father Noah and told his brothers, they walked into Noah's tent backwards to cover him, being careful not to look (Genesis 9:20-27). While commentators disagree on precisely what Ham was guilty of, Noah's severe reaction makes clear that his actions or attitude were highly inappropriate. Presumably, choosing to look at and tell others of his father's nakedness demonstrated a disrespect for his sexual sanctity and privacy. This principle has application both to those who display their nudity to others and those who delight in gazing at the nudity of others.

The Sin of Gender Dilution

In addition any form of gender dilution, including transvestism, can be addressed in the light of clear principles contained in the law.

> A woman must not wear men's clothing, nor a man wear women's clothing, for the LORD your God detests anyone who does this (Deuteronomy 22:5).

The point of this verse is not that women should only wear dresses. In that culture men commonly wore full-length robes. The point is this: In whatever culture you live, dress in such a way as to reflect your God-given gender, not deny it.

The same truth is suggested in the hair length issue of 1 Corinthians 11. Let your hair, your clothing, everything about you affirm your sexual identity (always with modesty). Paul left us not simply a cultural practice but an abiding cross-cultural principle as valid and important today as it was then: *Outwardly identify yourself according to your gender.*

God opposes the unisex movement; he is against the confusion of the sexes. Scripture clearly affirms male-female equality (Galatians 3:28), but it just as clearly affirms male-female differentness—and the importance of society upholding those differences. As long as their children are under their care, it is the responsibility of parents to see that this principle is implemented in their appearance. Sexual equality does not mean sexual sameness.

The public denial of one's God-given sexual identity, normally not even addressed in discussions of sexual deviations, is distinct enough to be considered a fifth category of Old Testament sexual sin, though it doesn't involve a specific sexual act.

In the light of these principles and others, it seems clear that no believer should identify himself with a cause, group, or proposed legislation that desires to minimize or eliminate sexual differences; that confuses equality with sameness; that denies male-female interdependence; that pits one gender against the other; that resists or usurps God-given role differences in the home and church; that excuses or condones hetero- and homosexual immorality; that views children as burdens and abortion as a personal right to remove those burdens.

The feminist movement appears to do all of these. The hotly debated Equal Rights Amendment would do at least some of them.

The Anatomy of Sexual Sin

In Galatians 5, Paul epitomizes the Christian life as the choice to live under the control of God's Spirit as opposed to the control of the sinful nature or flesh:

> So I say, live by the Spirit, and you will not gratify the desires of the sinful nature. For the sinful nature desires what is contrary to the Spirit, and the Spirit what is contrary to the sinful nature (Galatians 5:16-17).

He then illustrates and contrasts these two powerful spiritual forces, citing the acts of the sinful nature (vv. 19-21), followed by the fruit of the Spirit (vv. 22-23).

It is highly significant that the first three acts of the sinful nature listed by Paul have definite sexual implications. Moreover, there appears to be a deliberate progression of evil from sexual immorality to impurity to debauchery. The first speaks of immoral sexual behavior, the second of a degraded personality, and the third of unbridled depravity. This concept of debauchery is developed in several New Testament passages. One scholar describes it this way:

> i.   It is wanton and undisciplined action. It is the action of a man who is at the mercy of his passions and impulses and his emotions, and in whom the voice of calm reason has been silenced by the storms of self will.
>
> ii.   It has respect neither for the persons nor the rights of anyone else. It is violent, insolent, abusive, audacious. Any thought and any sympathy for the feelings of others has ceased to exist.
>
> iii.   It is completely indifferent to public opinion and to public decency. A man may well begin to do a wrong thing in secret; at the beginning his one aim and desire may be to hide it from the eyes of men. He may love the wrong thing, and he may even be mastered by it, but he is still ashamed of it. But it is perfectly possible for him to come to a stage when he does openly and blatantly that which he did secretly and in concealment. He may come to a stage of sin where he is so lost to shame that he no longer cares what others see, and what they may say, or what they may think. The terrible thing about *aselgia* [debauchery] is that it is the act of a character which has lost that which ought to be its greatest defence—its self-respect, and its sense of shame.[2]

Not just the ancient but the current social manifestation of all these works of the flesh is obvious. Sexual immorality and degraded character are evident everywhere. Utter debauchery is seen in the bragging about adulterous exploits, the flaunting of homosexual lusts, and the filling of streets, books, stages, and screens with the grossest of sexual perversions. The works of the flesh have worked their way from a first century epistle to the very heart of twentieth century America.

Remember, Paul began his list of the acts of the sinful nature with sexual sins because "he lived in a world in which such sin was rampant, and in that world Christianity brought men an almost miraculous power to live in purity."[3] We must not forget that power is still with us today.

Chapter 12, Notes

1. William Barclay, *Flesh and Spirit* (Grand Rapids, Mich.: Baker Book House, 1976), 27.

2. Ibid., 32-33.

3. Ibid., 28.

Chapter 13

Lust: The Battle's in Your Mind

*T*he sex drive is powerful. Many say it is just another urge, like hunger and thirst, and sexual intercourse just another biological function. Animals eat, drink, sleep, excrete, and copulate, and people are animals, so . . .

But Paul tells the Corinthians something different:

> Food was meant for the stomach and the stomach for food; but God has no permanent purpose for either. But you cannot say that our physical body was made for sexual promiscuity; it was made for the Lord, and in the Lord is the answer to its needs (1 Corinthians 6:13, Phillips).

Paul insists that the analogy between satisfying our hunger for food and indulging our sexual desires is invalid. "Natural" does not always mean "right." While other urges exist for our physical maintenance, sex does not. We will die without food and water. We will not die without sex. Sex is never an emergency, immorality never a necessity. Lust, however, tells us otherwise.

What Is Lust?

Lust is a consuming, often obsessive passion that focuses on some attractive object. The object itself is often morally neutral but becomes a tool for lust's evil. Food, alcohol, drugs, money, clothes, power, entertainment, fame—any of these can be objects of lust.

Lust is not bad because it is intense. A man can have an intense desire to live for Christ, study God's Word, lead his family, or serve his country.

Lust is not bad because it is sexual. Intense sexual longings and even visualizing sex are appropriate in marriage. Sexual desire and lust are by no means synonymous. Lust is sexual desire toward that which violates God's standards and which is cultivated, bred, and allowed to exercise a controlling force upon the mind.

Lust is obsessive. It is a preoccupation with that which God has not intended for us. And since there is no contentment apart from God and his will, there is no contentment in lust. Like a thirsty man who drinks salt water, lust, no matter how much it is indulged, is never satisfied. It feeds itself, pumping itself up to new levels of intensity. It leads to a frustrating frenzy and sometimes becomes increasingly violent as it fails to find satisfaction.

Lust is a controlling force, one that enslaves the mind and shackles the soul. Paul spoke of those whose god is their stomach (Philippians 3:19). Appetites God created for our good become tools for evil when they dominate our lives.

What Does Scripture Say about Lust?

Sexual lust is condemned in the Old Testament. As we briefly noted in the previous chapter, the tenth commandment prohibits the coveting of another person's marriage partner (Exodus 20:17). In vivid detail Proverbs repeatedly warns against the lust toward immorality, saying it is the fool who gives in to lust and the wise who resists it (Proverbs 2:16-19; 5:1-23; 6:23-29).

We can learn a great deal about lust through the examples, primarily negative, of Samson and Delilah, David and Bathsheba, and Hosea and Gomer.[1] The prophets' picture of Israel as God's unfaithful wife also portrays the ugliness of lust and immorality (Jeremiah 3, Ezekiel 16).

But the key to the entire biblical teaching on lust is found in Jesus' Sermon on the Mount:

> "You have heard that it was said, 'Do not commit adultery.' But I tell you that anyone who looks at a woman lustfully has already committed adultery with her in his heart" (Matthew 5:27-28).

Jesus begins by stating what was common knowledge to his hearers—the Old Testament injunction to refrain from adultery. However, he immediately moves to the moral root of the command. Sexual purity is much more than mere abstinence from physical immorality. It is an inner righteousness, a purity not merely of the body but of the mind.

Jesus is not being unreasonable here. He is not condemning us for temptations that come our way independently of our wills. He is simply saying there is no excuse for mentally indulging in a fantasy that if physically acted out would constitute immorality under Old Testament law.

I have heard people say of their lustful thoughts, "It's not my fault. I can't help it." Often we *are* at fault for allowing certain temptations to come our way in the first place. By our carelessness we invite opportunities to sin. If we exercised wisdom and discretion we could avoid a great deal of the temptation that comes our way.

Sometimes, however, we really *can't* avoid sexual temptation. We must realize that Christ does not condemn either the temptation or the initial prompting toward sin, but the *mental surrender* to sin's prompting. Lust is not something that just happens. It is a choice, an act of the will to mentally give in to sexual temptation.

Martin Luther said it best: "You can't keep the birds from

flying over your head, but you *can* keep them from making a nest in your hair." We can't keep all sexual temptations from coming our way. But we can keep them from taking up residence in our minds.

It's What's Inside that Counts

The Pharisees must have been appalled at Jesus' broadening of the Old Testament command. While they prided themselves on their outer righteousness, Jesus attacked their inner rottenness. He goes on to make his comments about lust even more severe—

> If your right eye causes you to sin, gouge it out and throw it away. It is better for you to lose one part of your body than for your whole body to be thrown into hell. And if your right hand causes you to sin, cut it off and throw it away. It is better for you to lose one part of your body than for your whole body to go into hell (Matthew 5:29-30).

Through a tragic misinterpretation of this and other passages, some sincere Christians early in church history emasculated themselves in an attempt to conquer the sin of lust. Mutilating the body is desecrating God's temple; it is *not* the answer to lust.

What was Jesus saying, then? He refers to the eye and hand in Matthew 5 for specific reasons. The eye represents the gate through which mental input is received and thoughts developed. The hand speaks of the action or behavior taken in conjunction with the thoughts of the mind. The right hand and right eye are mentioned because, for most people, these are the dominant and most useful. The point is, even our most valued bodily members, *if* they were the cause of sin, ought to be eliminated ("cut off and thrown away," so to speak). The mention of hell is a stern reminder that sin will be punished by a holy God. There are eternal implications to our present thoughts and actions.

Jesus is saying that whatever the true source of sin is, it *must* be severely dealt with. But are the members of our body the true source of our sin? The clear answer of Scripture is no. The eye and the hand are only avenues or instruments by which temptation is encountered and sin is committed. The true enemy is the flesh, the sinful nature that propels us toward rebellion against God (Romans 7:4-25; 8:1-14; Galatians 5:13-26).

The problem of sexual perversion is within me. The fundamental problem is one of my heart and mind, not my body. Consequently, radical steps must be taken to purify my mind. Only then can I control my eye, a medium through which temptations come, and my hand, an instrument by which sin is committed. True righteousness is measured by our hearts and minds, not merely our behavior. The problem is inside us, and only by conscious choice based on our new identity in Christ, can we overcome it.

> Put to death, therefore, whatever belongs to your earthly nature: sexual immorality, impurity, lust, evil desires and greed, which is idolatry (Colossians 3:5).

Our Fathers the Pharisees

The Pharisees were a curious lot, and we miss much if we fail to see ourselves in them. On the one hand, they over-extended the law, adding their petty rules and regulations and going far beyond what God intended. On the other hand, they fell far short of the true meaning of the law. They thought the key to righteousness was doing certain things and abstaining from other things. They lived by a check-list morality—a superficial list of do's and don'ts that focused on the externals and ignored the heart.

How many of us are like the Pharisees, taking pride in our purity and looking down our noses at the sexually fallen when all the while our own minds are sexual sewers through which a disease-ridden torrent of filth daily flows? When I have lustful thoughts I might well ask myself, "If I had the opportunity to go to bed with this person without being found out or punished in any way, would I do so?" It is often not genuine righteousness that keeps us from certain physical sins but fear, shame, and lack of opportunity (any and all of which we should be grateful for).

Sexual sin always begins in the mind, though it does not always end there. Not all lust results in physical adultery, but all adultery is the fruit of lust. Jesus went to great lengths to teach the Pharisees it is the inside of man, not the outside, that constitutes his true state before God (Matthew 15:1-20; 23:1-39).

> "For out of the heart come evil thoughts, murder, adultery, sexual immorality, theft, false testimony, slander. These are what make a man 'unclean'" (Matthew 15:19).

The problem with lust, then, is not just that it may lead us to sexual sin. The problem with lust is that it *is* sexual sin. Immorality in the mind is real immorality.

Is Lust *Really* Adultery?

Is Jesus saying there is no difference between adultery of the mind and the physical act of adultery? No. He is saying that both are sins, both are sexual sins, and both are a form of adultery.

On the other hand, we must realize that Scripture does treat physical immorality with particular severity, partly because it involves another person in sin. In the Old Testament, sexual immorality was punishable by death; in the New Testament, it disqualifies (for a season, anyway) a man from church leadership. If every lustful thought produced these two results, everyone would have been executed in Old Testament times, and there would be no qualified church leaders in New Testament times!

Jesus' point is certainly *not*, "If you sin in your mind you may as well go ahead and do the same sin with your body, because it doesn't make any difference." Rather, he is saying, "If you think you're righteous because you have abstained from a certain physical sin, you're absolutely wrong. You're held accountable to God for your mind as well as your body."

This is precisely the thought expressed by the apostle John

when he said, "anyone who hates his brother is a murderer" (1 John 3:15). He is not saying there is no difference between hatred and actual murder, but he *is* saying hatred is unrighteousness—the very kind of unrighteousness acted out when a murder is committed.

The Anatomy of Lust

One morning I spoke to a group of Christians on a secular college campus. My subject was "The battle for sexual purity." As I walked through the student lounge, I could hardly believe the photographs and paintings that covered the walls. Many were not just suggestive but blatantly lewd—pornography disguised as art. Knowing that many of the students I would speak to spent time in that lounge every day, I decided to use it as an illustration. As soon as I did, every head in the room nodded in recognition.

The presence of those pictures waged a continuous war against their minds. Some, I'm sure, were winning the war. Others, no doubt, had lost it already. I have before me a letter written by one of those young people in response to my presentation that day: "Sexual purity of the mind is the hardest thing for me to deal with. Being a Christian takes tremendous self-control, doesn't it?"

Self-control is the neglected fruit of the Spirit (Galatians 5:22-23). We hear much more about love, joy, and peace. But we'll never experience sexual purity until we learn self-control, which is always a matter of the mind.

Love or Lust?

Lust is the counterfeit of love. Satan wants nothing more than that we should fail to see the difference between the two. At its root, lust is absolutely selfish; it uses another to gratify itself. Love, on the contrary, always acts in the best interests of the other person. "Love can always wait to give—lust can never wait to get."

C. S. Lewis said it well:

> We use a most unfortunate idiom when we say, of a lustful man prowling the streets, that he "wants a woman." Strictly speaking, a woman is just what he does not want. He wants a pleasure for which a woman happens to be the necessary piece of apparatus. How much he cares about the woman as such may be gauged by his attitude to her five minutes after fruition (one does not keep the carton after one has smoked the cigarettes).[2]

Just as gluttony is the misappropriation of a good thing (the appetite for food), so lust is a misappropriation of the God-given sexual drive. The problem is not with food or sex nor the appetite for food or sex. The problem comes in elevating these desires over God's purpose in creating them and using them to serve self rather than him and others.

Hedonism makes the pursuit of pleasure the highest goal of life. The senses are satiated, the appetites engorged. The emphasis is upon pleasure at the expense of responsibility. It is here that the mind so often rationalizes: "To refuse sexual gratification is like refusing to enjoy a sunset or partake in a delicious meal. It is denying a part of myself."

How little we understand the ugliness of sin. How little we understand Christ's words, "If anyone would come after me, he must deny himself . . ." (Matthew 16:24). Self-denial—exercising control over one's desires—cuts hard against the grain of current philosophy. Yet it is at the heart of a Christ-centered lifestyle.

Is Lust a Woman's Problem?

Some believe that sexual lust is strictly a man's problem. The truth is many women, especially those who have been sexually active, feel strong sex drives, as strong as most men. Others do not, but are nevertheless vulnerable to another form of lust.

A woman may be disillusioned with her husband. She sees him as an overweight slob who is as boring as he is demanding.

So she sinks into the world of romance novels, soap operas, and women's magazines that speak wistfully of some wonderful man out there made just for her. Perhaps she even knows someone who fits this bill—the man next door, her best friend's husband, her boss, her doctor, or even her pastor.

Gradually and quietly she transfers her affections away from her husband to another man, whether real or imagined. Slowly but surely her mind is drawn to a fantasy world in which explicit sexual thoughts may or may not be present. But either way, she has succumbed to lust by becoming preoccupied with that which God has not intended for her.

Such a woman is looking for love, attention, romance—someone who makes her feel good about herself. When she finds him, she falls for what J. Allan Petersen aptly calls "the myth of greener grass."[3] In the end, her obsession with the forbidden fruit of an exciting relationship proves just as deceptive and disastrous as any man's sexual lust.

The Spiritual Roots of Lust

We are mistaken if we believe that every sexual sin is motivated by the lust for sexual pleasure. In fact, I have known people who *hate* sex that have nonetheless had repeated affairs. They were searching for something significant—and were willing to put up with sex if it could help them find it. The truth is that beneath the sexual drive is the desire not just for pleasure but personal relationship. None of us wants to be lonely. All of us, male or female, want more than faceless trysts and one night stands. We want truly meaningful and lasting intimacy.

Sex was designed by God to express and cultivate meaningful marriage relationships, and sex outside of marriage counterfeits that same purpose effectively enough that for a short time it appears to be real. Though it leaves a person cold and lonely, the memory of the fleeting fulfillment drives one back again with the hope that this time it will last.

Sex involves much more than physical urges. It is not just biology but psychology and, in the final analysis, theology.

Augustine said, "Thou hast made us for Thyself, O God, and the heart of man is restless until it finds its rest in Thee." We are all searching to meet our deepest needs—to be someone and to be loved by someone. Psychologist Larry Crabb labels these needs significance and security. They are real and legitimate needs, and every behavior is an attempt to somehow meet them. God intends that they be met in himself as our Creator and Savior. When they are not met in him (our choice, not his), we are left with a God-shaped emptiness and a compulsion to fill that emptiness somehow somewhere with someone.

Meanwhile we experience the personal pain of being unfulfilled. "There is no better anesthetic for personal pain than sexual intimacy."[4] But, like any anesthetic, it wears off and the pain returns. Those who seek relief from their pain are tempted to dull it by a brief sexual encounter, whether fantasized or real, that not only fails to solve their basic problem, but brings them a whole truckload of new problems to complicate their life, increase their pain, and push them to repeat the downward spiral. Traced to its roots, sexual lust is not a physical but a spiritual problem.

Sexual Sin Is Never "Out of the Blue"

Doug was a seminary student preparing for the ministry. One night he had an argument with his wife. Upset, he left home, drove to a nearby restaurant, and tried to think things through over a cup of coffee. Soon Doug was engrossed in conversation with a young woman in the next booth. A few hours later, he was in bed with her.

Doug came to me ashamed and distressed. "How can I tell my wife? Will she ever forgive me?" he asked. "It was so sudden—there was no warning. *Why did God let this happen?*"

Mike is a successful executive, church leader, and family man. One day he met an attractive woman in an elevator and thought she was flirting with him. Before he knew it, Mike asked her to come into his office and undress in front of him. Fortunately she refused. But Mike was shocked at what he had done (and might have done had she complied). "What is happening to me?" he asked. "How could I do something like this?"

From appearances it seemed that Doug and Mike fell into sexual sin suddenly, without warning. But that was not the case.

Doug had worked nonstop to put himself through seminary. He came to subtly resent Joan, his wife, seeing her and the children as obstacles to his goal of graduating and entering the ministry. It had been two years since he had spent any meaningful time alone with Joan or communicated on other than a superficial level. Their relationship was stale, but both lacked the time or energy to change it.

When Joan and the children were visiting relatives, Doug took an evening break from his theology paper to get some fresh air. He ended up at an X-rated movie. Afterwards, every time he had sex with Joan he pretended she was a woman from the movie. He felt guilty, yet it didn't appear to do any real harm.

What happened to Mike actually began years before he asked that girl to undress in his office. He had a problem with lust. Far worse, he failed to recognize or deal with that problem. On his lunch hour Mike often stopped by a convenience store to buy a paper or pack of gum. Invariably he wandered to the magazine rack and paged through *Hustler* or *Penthouse*. He never intended to (so he told himself). But he always did.

The same mind that wanted to serve Christ permitted itself to indulge in lustful fantasies. One day Mike's mind, programmed by the immoral images he had fed it, prompted him to immoral action.

Sexual sin never comes out of the blue. It is the predictable result of a long natural process in which a mind susceptible to sin is granted unguarded exposure to immoral input.

It's All in Your Mind

"Sow a thought, reap an action; sow an action, reap a habit; sow a habit, reap a character; sow a character, reap a destiny."

We are what we think. Today's thoughts are the stuff of

which tomorrow's character is made. Temptation may come suddenly, but sin does not. Neither does moral and spiritual fiber. It is the result of a process—a process over which we *do* have control. The best way to guard against tomorrow's sexual temptations is to cultivate a pure mind today, a mind saturated not in the world's input but in God's.

Our sexual morality is the sum of a continuous series of choices, decisions, and actions, including all those tiny indulgences and minuscule compromises. Like a photographic plate accumulating light to form an image, our mind is the cumulative result of all we expose it to—whether godly or ungodly.

Male or female, young or old, Christian or non-Christian, all of us face a battle for sexual purity. The enemy is lust, the stakes are high, the reward is the peace and pleasure of purity.

And the battle is in our minds.

Chapter 13, Notes

1. Mel White examines these instructive episodes in his book, *The Other Side of Love* (Old Tappan, N.J.: Fleming H. Revell Co., 1978).

2. C. S. Lewis, *The Four Loves* (New York: Harcourt Brace Jovanovich, 1960), 134-35.

3. J. Allan Petersen, *The Myth of Greener Grass* (Wheaton, Ill.: Tyndale House Publishers, 1983).

4. Lawrence Crabb, *The Marriage Builder* (Grand Rapids: Zondervan Publishing House, 1982), 89.

Chapter 14

Masturbation: Right or Wrong?

*T*wo rife issues must be addressed in light of Scripture's teaching on lust: masturbation and premarital sexual fondling (petting). This chapter concerns the first, the next chapter the second.

Masturbation is the stimulation of one's own sex organs in an attempt to find sexual pleasure or release.

Is masturbation a sin? Christians are divided on this issue. One camp says masturbation is obviously a sin in that it is a form of sexual activity outside of marriage. Others say it is not a sin but not the ideal either. Still others believe it is a God-given method of relieving sexual tension.

Does the Bible Say Anything about Masturbation?

Contrary to persistent myths, masturbation does not cause sterility, brain damage, acne, or hair on the palms. These scare tactics were once widely believed—and too often propagated by religious leaders.

Masturbation used to be labeled onanism after the supposed masturbation of a man named Onan (Genesis 38). I remember as a young Christian in high school reading a book that warned against masturbation and referred to this passage as definitive proof of its evil (it was particularly significant since God struck Onan dead for what he did).

I went to Genesis 38:8-10 fully expecting a statement condemning masturbation. Instead, I found a passage that has nothing at all to do with masturbation. The issue instead was Onan's disobedience in refusing to raise up children for his deceased brother, which he was bound by law and family loyalty to do.

Another common proof text against masturbation was Micah 2:1, directed against "those who plot evil on their beds" —a passage that has even less bearing on the subject than Genesis 38.

Both of these passages stand as embarrassing monuments to our ability as Christians to twist, distort, and strip Scripture from its context to prove anything we want.

But a caution is in order here: Because Scripture has been misused to condemn masturbation, it does not follow that masturbation is therefore right. If we do oppose masturbation, we must do so only for good reasons based on carefully interpreted passages and clear biblical principles. To say masturbation is wrong because it does harm to the temple of the Holy Spirit (the body) carries no weight—it is *not* physically harmful. To say it is wrong because it is sexual or brings pleasure is as revealing an argument as it is faulty—it exposes an unbiblical assumption that anything sexual or pleasureful is sin.

What Makes It Right or Wrong?

Is masturbation inherently sinful? No it is not. Can masturbation be sinful? Yes it certainly can. The bottom line in evaluating masturbation is the issue of the previous chapter—lust.

When masturbation takes place, as it often does, in conjunction with mental images that depict a sexual situation forbidden by the Word of God, then, according to Jesus' words in Matthew 5:27-28, it is wrong. The essential problem is not that the body is being stimulated by its owner but that the mind is engaging in lustful thoughts.

I know one man who says he occasionally masturbates purely for the release of a physical pressure but with no sexual thoughts at all, moral or immoral. My conversations with many others indicate this man is the exception not the rule. Yet I cannot fault him with any clear scriptural precept or principle. His masturbation does not involve lust and is apparently neither obsessive or excessive.

Though masturbation is an ancient practice, Scripture says nothing directly about it. Certainly this is not because the Bible doesn't address personal problems or is hesitant to deal with sexual sins. If masturbation, in and of itself, is a sin, it is hard to understand why it is never addressed in Scripture.

The issue of the thought life and the matter of lust, however, are strongly addressed in the Bible. That is why the masturbation issue must ultimately stand or fall on each individual's response to the question, "Does it create or reinforce lust?"

Some argue that masturbation can actually help reduce lust by decreasing sexual pressures. But in the long run satisfying lust never diminishes lust, it only reinforces it. A drug addict experiences temporary release from his drug lust when he gets a fix, but his long term problem is made worse not better.

One book written for Christian young people says, "The only way masturbation can have a negative effect is if it causes a person to become withdrawn."[1] While isolationism is sometimes a bad side effect of masturbation, it is by no means the only or primary danger. Masturbation can become an obsessive and enslaving habit fueling and refueling the fire of one's lust and lowering people to sex object status. It can become entangled with the obsessive consumption of pornography and lead to increasingly perverse fantasies and desires—and possibly aggression against the opposite sex.

Masturbation can have other side effects if done in anyone else's presence. One Christian student told me of masturbating with his brother in their early teens. He felt it contributed significantly to his present homosexual desires and practices. Another confessed that throughout high school he had often engaged in group masturbation with some of his football team-mates. He was now consumed by a deep and irrational fear that as a result of this practice he would someday become a homo-sexual. That prospect sickened him, yet he was convinced it was inevitable.

To say masturbation is less than ideal is true enough. It is, as John White says, "sex on a desert island."[2] It lacks the rela-tional and reciprocal dimension God intended for sexual ex-pression.

Yet masturbation appears also to be a natural part of adoles-cent self-discovery, particularly among boys, who must deal with a seminal buildup that creates an involuntary urge toward release. It takes time to adjust to the sexual awakening puberty brings. Failure to refrain from masturbation during this period may indicate immaturity but not necessarily sin.

I do not mean to imply it is impossible to control masturba-tion. Some manage to stop masturbating altogether. Often if one sets short-term goals—say, not masturbating for two weeks or a month—it becomes much easier to control. Like all habits, mas-turbation can be controlled.

It's Not the Central Issue of Life

Sometimes Christian parents panic when they discover their children masturbating and instill a sense of fear and guilt that reinforces rather than solves the problem. By taking it in stride and calmly discussing the dangers, parents can help their children appreciate the beauty and naturalness of their sexual awakening while also appreciating the challenges it presents.

Too many Christians, especially young people, allow the masturbation issue to become the focus of their lives. A female Bible college student sent me a lengthy letter in which she de-scribed her agonizing struggle with masturbation. Like count-less other Christians, this sincere Christian girl suffered from nagging guilt and a constant sense of spiritual defeat because of this ongoing problem. I wrote back that while she needed to work on the problem if it involved lust, I simply could not believe God has no plan for her until she stops masturbating forever.

I know of one youth director who treated masturbation as the most critical issue in the Christian life. He referred to it as "the problem," and whenever he saw one of the young men in his youth group he would say, "How are you doing with the problem?" I consider this not only unnecessary but unhealthy and reflective of an obsession on the man's part that could easily be passed on to the boys.

We only add to "the problem" when we act as if someone's spirituality is all wrapped up in the issue of masturbation. Such attitudes result in more pressure and magnified guilt and lead to continuous failure and a deeper sense of inadequacy and despair. The person involved often gives up and is driven to the very behavior he is being condemned for.

As a result of seeing this harmful self-condemnation, Dr. James Dobson has taken an uncondemning approach to masturbation among the young. Provided we do not overlook the issue of lust—and are careful not to rationalize a habit that we should take reasonable efforts to control—I think this is a positive move that will save many young people a great deal of self-condemnation. It will free up mental and emotional energy that would be better channeled into cultivating their relationship with God.

Chapter 14, Notes

1. Steve Clapp, *A Christian View of Youth and Sexuality* (Sidell, Ill: C-4 Resources, 1981), 37.

2. John White, *Eros Defiled* (Downers Grove, Ill: InterVarsity Press, 1977), 33.

Chapter 15

Premarital Intimacy: Where Should the Line Be Drawn?

*P*remarital sexual fondling (or petting as it is often called) refers to any intimate sexual activity between two unmarried people that falls short of actual intercourse.

In some cultures this activity is virtually nonexistent. A boy and a girl are under the strict supervision of their parents, are not allowed to choose each other as partners, and are permitted almost no time together alone before marriage. Furthermore, their marriage often takes place shortly after puberty, allowing little time in which sexual desires can exist without a legitimate avenue of fulfillment.

Our own culture is the opposite of this in every respect. The average age of puberty has measurably decreased in recent years. Puberty is now reached somewhere between the ages of twelve and sixteen. Since the average person is over twenty before he or she is married—often considerably older—there is a significant time gap between sexual maturity and the appropriate context in which sexual needs can be met.

Furthermore, young people in our society have much freedom to spend time alone with the opposite sex. Coupled with their mobility, money, and a large amount of leisure—not to mention their constant bombardment with sex through media and music—it is almost inevitable that their sex drives will be activated and experimented with. Often this leads to fondling, and frequently it is followed by sexual intercourse.

(While I am focusing mostly on young unmarrieds, I am well aware that many readers are older unmarrieds. While the references to youth and parents may not be pertinent to you, the biblical principles and many of the practical considerations are. I encourage you to read with this in mind.)

As we have already seen, Scripture is clear that premarital sex (fornication) is wrong. The real moral issue for most Christian singles is petting: "How far can we go without sinning?" Some feel the freedom to engage in every form of sexual activity short of intercourse itself, leaving themselves with only a technical virginity.

Though it may be natural for a young person to experiment with sex drives, petting is also experimenting with a person. Some speak of sexual experimentation before marriage as if they were speaking of dissecting a frog in biology class. Actually, a closer parallel would be dissecting your lab partner. As we have stressed, sex is far more than something you do. It is someone you are.

The Stages of Sexual Intimacy

Where does an unmarried couple draw the line? Can they hold hands, hug, kiss? Can they go further? Scripture does not directly address these levels of physical contact. The key to answering these questions is to determine what level of physical activity results in the sexual arousal of one or both partners in the relationship. The key question is, "At what point does the body begin to prepare itself for intercourse?" Surely the God who forbids intercourse outside of marriage does not advocate any physical activity which he himself specifically designed to prepare the body for intercourse.

When a parent tells his child not to play on the freeway, it is safe to assume he does not want the child to walk down to the freeway and dangle one foot over the edge. An obedient child does not try to get as close as he possibly can to disobedience (even the question "How far can I go?" implies a desire to live as close to disobeying our Father as we can). Then there is the safety factor. Once by the freeway the temptation to cross it may be too great, or the child may forget, stumble, or be pushed.

Though no universal point exists where every person's body begins to prepare for intercourse, a couple who would abstain from premarital sex should likewise abstain from all physical activity that propels their bodies and emotions toward sexual climax. If they pursue such activities, their natural healthy sex drives will tend to degenerate into lust.

Once set in motion, sexual desires escalate and so do levels of physical intimacy.

> God has made sex so that it is progressive and leads ultimately to intercourse and its climax in orgasm. This includes a built-in "law of diminishing returns" which demands more and more, with an increasing crescendo of arousal and excitement until there is a place where the will no longer effectively functions and the emotions take over completely.[1]

When have I gone too far in a physical relationship before marriage? When my heart is pounding like a jackhammer and my hormones are flowing like water through a firehose, it's a pretty strong clue that I have gone too far already! At such times, my body neither knows nor cares about my Christian convictions. Instead of trying to figure out how to derail a fifty ton locomotive traveling at high speed, wisdom suggests we would do better to stay off the train and avoid the crisis in the first place.

Any sexual stimulation of one partner by the other is actually foreplay—the very same thing marriage partners do to prepare each other for intercourse. Foreplay without intercourse is like warmups without a race or a preface without a book. It is incomplete. Worse yet, it is unnatural and frustrating.

When it comes down to it, petting must always be either fornicative or abortive. That is, it will either lead to intercourse—which is fornication when outside of marriage—or it will have to end prematurely, in some way other than God intended.

Illusions of Intimacy

Sexual encounters outside of marriage, whether or not they include intercourse, give an illusion of intimacy that can be mistaken for the lasting commitment that makes a marriage work. Too many young people end up getting married because of their sexual involvement (even apart from pregnancy). I have often seen girls lose their objectivity about a boy because they have gone too far with him sexually. Because they cannot abide the thought of being promiscuous, they convince themselves that this is the one they should marry (they haven't given themselves to just anybody). They end up pushing for a marriage built on a faulty foundation—one that statistically will probably result in divorce.

Dating and engagement are the times to explore each other's mind and spirit, not each other's body. When a couple becomes preoccupied with the physical, they neglect mind and spirit and consequently make poor choices.

> Petting is playing at love. It makes the more genuine expressions of love seem dull and stereotyped, unreal and unsatisfying. It dulls the finer sensitivities of true love. Many young people have failed to recognize true love and a properly restrained lover because petting has prompted the false expectation that true love is always aggressive and free in initiating familiarities.[2]

A Christian Defense for Petting?

Despite this, some material written for young people endorses "responsible" premarital sex. (Are there responsible ways to disobey God?) Particularly alarming are some books written for Christian teenagers. One of these states, "Petting should be reserved for serious relationships." The same book affirms, "It is wise not to do a lot of petting below the waist unless you have decided that you want to bring each other to orgasm." The author goes on to propose oral sex as a method by which a couple can avoid premarital intercourse.[3]

Another Christian author, in a chapter entitled "Responsible Petting," says this:

> Petting can be a delicately tuned means of mutual discovery. It need not be a cheap way of having the thrills of starting out toward intercourse without the derring-do to finish it. Petting can be an end in itself. It can be a process in which two people explore each other's feelings with no intention of having intercourse. Communication can take place that conveys personal closeness and sharing, with flexible but recognizable limits. It demands, of course, a sophisticated sense of appropriateness if it is not going to trap the players in a fondling game that goes beyond the implicit limits of their relationship. And this in turn calls for education of young people in responsible relationships. Thus petting is a tender route that *could* lead to coitus, but need not intend to go that far. It has many natural exits, each of which is marked by invisible signs that signal the place to stop, according to the amount of involvement that the two players have with each other as persons. It is not a cataract that carries partners over the falls of passion unless they halt the plunge and suffer the lesser fits of frustration. It is an adventure in personal understanding and intimacy that calls for control and discipline.[4]

Such teaching provides an obvious moral justification for virtually any level of sexual stimulation outside of marriage. When wanting to become sexually involved, most young people will quickly conclude that they are indeed sophisticated and that theirs is a responsible relationship in which petting can be tender and a delicately tuned means of mutual discovery. For them, no doubt, petting can be an adventure in personal understanding, not a cheap way of having thrills. Indeed, if we bought this author's reasoning, any couple abstaining from petting would appear to be destined to a shallow relationship.

In the flush of hormonal torrents, any mind, young or old, can act out its lust and easily rationalize it with this sort of deceptive terminology. Twice the author uses the word "intention" or "intend," saying that the couple need not plan on having intercourse just because they are petting. The fact is—I say this as a counselor and former youth pastor—among Christians premarital sex is rarely planned, at least the first time. What is originally intended by the petting quickly becomes beside the point when one is in the midst of it.

I do not agree that petting "has many natural exits, each of which is marked by invisible signs." What are invisible signs— are they like inaudible noises? How does one see an invisible sign, or know when he has seen one? Since petting is a physiological and emotional preparation for sexual intercourse, it will inevitably propel itself toward sexual intercourse. While there are exits, they are the very opposite of natural.

Instead of talking about intentions in petting, we should talk about probable *results*. A man on a diet can go into a doughnut shop with the intention of only having coffee. The probable result, of course, is that he will also have several doughnuts. If we permit intentions to be the bottom line of morality, we are in sorry shape indeed. My counseling experience indicates that the Christian community is full of unintentional adulteries, unplanned fornications, and unpremeditated sins of every variety.

I believe that we as Christians (and especially as Christian leaders) must be careful not to provide for ourselves and others —particularly our young people—any grounds for rationalization that emboldens them to pursue activities that range from unwise to immoral.

Practical Precautions to Avoid Premarital Fondling

What steps can an unmarried person take to cultivate meaningful relationships while avoiding sexual intimacy? I offer these guidelines not only to young people but to their parents and youth leaders, who are often in the best position to communicate them.

First, each person must determine at what point his body begins to prepare for intercourse and make sure he does not engage in any physical contact which brings him to that point or beyond. Then this needs to be written down as a standard and diligently adhered to. If you think it is hard to set standards and keep them, it is much harder once the line is crossed to back up and start over. It is still possible, however, and those who have done so should ask God's forgiveness and recommit themselves to their original standards.

Becoming accountable to a parent, pastor, or other respected authority can be very helpful. Share your standards with them, and ask them to ask you from time to time how the battle's going.

In dating, focus on conversation not physical contact. Above all, avoid set-ups like the plague. A car on a lonely road, a couch in a house where everyone is gone or asleep, large gaps of unplanned time, being out late, and being in each other's bedrooms are clear invitations to immorality.

Remember that your youthfulness involves strong sexual desires but often neither the wisdom nor experience to effectively control them once they are set in motion. This is why Paul said to Timothy, a young pastor, "flee from youthful lusts" (2 Timothy 2:22, NASB). Be aware of your vulnerability—don't overestimate your ability to resist temptation.

If you and your parents have discerned before God that it is his will for you to be married and you are wearing down in your battle for sexual purity, you should marry soon (1 Corinthians 7:9). If this is impossible or if you are otherwise unready or unwilling to be married, you should back off in your relationship. It is asking for trouble to maintain an intimate relationship over a long period of time when you are losing the battle for sexual purity.[5]

Remember, difficult as all this effort to please God is, it will bring great reward in the future: "A man reaps what he sows. . . . Let us not become weary in doing good, for at the proper time we will reap a harvest if we do not give up" (Galatians 6:7,9).

Chapter 15, Notes

1. David Seamands, "Sex, Inside and Outside Marriage," Gary Collins, ed., *Secrets of Our Sexuality* (Waco, TX: Word Books, 1976), 157.

2. Dwight Small, "Dating: With or Without Petting," *Essays on Love* (Downers Grove, Ill: InterVarsity Press, 1968), 20.

3. Steve Clapp, *A Christian View of Youth and Sexuality* (Sidell, Ill: C-4 Resources, 1981), 39, 41, 42.

4. Lewis Smedes, *Sex for Christians* (Grand Rapids: William B. Eerdmans, 1976), 151-52.

5. For a discussion of this and other dangers of lengthy engagements, see Randy C. Alcorn, "How Long Is Long Enough," *Moody Monthly,* June 1983, 20-23.

Chapter 16

The Consequences of Sexual Sin

"**W**hy shouldn't single people get in on sex?" The question came from the audience of a popular television talk show and was directed at the panel of three Christian authors and their wives.

"We're not saying that unmarried people can't get a kick out of sex," came the reply. "We're just saying we believe in God's commandments. They're written on stone, and you can't break them without them breaking you!"

The Law of the Harvest

Violating God's sexual standards is like violating the law of gravity—it has a way of catching up with you. The laws apply regardless of who believes in them and who doesn't. The unbeliever lives in the same moral universe—*God's universe*—as the believer and is therefore liable to the same moral laws (one need not believe in the law of gravity to be subject to it).

> Do not be deceived: God cannot be mocked. A man reaps what he sows. The one who sows to please his sinful nature, from that nature will reap destruction; the

one who sows to please the Spirit, from the Spirit will reap eternal life (Galatians 6:7-8).

The Christian who treats sex with proper sanctity, elevating it in marriage and rejecting it outside, will be blessed and rewarded by God. The believer who plays with sex, takes it lightly, and compromises God's principles opens up a Pandora's box that floods his life with a wave of evils he never imagined. Those who try to get the best of both worlds end up with the worst of both.

Scripture doesn't deny sin's attractiveness or its pleasures. It simply says those pleasures are fleeting while their consequences stick like glue. Viewed from the long haul, sin is *always* a raw deal.

Words to the Wise

After warning his son not to lust after an immoral woman, Solomon asked two rhetorical questions:

> Can a man scoop fire into his lap
>   without his clothes being burned?
> Can a man walk on hot coals
>   without his feet being scorched?
>   (Proverbs 6:27-28)

The obvious answer is *no*—consequences are inescapable.

In case the point of the illustrations was missed, Solomon brings it home:

> So is he who sleeps with another man's wife;
>   no one who touches her will go unpunished.
>   (Proverbs 6:29)

There is no disparity here between the testaments. The New sounds the same warning as the Old, directed right at believers: "God will judge the adulterer" (Hebrews 13:4).

Throughout Proverbs a special emphasis is placed on the consequences of sexual sin:

For the lips of an adulteress drip honey,
　　and her speech is smoother than oil;
but in the end she is bitter as gall,
　　sharp as a double-edged sword.
Her feet go down to death;
　　her steps lead straight to the grave.
　　　　　　(Proverbs 5:3-5)

The alluring centerfold, packaged to sell, is Satan's lure and bait. She is the glossy tabloid equivalent of the same adulteress Solomon spoke of centuries ago:

I find more bitter than death
　　the woman who is a snare,
whose heart is a trap
　　and whose hands are chains.
The man who pleases God will escape her,
　　but the sinner she will ensnare.
　　　　　　(Ecclesiastes 7:26)

Not Just Wrong But Stupid

A friend and I had to confront a man we dearly loved who was living a lie. At one point my friend said to him, "What you're doing is wrong. And it's not only wrong, it's just plain stupid!" He was so right. In God's moral universe, governed by the law of the harvest, whatever is right is smart and whatever is wrong is stupid.

But a man who commits adultery lacks judgment;
　　whoever does so destroys himself.
Blows and disgrace are his lot,
　　and his shame will never be wiped away.
　　　　　　(Proverbs 6:32-33)

"You may be sure that your sin will find you out," Moses warned (Numbers 32:23). Sometimes this judgment of God will come only after we have left this world. More often, though, it touches us in this life as well.

Biblical Examples of Immorality's Consequences

The Bible has numerous examples of sexual sin and its consequences. Genesis records sexual sin in the lives of the people of Sodom (19:1-29), Lot and his daughters (19:30-38), Shechem (34:1-31), Reuben (35:22), Judah and Tamar (38:1-26), and Potiphar's wife (39:1-20).

Consider the consequences of these sexual sins. Sodom and Gomorrah were obliterated by God's judgment. The incest of Lot and his daughters produced two nations: the Moabites and the Ammonites, wicked people who plagued Israel for many generations. Revenge on Shechem's rape of Dinah resulted in the murder of every man in his city. The sins of Reuben and Judah brought shame to the house of Jacob. The uncontrolled lust of Potiphar's wife sent Joseph, an innocent man, to prison.

Samson was God's man of the hour, but his lust after beautiful but unrighteous women led directly to his tragic downfall (Judges 14-16). Not only Samson but his entire nation suffered because he satisfied his desires rather than obeying God's word.

David was as godly a man as Scripture portrays, yet 2 Samuel 11 documents the lust that brought him catastrophe. What began as relief from boredom ended in adultery. Actually, it didn't end there. David attempted to circumvent the consequences of his adultery—to cheat the law of the harvest—by covering up. In doing so his sin of adultery expanded to the murder of a righteous man and the death of David's infant son.

David's model of immorality was not lost on his family. When David's son Amnon lusted for his half-sister Tamar, he took what he wanted, just as his father had. This prompted Absalom's murder of Amnon, followed by David's banishment of Absalom. That in turn led to the bitterness that divided David and Absalom and eventually divided the nation.

The final blow was the death of Absalom, for whom David grieved inconsolably (2 Samuel 18:33). Three sons dead, his daughter raped, his family name disgraced. David fulfilled his own words by paying for his sins four times over (2 Samuel 12:6).

True to form, even Solomon, the son in whom David put most hope, eventually let his devotion stray from God to ungodly women. In trying to please his seven hundred wives and three hundred concubines, Solomon built altars to their false gods and brought divine judgment on himself and all Israel (1 Kings 11:1-13).

Sometimes God's judgment on sexual sin is immediate and obvious. Paul warned the Corinthians to learn from the example of Israel in Moses' day: "We should not commit sexual immorality, as some of them did—and in one day twenty-three thousand of them died" (1 Corinthians 10:8). When twenty-three thousand people in one place are struck dead for sexual sin (among other things), the message is not a subtle one.

The Physical Consequences of Sexual Sin

Traditionally, books on Christian morality have stressed heavily the possible physical consequences of sexual sin, specifically unwanted pregnancy and venereal disease. Yet these are not the fundamental reasons for abstaining from extramarital sex. Pregnancy can often be avoided through birth control, and most venereal diseases, while serious, can be medically treated. Pregnancy and venereal disease are not sins and never have been. They are only possible consequences. Immorality is the sin.

How many people have acted immorally but have been lucky enough or, worse yet, deliberate enough to have avoided pregnancy and venereal disease? Some frown at the pregnant unmarried teenager while smiling at the wonderful young couple in the youth group who, unknown to anyone, behind closed doors are using contraceptives or have had an abortion. (Admire the unwed mother for her courage—she did not have to carry that child.)

Pregnancy and venereal disease are only possible consequences of immorality. Avoiding them while having illicit sexual relations may demonstrate foresight but not morality.

Mental and Emotional Consequences of Sexual Sin

Amnon thought he was deeply in love with Tamar. Yet what he thought was love turned to bitter hatred and disgust after he had raped her (2 Samuel 13:15). Lust, disguising itself as love, often reflects disdain, not commitment, once it is gratified. Many young girls who have sexually surrendered to their boyfriends have learned the "Amnon effect" the hard way. Promises of lifelong love and commitment flow freely in the heat of passion but often turn to indifference and even contempt.

One afternoon I spoke to a large class of high school seniors in a public school. "Why should I stop having sex with my boyfriend?" asked one girl. "He loves me, and I know he'll marry me."

"How do you know?" I replied. I shared from experience and research that a high percentage of engagements are broken off, and the majority of people who consider themselves practically engaged do not end up marrying each other. Even the term "premarital sex" is a misnomer because it assumes marriage will take place (either to this person or another). Often it does not.

"But even if he does marry you, will he be faithful?" I asked. "Obviously, he believes in sex outside of marriage. Otherwise he wouldn't go to bed with you now. If he doesn't limit sex to marriage now, what makes you think he will once the two of you are married? Will you ever be able to really trust him, or he you?"

Another consequence of sexual sin is the comparison trap. In a sense we are programmed with each sexual encounter. A man may remember a partner who was more sexually aggressive or more physically attractive. A woman may remember a man who was more sensitive or had a better physique. Comparison can be deadly.

My wife and I are indescribably thankful that we have no one to compare each other to as sexual partners. Couples who marry as virgins have much to be grateful for. Those who have come to Christ from morally loose backgrounds will usually be quick to tell you the same.

Immorality permanently taints some people's view of sex. Their first sexual encounters came in the back seat of a car or on a living room couch, where both hearts fluttered every time the wind blew or the door rattled. In such cases, sex may be inseparably linked to feelings of fear and guilt. Eventually, some who choose to enjoy sex outside marriage cannot enjoy it *inside* marriage.

Extramarital sex lends itself to shallow relationships. The focus is on the body, not the real person. Sexual involvement produces more sweat but less conversation. One disillusioned young man told me of his relationship with a girl: "I wanted something meaningful, but all I got was sex."

Many young people try to prove their love by sexual surrender. But when a relationship has no more unexplored dimensions, boredom usually sets in along with loss of respect. Sexual compromise is actually the surest way to end a good relationship. Ironically, it is also an effective way to prolong a bad relationship—many people end up marrying the wrong person because of their sexual involvement (a disastrous consequence that affects the rest of their lives).

The Spiritual Consequences of Immorality

While the physical consequences of immorality may be circumvented, the spiritual consequences are inevitable. Antibiotics will prevent or cure some venereal diseases. The pill will lower the chances of pregnany. Abortion is a way out of an unwanted pregnancy. But no scientific or medical breakthrough ever changes the fact that I will answer to God for my moral choices. Medical science may eliminate some consequences of my sin, but it cannot remove my accountability to God.[1]

It was to religious people that God said,

> "When you spread out your hands in prayer,
> I will hide my eyes from you;
> even if you offer many prayers,
> I will not listen" (Isaiah 1:15).

When the adulterous people of Israel sought God they would not find him, he said, for he would withdraw himself from them (Hosea 5:6). Similar statements are found throughout the Old Testament.

To those living in immorality, here is the message: Husband, don't bother praying at meals—God isn't listening. Wife, don't lead out in prayer at a women's Bible study—God won't hear you. Young couple, don't pray that God will bless the wedding ceremony—his ears are deaf to you. Pastor, don't ask God's anointing on Sunday's sermon. If you are living in sexual sin, there is one prayer he is waiting for—the prayer of sincere confession and repentance. He longs for you to start fresh with him again.

"I wanted to pray that I could share the gospel with my friend. But I knew God wouldn't hear me because of what I was doing." This young man was sexually involved with his girlfriend. Without knowing the Scripture quoted above, he sensed his prayers were being blocked by his sin. He was right. By the grace of God he repented, and God was once again pleased to hear and answer.

Our sexual lives cannot be isolated from our spiritual lives. The believers in Corinth tried to separate the two. They still participated in the idolatry and immorality they grew up with and thought they could somehow remain spiritually unaffected by it. Paul told them they were wrong (1 Corinthians 6:12-20; 10:14-22). God is concerned with what I do with my body, for it is the temple of my spirit—and his.

The Effects of Sexual Sin upon Family and Church

We would like to think that if our sexual sin has consequences, at least we alone will bear them. But this is simply not the case.

No doubt some resented the fact that one man, Achan, caused thirty-six men to die because of his sin (Joshua 7:1-26). Perhaps some questioned too why his whole family was put to death for that sin. We may not understand why, but surely we must learn the lesson that the sins of one can bring terrible consequences on others.

Cindy was twelve years old when her father, a church leader active in evangelism, committed adultery with a woman in the church (his wife's best friend) and left his family. Deeply hurt, Cindy's godly mother remarried hastily and unwisely. In fact, she married a non-Christian.

The whole scandal was well known throughout the small community, and Cindy had to live with looks of pity and scorn whenever she walked through town. Though a Christian today, Cindy has been through a long series of bad relationships with men, including repeated sexual compromises. Though she is fully responsible for her actions, she is also reaping what her father sowed (Exodus 20:5).

A man formerly active in Christian work resigned because of his homosexual activities. I asked him, "What could have been said to you that might have prevented your first involvement in homosexuality?" After carefully thinking he said, "If someone could have helped me envision the tragedy it would bring to my ministry and the disgrace it would bring to Christ's name, I might never have done it. I have forfeited great ministry opportunities that may never come my way again."

Every church, every Christian organization that harbors sin, sexual or otherwise, simply *cannot* experience the fullness of God's blessing. "A little yeast works through the whole batch of dough" says Paul (1 Corinthians 5:6). His command to the entire Corinthian church was to remove the man guilty of sexual sin lest his presence contaminate others in the body as well as bring them all under God's judgment.

The Effects of Sexual Sin on the World

Perhaps there is no more tragic consequence to the sexual sin of Christians than its effect on non-Christians. Nathan said to David, in the wake of his sexual sin, "by doing this you have made the enemies of the LORD show utter contempt . . ." (2 Samuel 12:14).

Nonbelievers, both the sincere and the insincere, look at immorality among Christians and simply conclude that we are hypocrites and no different than the rest of the world.

Sometimes, unfortunately, they are right.

While God is working to bring people to Christ through the love and holiness of his people, Satan will do all in his power to rob the church of her purity and consequently of her effective witness to the watching world. Only when the people of God confess and repent will they have a credible and effective witness to the non-Christian world (Psalm 51:10-13).

CONCLUSION

If we would only rehearse in advance the consequences of immorality, we would be far less prone to commit it.

When I turned eighteen, my friends threw a surprise birthday party for me. They gave me two cakes, covered with delicious frosting and beautiful decorations. But when I was given the knife to cut them reality set in. I had been deceived. What appeared to be mouthwatering cakes turned out to be two Sears catalogs covered with frosting.

The gift was not what it seemed. In that case it was funny. But when we fall for Satan's lies about sex, there is nothing funny about it. This world is filled with disillusioned and bitter people who have run into a brick wall at the end of a dark alley marked "Sexual Freedom." Despite our rationale for violating God's will, the law of the harvest stands—what we plant, we will reap.

But we should likewise never forget that the law of the harvest applies as much to the rewards of righteousness as to the consequences of sin. If we plant sexual purity today—difficult though it be—in another season we will reap a rich harvest.

Chapter 16, Notes

1. I highly recommend for all young women Lissa Halls Johnson's *Just Like Ice Cream* (Palm Springs, Calif.: Ronald N. Haynes Publishers, 1982). This outstanding "romance novel" puts in realistic story form the tragic consequences in a girl's life as she watches her storybook romance turn into a nightmare of sin's consequences. But even then, the grace of God is there to help her.

Chapter 17

Forgiveness for Sexual Sin

"*M*ore than anything, I want to feel clean. I want to *be* clean," Terry sighed.

Terry was raised in a Christian home. But for twenty of his forty years he'd lived a life of homosexual promiscuity with hundreds of sexual partners.

The good news is that people like Terry—people like you and me—*can* be clean. Forgiveness and moral cleansing come from asking and accepting Christ's provision for our sin.

Jesus and Sexual Sinners

Jesus loved and forgave sexual sinners. The gospels take pains to tell us that. He lived in a culture that mercilessly stigmatized immoral women. Branded as sinners of the worst kind, these women carried a life-long scarlet letter. Yet Jesus reached out and touched their lives, among them the Samaritan woman of John 4, the adulterous woman of John 8, and the immoral woman of Luke 7.

"Neither do I condemn you," he said to the adulterous woman. "Go now and leave your life of sin" (John 8:11).

Of the immoral but repentant woman Jesus said, "Her

many sins have been forgiven—for she loved much. But he who has been forgiven little loves little." "Your sins are forgiven," he assured her. "Your faith has saved you; go in peace" (Luke 7:47-50).

Sexual sin is serious, but it is not beyond Jesus' grace and power to forgive. He outraged the chief priests and elders by telling them, "the prostitutes are entering the kingdom of God ahead of you" (Matthew 21:31).

Jesus not only forgives sexual sin, he understands sexual temptation:

> For we do not have a high priest who is unable to sympathize with our weaknesses, but we have one who has been tempted in every way, just as we are— yet was without sin. Let us then approach the throne of grace with confidence, so that we may receive mercy and find grace to help us in our time of need (Hebrews 4:15-16).

How Much Can God Forgive?

The parable of the unmerciful servant (Matthew 18:21-35) teaches us two things about sin: first, it is infinitely beyond our capacity to repay, and second, it is infinitely greater than any offense we have suffered—or could suffer—at the hands of others. Without a penetrating perspective of ourselves as impoverished sinners, we cannot appreciate God's grace and cannot truly forgive others as we should.

The forgiveness of God is a prominent theme throughout Scripture, one that should invoke from us expressions of wonder and praise. I cite here a single passage from each testament. There are countless others.

> The LORD is compassionate and gracious,
>> slow to anger, abounding in love.
> He will not always accuse,
>> nor will he harbor his anger forever;

he does not treat us as our sins deserve
　　or repay us according to our iniquities.
For as high as the heavens are above the earth,
　　so great is his love for those who fear him;
as far as the east is from the west,
　　so far has he removed our transgressions from us.
As a father has compassion on his children,
　　so the LORD has compassion on those who fear
　　　　him;
for he knows how we are formed,
　　he remembers that we are dust.
　　　　　　　(Psalm 103:8-14)

What, then, shall we say in response to this? If God is for us, who can be against us? He who did not spare his own Son, but gave him up for us all—how will he not also, along with him, graciously give us all things? Who will bring any charge against those whom God has chosen? It is God who justifies. Who is he that condemns? Christ Jesus, who died—more than that, who was raised to life—is at the right hand of God and is also interceding for us. Who shall separate us from the love of Christ? Shall trouble or hardship or persecution or famine or nakedness or danger or sword? . . . No, in all these things we are more than conquerors through him who loved us. For I am convinced that neither death nor life, neither angels nor demons, neither the present nor the future, nor any powers, neither height nor depth, nor anything else in all creation, will be able to separate us from the love of God that is in Christ Jesus our Lord (Romans 8:31-39).

What is the bottom line of God's forgiveness? He has seen me at my worst and still loves me; because he knows everything I've ever thought or done, there are no skeletons in my closet;

his love for me cannot be earned and therefore cannot be lost; and I am totally secure in his unconditional work of grace for me.

Christ not only removes my condemnation and considers me innocent, he declares me *righteous*. I am as acceptable, yes *commendable*, to the Father as Christ himself (2 Corinthians 5:21). God is totally and irreversibly satisfied with me because he is totally and irreversibly satisfied with Christ's work on my behalf (1 John 2:2; 4:10).

Paul gave the Corinthians this bad news:

Neither the sexually immoral nor idolaters nor adulterers nor male prostitutes nor homosexual offenders nor thieves nor the greedy nor drunkards nor slanderers nor swindlers will inherit the kingdom of God (1 Corinthians 6:9-10).

But he didn't stop there:

And that is what some of you were. But you were washed, you were sanctified, you were justified in the name of the Lord Jesus Christ and by the Spirit of our God (6:11).

This is a matter of transformed identity—in Christ, we are no longer who we used to be. "Therefore, if anyone is in Christ, he is a new creation; the old has gone, the new has come!" (2 Corinthians 5:17). I am Christ's bride, clothed in "fine linen, bright and clean" (Revelation 19:7-8). *Clean*—the very thing Terry, my tired and defeated homosexual friend, longed to be.

Then What about the Consequences?

One of the hardest questions we face is how to reconcile two paradoxical scriptural principles: forgiveness for sin and having to live with the consequences of sin. We must face the fact that the Bible clearly teaches both, and we must believe both even if we do not understand how they can both be true.

Christ took upon himself the *ultimate* consequences of my

sin—eternal death. This I will never have to experience. But the unpleasant fact remains that in this life there are still consequences for some of the very sins he has removed from me.

If I drank a bottle of wine, got in my car, drove seventy miles an hour in the rain, and hit and killed a ten-year-old girl on her bicycle, would God forgive me if I repented? Of course. Would his forgiveness bring the girl back to life? Of course not. Nor would it save me from prosecution and possible imprisonment.

Christ's blood cleanses us from sin's guilt, but it does not remove all of sin's consequences. God can forgive me for premarital sex, but I can never be a virgin again. God can forgive me for a homosexual relationship, but I might still contract a venereal disease that may plague me the rest of my life.

Being forgiven doesn't change our accountability for what we've done. Repentance doesn't alter the laws of biology that affect pregnancy, the forces that cause venereal disease, or even (automatically) the emotional trauma related to guilt. God may supernaturally remove these things if he chooses, and no doubt he sometimes does. It appears that far more often, however, he does not.

Forgiveness of sin is real. Consequences for sin are also real. Neither invalidates the other.

Whenever I teach this concept, I invariably receive some strong negative reactions. No matter how I stress forgiveness, people become upset, thinking I am saying Christ's blood is not enough to take away our sins.

In a Bible college class, several students were vigorously arguing with me that forgiveness is not *really* forgiveness if any consequences still have to be faced. One elderly lady in the class raised her hand and rescued me (possibly from being stoned!). Speaking in a hoarse and raspy voice, she said, "For forty years I smoked three packs of cigarettes a day. When I became a Christian ten years ago, I stopped. Call it a sin or just a bad habit, Christ forgave me for it and I gave it up. But listen to my voice. And take my word for it, my lungs are black. I have no trouble

at all understanding that we have to live with some consequences, even after God forgives us."

But don't I pay for my sins when I face consequences for
them?

No, not in any redemptive sense. Christ went to hell for us
on the cross; he does not want us to go through hell later *or* now.
He is there to help us face the natural consequences of our sin
and even enrich us through them.

Mary, a Christian woman who committed adultery, said:
"What I've done is too bad to expect forgiveness. Certainly my
husband can't forgive me, and I don't believe God can either. I
must suffer for it myself. There is no other way."

Mary knew her Bible—but she did not understand it. To
live in a self-imposed purgatory or to inflict it on others says
Christ's work is insufficient and implies a worthiness and capacity of our own to pay off our debt. Attempts at self-atonement
are as prideful as they are pitiful.

Mary is still living in a prison, groaning under her captiv-
ity, yet all the while holding in her hand the key (Christ's redemptive work) to unlock the chains and bars that hold her. As
for her sexual sin, her refusal to accept Christ's forgiveness will
not give her strength to avoid it. Far more likely, it will prompt
her to repeat it.

Many believers are like Mary, laboring under such guilt
that they "unconsciously arrange their lives—even to the point
of choosing poor marriage partners or unworthy occupations—
so they can punish themselves."[1]

Christ paid the debt for our sins. He did it once and he did
it right. We must accept his atonement, not try to repeat it.

Living with Our Failures

Yet how *can* we live with ourselves when we have sinned
against God and failed to live pure lives? First, by realizing that
growth is often achieved through picking up the pieces after we
have miserably failed. Scripture does not say a righteous man
never falls. It does say "though a righteous man falls seven

times, he rises again" (Proverbs 24:16). Whenever we fall we have opportunity to learn a lesson about the sufficiency of Christ. Self-sufficiency is the great enemy of faith. Failure is the great enemy of self-sufficiency.

Some of the healthiest people in this country are former heart attack victims. Because they took their heart attacks seriously, they began to eat right, exercise regularly, and live as healthy lives as possible. Some of them are accomplished marathon runners. Many will long outlive their friends who never experienced their trauma—and were therefore never shaken into changing their lives.

Likewise, some of the most spiritual people I know once lived in immorality. There *is* forgiveness, deliverance, and new life for anyone, regardless of his or her background. In fact, God views such backgrounds as opportunities to display the extent of his grace and life-changing power.

A Warning to the Presumptuous

Those who understand God's grace understand that this does not mean we should seek to fall into sin—"Shall we go on sinning so that grace may increase? By no means! We died to sin; how can we live in it any longer?" (Romans 6:1-2). The grace of God should never lead to presumption, indifference, or dropping our guard against temptation. In fact, it should have the opposite effect (Titus 2:11-12).

Not only does sin have consequences, but each time we sin we reinforce a pattern that becomes harder and harder to break. If we persist in sin with the thought that one day we will get right with God, we should remind ourselves that God may still be there to forgive and restore . . . but *we* may not be.

What about Guilt Feelings?

More and more Christians are adopting the position of secular psychologists (who *are* occasionally right, of course) that all guilt feelings are harmful. Whether or not this is true depends on one's definitions of "guilt" and "guilt feelings."

In one sense, only those with a seared or desensitized conscience never feel any guilt. Mass murderers, for instance, sometimes have no guilt feelings at all. Obviously, an absence of guilt feelings is no guarantee of spiritual or mental health.

There is what *could* be called a feeling of guilt that often accompanies the convicting work of the Holy Spirit. It is a sorrow for true guilt (unrighteousness) that leads to repentance (2 Corinthians 7:9). Whether or not this should be called a guilt feeling is not all that important. What is important is that there *is* such a thing as true moral guilt (as many secular psychologists do not acknowledge), and that guilt must be somehow perceived in order to be dealt with. We should therefore be grateful for a guilt feeling *if* it does in fact stem from true guilt, *if* it flows from a mental perception of that guilt, *if* it prompts us to take the God-given measures to deal with that guilt, and *if* it subsides once the true guilt is removed.

David expresses deep feelings of guilt (Psalm 32:3-5; 51:3-4) and attributes them to the heavy hand of God leading him to confession, repentance, and a fresh start.

Two common kinds of guilt feelings, however, are tragic—those rooted in true moral guilt, yet not leading to confession, repentance, and freedom from the guilt and its accompanying feelings, and guilt feelings stemming from false guilt.

Motivator or Demotivator?

Often children who have been sexually abused, especially in incestuous relationships, feel overwhelmingly guilty. Some people feel guilty just for struggling with sexual temptation, which itself is not sin. An adolescent may be consumed with out-of-proportion guilt because he seems unable to stop masturbating. Some people feel guilty about everything—and are spiritually paralyzed because of it.

Unresolved guilt feelings are demotivating. A coach who demeans and belittles doesn't bring out the best in most of us. On the contrary, he makes us feel like quitting. Likewise, residual guilt feelings (those left after confession and forgiveness) do not inspire us to better behavior but to worse.

Discouragement never fosters accomplishment. The cycle of defeat in many Christians is as predictable as it is devastating: we fail, feel guilty, try to offset our guilt by making new resolutions, then fail again and feel more guilty than ever. After the cycle repeats itself again and again, many of us just give up. "Why try any more when you know you'll fail?" The result is an endless vortex in which we love God but trust God too little, and hate ourselves but trust ourselves too much.

Like a dark cloud, guilt feelings hover over us, sapping us of spiritual energy. False guilt feelings, or guilt not dealt with, can drive us to depression and suicide, and more often to a paralysis of the will that results in a defeated Christian life.[2]

What to Do When I Sin

What steps should I take in order to deal with sin? First, *I must admit my sin to myself*. I need to call sin sin, not just a mistake or a little slip, and quit rationalizing and making excuses. Jesus died for our sins, not our excuses for our sins.

Second, *I must confess my sin to God*. Since he knows about it already, the purpose is not to inform him. It is to verbally agree with God that what I have done is in fact sin.

Third, as a part of my admission and confession, *I must genuinely repent*. True confession is not a begrudging or flippant admission of wrong doing, but an expression of guilt, regret, *and* desire and intention to change. I have had people tell me they were sorry for adultery, yet refuse to quit seeing their lover. Actually, their sorrow is for sin's consequences, not for sin. They *admitted* something—but they confessed nothing.

Finally there is a place in the family and church to *confess my sins not only to God but to others* (James 5:16). Two cautions should be exercised in such confession: first, it is made to those who have actually been hurt by the behavior (this may or may not include a whole church body), and second, details should be shared only as necessary. God has no problem forgetting the details but people do. Why etch on their minds images that will be hard or impossible to shake?

I believe adultery is a sin that should be confessed to one's partner, but I have seen husbands and wives share details of adulterous relationships that left vivid pictures, deepened wounds, and increased bitterness. I know one pastor who took a young woman from his church out to lunch to confess—and ask her forgiveness for—his lustful thoughts toward her. Embarrassed but flattered, within a month the girl was having an affair with him. Unwise and undiscerning confession dishonors God and may actually compound the problem.

Forgive Others

If we have admitted, confessed, and repented of our sin, we have been forgiven by God whether or not we feel like it. But there is yet another dimension and evidence of forgiveness. If we have experienced God's forgiveness, it will be shown in our forgiveness of others. In the parable of the unmerciful servant, Jesus teaches that forgiving others is part and parcel of our own forgiveness (Matthew 18:21-35).

"You must forgive to be forgiven" is a foreign concept to many believers. Strange, since it is clearly assumed in the most often repeated passage in Scripture, the Lord's Prayer: "Forgive us our debts, as we also have forgiven our debtors" (Matthew 6:12). In fact, this is apparently the central emphasis of the prayer for it is the only aspect Christ elaborates on in the following verses:

> For if you forgive men when they sin against you,
> your heavenly Father will also forgive you. But if
> you do not forgive men their sins, your Father will
> not forgive your sins (Matthew 6:14-15).

"But how can I forgive my wife for committing adultery?" "How can I forgive my fiancé for pressuring me into premarital sex?" "How can I forgive my father for molesting me?" Without a doubt, sexual sins are among the hardest to forgive, but clearly they are not an exception to Christ's rule of forgiveness.

I have seen great miracles of rebuilding when one partner

has truly forgiven the other's adultery, and bitter tragedies when forgiveness was not sought or sought but not received. One of the most powerful miracles occurred when a thirty-year-old woman went back to her father and told him she forgave him for sexually abusing her when she was a child.

Forgiveness is a matter of choice not feelings. Yes, we may remember the facts, but we must not allow ourselves to dwell on them. The offense must be buried in the past and not exhumed in the present. It *is* possible to "forgive and forget" if we truly do forgive. But we will never forget what we choose to brood over, and if we brood over it we demonstrate we have not truly forgiven.

We must refuse to cater to our emotions or indulge our fatal tendency toward bitterness. We must not simply suppress resentment but confess it as sin. "Time heals all wounds" is an erroneous maxim. If we do not rehearse others' offenses, if we do not indulge our vengeful tendencies, then time will bring healing. But time never heals the cancer of bitterness—it only allows it to grow.

"Can we really forgive those who continue in sin?" We should never excuse them, defend them, or guard them from the consequences of their sin. We can't always eliminate our pain. But we can release them—and ourselves—from our bitterness or resentment.

Forgiveness is not unrealistic. A woman whose husband continues over a period of time in unrepentant adultery is not to pretend nothing is happening. She might take steps that include separating herself and the children from him. Certainly, she must let him see that continued sin will take its toll. To whitewash his sin hurts him as much as herself and the children. She should forgive him "seventy times seven," but that does not mean when he continually rips the fabric of their marriage she will be a party to his sin by keeping up the front of an unbroken home.

It *does* mean, however, that she will pray for his repentance and offer restoration if it comes. It also means that—

realizing she cannot control him and he will answer not to her but to God—she will surrender to God her claim on his life. Even if he never repents and she never lives with him again, she is called upon to offer him forgiveness. It is painful yet possible for us to forgive the worst offenses.

Moving on from Past Sins

"I wish I'd wake up and the nightmare would be over. I wish so much I'd never been unfaithful." Helen was sincere. But, like many of us, she needed to leave her past—and the sin of her past—and move on. Once confessed and repented of, sin should be put behind us.

When I was a boy, I had a golden retriever named Champ. Whenever we gave him a bone, he'd chew it till it was bare, then take off to bury it. But once it was buried, he would never let it lie. Every day, sometimes several times a day, he would make his rounds, going to every buried bone—dozens of them—and digging them up to chew on some more. Then he'd bury them again, only to repeat the process till the day he died.

Unlike my dog, God buries our sins and lets them lie; he never digs them up. Like my dog, however, sometimes we do. We dig up old sins, chew on them, confess them again, and bury them—but in a shallow grave whose location we memorize for convenient access. We do this not only to ourselves but others. We piously say "I forgive you," but dig up old sins to chew on at our pity parties, wave in front of others as gossip, or use as weapons of revenge or tools to barter and manipulate. In doing so, we become obsessed with sin instead of the Savior. We give more credit to its power than to his.

Once confessed, sins should be forgotten. We should choose to dwell on them no longer.

> Forgetting what is behind and straining toward what is ahead, I press on toward the goal to win the prize for which God has called me heavenward in Christ Jesus (Philippians 3:13-14).

Chapter 17, Notes

1. Bruce Narramore and Bill Counts, *Freedom from Guilt* (Eugene, Ore.: Harvest House Publishers, 1974), 12.

2. See Narramore and Counts, *Freedom from Guilt,* for a fuller development of this concept.

PART 4

WHAT CAN WE DO TO PROMOTE SEXUAL PURITY?

Chapter 18

What We Can Do in the Family

*T*he individual believer needs to remove sources of sexual temptation, avoid temptation, and run from temptation—"flee from sexual immorality" (1 Corinthians 6:18). When he cannot remove it, avoid it, or run from it (usually he can), he must dig in his heels, call upon the purity of his new identity in Christ (Colossians 3:1-14) and the power of the indwelling Spirit, and stand firm with his God-given armor, wielding "the sword of the Spirit, which is the word of God" (Ephesians 6:17). All this he must do quickly, since it is most true of sexual temptation that "he who hesitates is lost."

No one can become prepared for such a battle on short notice. Prior to the confrontation the mind must have been exposed to God's Word, the life planted in a climate of spiritual growth that includes Bible study, prayer, and Christian fellowship. The believer who isolates sexual temptation from the whole of his life in Christ is doomed to failure.

There are a few books that deal with sexual temptation, and many that deal with temptation in general. Some of these offer help to the individual Christian. Too often, however, the believer is addressed as just that—an individual. He is seen as fending for himself in the sexual wilderness, isolated from the major formers and reinforcers of identity—his family, his church, and his society.

In these final three chapters we will examine what the family and church can do for the believer to cultivate his sexual purity, and what believers together can do for the sexual-moral welfare of our society.

WHAT PARENTHOOD IS ALL ABOUT

When my daughters were two and four, I took them out for breakfast at a restaurant. On the way back to the car, I was surprised to see they both had toothpicks in their mouths. Reaching to my mouth, I found I too had a toothpick. Unconsciously, I had picked it up at the counter after paying. It's a habit, something I always do but never think about. And almost as second naturedly as I, my little girls—who didn't even know what a toothpick was for—imitated my action.

There, in miniature, is parenthood. Children pick up on everything we do, consciously or unconsciously. Sometimes it's amusing. Sometimes it's scary.

As one family watched television together an immoral scene came on the screen. Being good Christian parents, mom and dad asked the children to leave the room (that is, unfortunately, more than many parents would do). But they themselves kept watching. What lesson did the children learn?

"I can't watch garbage but mom and dad can. When I grow up, I can watch garbage too because garbage is okay for big people."

A Christian father can say "Sex outside of marriage is wrong," but when his son sees him leering at a woman at the beach or on television or in a magazine, a whole different value system is taught—the parent's *real* value system, not the one he professes. Sometimes your children may fail to listen to you. Rarely will they fail to imitate you.

Develop a Strong Marriage

The quality of your family life will not rise above the quality of your marriage. The greatest sexual legacy you can give your children is to show them a good marriage, to daily demonstrate loyal love for your spouse. My wife excels at this. She is always building me up in our children's eyes, showing respect and appreciation for me, as I do for her. This is never lost on the children.

Good cross-sexual relationships build good cross-sexual relationships. It's hard for a teenage girl to know what to look for in a guy when she (and most likely her mother) doesn't respect her dad.

Make improving your marriage a project. Buy one of the myriad of good books on communication and strengthening your marriage. Attend a marriage encounter weekend. Ask your pastor's help in strengthening your marriage.

Spend time together alone. Go out on dates. Put each other in your appointment books. Have someone you trust watch your children, then focus on each other for the evening.

Communicate. Share the little things and the big. Take an interest in each other's day. Talk about God. Read Scripture together. Pray together. Share your needs, your joys and sorrows, frustrations, plans and dreams.

When you're experiencing this kind of intimacy, it spills over into every facet of the family. It creates a climate in the home that is a tribute to sexual (male-female) relationships.

Being affectionate with your spouse not only expresses and enhances your intimacy, it teaches your children how special the ultimate male-female relationship can be. It says "touching is good," and "touching in marriage is the most special of all." Obviously, discretion is important. But your children need to see that affection flows out of commitment—that physical intimacy and marriage are two sides of the same coin despite what the rest of the world is telling them.

The husband and wife's sexual relationship is important as a cultivator of intimacy *and* a guard against immorality. That's why Paul says to the married: "Do not cheat each other of normal sexual intercourse" (1 Corinthians 7:5, Phillips).

Train Your Children

Both testaments make clear the parental responsibility to train children in the way of righteousness (Deuteronomy 6:1-9; Ephesians 6:4). Parents should first of all seek to cultivate a love and devotion to God in their children. Second, they should train them in moral principles, especially the principles of choice and consequence, wisdom and folly. In Proverbs, Solomon teaches his son practical moral principles including guidelines for sexual purity.

Children should be taught correct values, how to recognize conflicting values, and how to resist the temptations they present. They should be taught to value the inner person, not just the outer. First Peter 3:1-6 suggests mothers need to teach their daughters a great deal more than how to look in a mirror, put on makeup, and win the attention of boys.

> Charm is deceptive, and beauty is fleeting;
> but a woman who fears the Lord is to be praised.
> (Proverbs 31:30)

We need to put less emphasis on projecting images and more on cultivating character. Beauty is easily lost; character is an investment in eternity.

Children should be taught to love righteousness and hate sin. Too often Christian families declare a truce with sin and live in a state of detente—tolerating unrighteousness and letting it gradually claim more and more territory in the home.

The kind of clothing worn by children is the responsibility of their parents, especially the father. Any man will tell you that the current crop of women's swimsuits communicates only one thing to men—regardless of a woman's motives in wearing them. There will be some years that for the sake of sexual purity, mother's and daughter's swimsuits—and perhaps father's and son's—will have to be out of style. Children are trained by the clothing their parents allow and encourage them to wear.

One of the greatest assets you can pass on to your child is self-control. If he does not learn it from you at an early age, when he's older he may never carry on the holy habits of Bible study, prayer, and church attendance. Without self-control, he will find it exceptionally difficult to resist temptations, sexual and otherwise.

Develop close family relationships. Spend time together. Don't just say your family is priority—*show* them they're priority.

A close family is an accountable family. By loving each other and having fun together you earn the right to caution, challenge, and confront when you see wrong attitudes and actions. Too many parents descend from Mt. Olympus just long enough to throw a few lightning bolts. The hit and run approach to morally training your children is a disaster.

SERVING AS YOUR CHILD'S SEX EDUCATOR

Sex education begins at birth. Parents are their children's most influential sex educators, for children will learn from what their parents say and don't say, what they do and don't do— whether right or wrong.

Every child receives a sex education. The only questions are: From whom? When? Where?

Developing Sexual Identity

The most fundamental aspect of sex education is modeling and teaching proper sexual identity—helping boys learn to be boys and girls learn to be girls, and like it that way.

> In some cultures homosexuality is practically non-existent. Usually in those cultures where homosexuality is rare, proper sex roles for men and women are clearly differentiated; men are trained into the masculine sex role and women into the feminine sex role with little, if any, overlap between the two sexes.[1]

We saw in previous chapters the severe gender confusion in America, fostered both by the feminist and homosexual movements. With these forces working against healthy sexual identities, parents must take more responsibility than ever to see that their children understand and appreciate their sexual identities.

Every child is born with a definite and nonnegotiable sexual identity. He is male, or she is female. The genetic code is indelible and unchangeable.

Though the child's sexual identity is sure, his sense or perception of that identity is not. Normally that sense of gender identity comes naturally, so long as his family provides a structure and model of proper gender roles.

Sexual perceptions do not begin at puberty but at birth. Parents naturally and subconsciously treat a boy in one manner and a girl in another. It is not a matter of preference but difference. It is both natural and healthy. This is not to say that parents in any sense determine sexual identity. It is already there. What they do—or should do—is cultivate and reinforce it.

Often we tell our daughters how glad we are that God made them girls. We tell them boys are wonderful, but we encourage them to thank God he made them girls. We give them positive reinforcement when they take good care of their dolls and encourage them to work with their mother around the home. We want to link their sexual identities and roles to hers and help them develop helpful skills. As their father, I treat them with tenderness and honor, respecting their privacy and taking great delight in their femininity (by fussing over them when they wear pretty dresses, for example). In our family, we elevate motherhood. While we will never discourage our girls from advanced education or a career, we want them always to know that no calling is higher than that of wife and mother.

There are innumerable ways—many of them subtle—we can either reinforce or confuse our children's sexual identities. I know of families, for instance, where a boy has been frequently dressed in his sister's clothes, sometimes for amusement and sometimes because "he grows out of his clothes so fast." Often parents who wanted a girl but got a boy will tend to treat him as a girl. One man's parents even admitted this to him. Not coincidentally, he has since taken up a homosexual lifestyle. Parents who confuse or dilute their children's distinct sexual identities are storing up a great deal of grief for both their children and themselves.

The Critical Role of the Father

Sexual identity studies clearly show that the father is the parent who most greatly influences the sexual development of the children. If he is absent, indifferent, weak, or hostile, it will adversely affect both his sons' and daughters' sexual identities, in some cases resulting in homosexual tendencies. Often a mother will try to compensate for her husband's hostility or distance from the children, or his lack of leadership, and end up playing a domineering role in the home, further confusing the children's sexual identities and role perceptions.

Christian fathers who find themselves constantly away from home should keep this in mind. Curtailing outside activities, business hours, or even finding another job might free up the critical time your children need to have with you.

When death or divorce leave children without a father, it is important that the children, especially boys, regularly spend time with positive male role models, perhaps a college age boy or man in the church.[2]

Parents should not live under a burden of guilt for the lifestyle choices their grown children have made. Homosexuality is not always as predictable as it might sound. Sometimes parents do a fine job raising their children and it still happens. Nevertheless, homosexuality is certainly much easier to prevent than to correct. If you see signs of or tendencies toward homosexuality in your children, the earlier you deal with them the better.

I know of several cases where parents have been concerned about their child's sexual identity and behavior and were told, both by friends and professionals, "don't be alarmed" and "that's just a passing phase." Too often the passing phase develops into a lifestyle. Certainly, not every act of childhood curiosity will lead to sexual perversion. While they should avoid becoming paranoid or overreacting, Christian parents *must* be perceptive to their children's psychosexual development and needs.

The Importance of Modesty

Family modesty is likewise an important part of sex education. By modesty I do not mean a negative sort of paranoia that faints or screams when a child sees a parent or sibling without clothes on. Modesty is a healthy attitude that says, "My sexual parts are special. God made them that way. They are so special that I respect them by covering them when other people are around . . . just like mommy and daddy do."

While there is nothing wrong with children seeing their parents and siblings unclothed from time to time at an early age, I recommend that nudity not become a habitual part of family life.

Remember that sex drives exist considerably before puberty. A mother who thinks her son is "just a little boy" might be surprised to know what he's thinking when he sees her naked. The importance of family modesty is intensified by the sad but real problem of temptation toward incestuous relations, especially of brothers toward their sisters and fathers toward their daughters.

Guidelines for Sex Education

Here are some guidelines that parents may find helpful in teaching their children about sex:

If you don't know the facts, don't be embarrassed—just find them out. In this sex-saturated culture, everybody thinks we should know everything about sex. But often we don't.

There are many fine resources for Christian parents including James Dobson's *Preparing for Adolescence,* Grace Ketterman's *How to Teach your Children about Sex,* and Wilson Grant's *From Parent to Child about Sex.* Ask your pastor and other parents for advice in what to say and how and when to say it.

Always teach sex in the context of values, responsibility, and marriage. When you teach your children anatomy, don't do it as if their sex organs are parts of a car engine. Relate them to their purpose.

Sex is so much more than biology. It is a matter of ethics and religion as well. If you create a tie between sex and marriage when your children are young, they will find it hard to conceive of sex having a place outside of marriage. And that's exactly as it should be. In contrast, sex education in the schools often isolates sex from its proper spiritual and ethical implications.

Know your child. Some children are sexually precocious, others are not. Some need to hear direct and to the point answers. Others respond better to a more subtle approach. You are the parent—no one is better qualified than you to discern what your child is ready to hear.

Answer your child's questions honestly. This may require some forethought. It is good to anticipate some of the questions that will be coming your way.

One of the classic questions is "Where do babies come from?" or "How does a baby get inside his mommy's tummy?" To a younger child you might explain it this way: "Mommy and daddy love each other so they hold each other close, and sometimes God decides to make a baby—part from mommy and part from daddy."

Tell them as much as they need to know now. A five-year-old does not need to see a diagram of sexual intercourse, nor does he need to be told "The baby's in mommy's uterus, not her tummy." Not every technical error needs to be corrected at an early age. Giving too much information too early may overwhelm a child. Discussing details of sexual intimacy can push a child to "grow up" sexually before his time (a major danger fostered by the media).

On the other hand, an eleven-year-old needs to know a great deal more than a five-year-old. If mom and dad don't explain sexual intercourse to him, someone else will very soon (if they haven't already) and probably not in the nicest way.

Still, the eleven-year-old doesn't need to know about matters such as premature ejaculation and birth control. In fact, things such as these would be better learned very shortly before marriage.

Unfortunately, the bombardment of sexual information (and misinformation) is so great that many twelve-year-olds know a great deal about sex. Once a child—whether too young or not—has learned something about sexual relations, parents need to be sure he has the right information and the right perspective.

Do not procrastinate. Too much too soon is one problem. Too little too late is another. It's too easy to wait for the right opportunity that never comes. Sometimes our children have already been misinformed or developed irrational fears about sex, and it's always harder to correct wrong thinking than to prevent it.

Don't try to calculate your child's exact date of puberty, then start telling him about sex the night before. It can be traumatic for boys to ejaculate and not understand what has happened, and even worse for girls to begin menstruating with no or only partial information. By the time some parents get around to telling their children about sex, their children know more than they do.

Remember, it's much easier to tell a twelve-year-old about sex than do what many Christian parents have done—had their first heart-to-heart talk about sex with their pregnant fifteen-year-old.

Do not come on too strong. It's best to spread things out, not dump the whole load of sexual knowledge at once. It's easy to overwhelm children not only with information but with emotions, especially negative ones. Difficult subjects like homosexuality need to be discussed with children as they get older.

But parents must be careful not to sound threatening or angry—they must be calm and remain approachable or their children will repress and hide their sexual questions and struggles for fear of rejection.

Be positive. Some parents tell their children about sex only because they have to. But they are so uncomfortable and tentative that, without meaning to, they communicate, "This is an unpleasant and shady thing we're talking about. I wish I was somewhere else, don't you?"

I know one girl who learned about menstruation through a note from her mother—passed under her bedroom door. This clandestine approach made a strong negative statement about female sexuality.

I don't mean to pick on mothers, but in premarital counseling my wife and I have talked with many young women whose Christian mothers have—usually not deliberately I'm sure—given them a negative view of sex. For a counselor to try to turn this around in the two months before the wedding is no easy task. In fact, it is usually impossible.

The most sensitive areas can be approached positively. A father can sit down with his son and talk about masturbation—how a lot of guys do it and it isn't so bad, but it could become a problem if you do it all the time and think about girls as sex objects. This is *so* much better than never saying anything or catching him and making him feel terrible about himself.

If you're positive about sex (this includes refraining from choking and turning crimson when the subject comes up), you will keep communication lines open, and your children will feel free to ask questions as they arise.

Of course, to speak positively about sex, you have to *think* positively about it. Perhaps a rereading of chapter 11 would be of help. Or if you need to work through some negative sexual freight from the past, see your pastor or Christian counselor—for your sake, your spouse's, *and* your children's. Remember what we said before—don't be ashamed to talk about what God was not ashamed to create.

Protect Your Children against Sexual Abuse

Sexual abuse of children is rising at an alarming rate. Parents must make all reasonable precautions to protect their children from such abuse.

Parents should regularly visit their children's schools, especially day-care centers. The same applies to scouts, clubs, and church groups. Parents should insist on their right to visit their children's activities at any time and at any place—and should deliberately make periodic unexpected visits.

Parents should check in on their children's play with each other, monitor their neighborhood activities, and know what goes on when their children are visiting neighbors, friends, and even relatives (the majority of child abusers are relatives).

Children should not be sent alone into public restrooms without reasonable precautions. When they are too young to resist or defend themselves, they should not walk long distances alone. Parents should teach them to resist lures from strangers, such as "Would you like a ride?" "Will you help me find my lost puppy?" "Can I take your picture over there?" and "Want to play a fun game?"

Children should be instructed to allow no one to touch their private parts, undress them, or undress in front of them.

Parents should be aware that father-daughter, stepfather-daughter, and brother-sister incest are the most common forms of sexual child abuse. Mothers must be particularly aware of family relationships. Fathers who struggle with sexual temptation toward their children should get help before they do permanent damage to their children and themselves.

Parents need to be sensitive to sexual abuse clues, including genital pain and rashes, depression, withdrawal, antisocial or regressive behavior, nightmares, and running away from home. Above all, children who say they have been sexually abused should be believed unless and until it is proven otherwise. Studies show that children rarely lie about sexual abuse.

Those with good reasons to suspect the sexual abuse of their children or other children should contact local authorities.

Often child abuse hotlines or services are found under "Family Services" or the "Human Services" section of the phone book. Any doctor, minister, school official, or government agency should be able to help you get in touch with the proper authorities. (Should you desire more information on this subject, contact the National Committee for the Prevention of Child Abuse, 332 South Michigan Avenue, Suite 1250, Chicago, Illinois 60604-4357.)

Exercise Parental Control

> There are overwhelming societal pressures on the young and on their parents to regard early sex as inevitable in our social climate.[3]

Parents *must* resist those pressures, or their children never will.

I'm alarmed at how many parents do not want to interfere in their children's lives. I believe most Christian parents today are not overprotective but underprotective of their children, at least when it comes to understanding and dealing with their developing sexual perceptions, values, and behaviors.

Parents *are* responsible to see that their children's friends are good influences. "Do not be misled: 'Bad company corrupts good character'" (1 Corinthians 15:33). Peer pressure is incredibly strong. It *is* our business to know about and provide direction for our children's relationships with others.

Parents are responsible for the school their children attend and what they're learning there. God entrusted your child to you not the school, whether public or Christian. It is *your* responsibility to see that they are taught what is right.

I've known Christian parents who wish their teenagers wouldn't bring home R-rated movies for their home videos, wish their daughters wouldn't wear suggestive swimsuits, and wish their sons wouldn't tell dirty jokes or listen to rock music that glorifies immorality.

Christian parents, we need to wake up. We must stop

wishing and start acting! God does not give us responsibility without corresponding authority.

"But I don't want my children to think I don't trust them." Trust is important, but it is never unrealistic. Parents don't trust their children to play on the freeway. It's not a matter of trust, just common sense and wisdom. Some parents trust their teenagers doing things I wouldn't trust myself doing.

Some parents trust their teenager to be in a car alone on a date till 1:00 A.M. Usually this is *neglect,* not trust. It is also the height of naiveté. What did *you* do when you were in a car with a date at 1:00 A.M.? Chances are, you weren't reciting Bible verses. How soon we forget.

"But my teenager is a Christian." Was your teenager born without glands? When he became a Christian did he develop green blood instead of red? If we parents give our young people this kind of freedom, we need to be prepared to share the responsibility for the powerful sexual temptations they will confront but may not yet be ready to resist.

Psychologist Henry Brandt's son was upset when his father didn't permit him to go out alone in a car with a girl. "What's wrong, Dad? Don't you trust me?"

"In a car—alone at night with a girl?" Brandt replied. "I wouldn't trust me. Why should I trust you?"[4]

Control the TV

The television is a good place to start exercising more positive parental control. Start by keeping record of every minute each family member (including mom and dad) watches television for one whole week. When you add up the total, you may be shocked or embarrassed into watching less.

Decide in advance how much television per week to watch—perhaps eight hours or five selected programs per week. Or choose two days a week when the television can be on, and keep it off the others. You can decide in advance which programs to watch and stick to the schedule you've determined. This will keep the television from being mindlessly flipped on and your brain flipped off.

"Fasting" from TV for a period of weeks or months helps keep it under control. Just try going a week without television in your home—to remind yourself of how pleasant life can be without it. Some people get rid of their televisions entirely. After the initial withdrawal symptoms, most are relieved and happy at all the time they have to do other things (like relating to each other, calling a friend in need, visiting a neighbor, and other forgotten practices of the pre-TV era). If you keep a TV, try keeping it in your closet. This way, it will take an intelligent effort to go and get it out.

Determine to watch only shows that uplift biblical values and turn them off when they don't. Discuss programs as a family. Why is this one good or this one bad? This will develop moral discernment in the whole family. Do *not* allow your children to pick any programs they wish—that is your responsibility.

Beware of using television as a babysitter—especially when the programming doesn't contribute to your child's spiritual and moral development. Provide alternatives for your child—like reading, projects, and healthy play. Even good TV programs watched too often encourage passivity and discourage meaningful play, interaction, and communication—essential to proper development.

Here's a radical idea—require that any family member spend one hour reading the Bible or engaging in a ministry for each hour watching television. Is it too much to ask that God be given equal time with ABC?

CONCLUSION

We parents can save ourselves and everyone else a lot of confusion if we recognize our God-given responsibility to teach our children about sex. We cannot and should not expect the schools, the media, or anyone else to do our job for us, even though they will if we don't (and they will try even if we do). Naturally, we'll make mistakes in educating our children about sex. But just giving it a conscious effort will put us far ahead of most parents.

Recently a sixteen-year-old girl spent the evening with our family. We were watching what seemed to be a good television program when a scene came on showing an unmarried couple obviously moving toward sexual intercourse. As I turned it off, she said, "That's not for me. I'm saving myself for my husband—whoever he'll be. My marriage present to him will be me. He'll be my first and only; that's the best I can give him."

I was proud of her. But even more, I was proud of her parents.

Chapter 18, Notes

1. W. Peter Blitchington, *Sex Roles and the Christian Family* (Wheaton, Ill.: Tyndale House Publishers, 1980), 139.

2. In his excellent book, *Growing Up Straight* (Chicago: Moody Press, 1982), Dr. George Rekers develops these and many other important aspects of raising children with proper sexual identities. I highly recommend this book for all, especially parents of young boys.

3. Jeane Weston, *The Coming Parent Revolution* (Chicago: Rand McNally and Co., 1981), 229.

4. Elisabeth Elliot, *Passion and Purity* (Old Tappan, N. J.: Fleming H. Revell Co., 1983), 147.

Chapter 19

What We Can Do in the Church

*T*he church is to challenge the world's morality, not mirror it. It is to be an oasis in a spiritual desert. Yet it is increasingly impossible, morally speaking, to tell where the world ends and the church begins.

STEMMING THE CHURCH'S MORAL DECLINE

Getting Our Heads Out of the Sand

What can the church do about its moral decline? First, we must be more aware. We can no longer afford to be naive. We must face the fact that beneath the squeaky clean Sunday morning exteriors are many hurting people, more than a few in mental and physical bondage to sexual sin. In too many churches the reality of such problems is ignored. We pretend they don't exist or only exist far away. Unless this changes, the church is destined to irrelevance, a fate worse than extinction.

Church leaders must realize that the reading and viewing habits of their people are not very different from those of their non-Christian neighbors. Furthermore, we must stop assuming that everyone in our churches knows what is right and wrong.

We need to teach the ABCs of morality. One man and woman from non-Christian backgrounds lived together in fornication for two years while regularly involved in an evangelical church. They never tried to cover it up, but not once did they hear the subject dealt with. Church leaders cannot presume people know what the Bible says is right and wrong. We must tell them.

Nor is it enough to tell only the youth groups about sex. Tell their parents. Don't just give junior high and high schoolers guidelines for resisting temptation. Give them to the whole congregation. Lust may begin in adolescence—it certainly doesn't end there!

After I preached several weeks on the subject of sexual purity, one man in our church told me, "Thanks so much. I had come to believe I was the only Christian who ever struggled with lust."

Helping Each Other in God's Family

Churches need to devote men's breakfasts, retreats, and other opportunities to developing camaraderie and accountability in living holy lives. Women's groups need to not only learn Bible content, but how to identify and resist the temptations to transfer their affection from their husbands to other men. The church's mature women are to teach the younger women to "love their husbands," to "be self-controlled," and to be "pure" (Titus 2:4-5).

The entire family, from children to adults, needs guidance from the church for their reading and viewing habits. I've found that using specific illustrations from magazines, novels, programs, and movies stimulates controversial, but usually very healthy, discussion.

Of course, we must do more than serve as censors by hitting on the "do nots" of sex. We must build a positive foundation. God's hatred of sexual sin should always be stressed in the light of his zeal to maintain the beauty and purity of marital sex.

We should recommend that our people read the Christian books that deal positively with sexual relations in marriage.[1]

Otherwise, they will read the bestselling secular books that are usually devoid of moral foundations. Clearly, the people in our churches *will* hear about sex—from everywhere. Then why not tell them what *God* says about sex and how they can have their questions answered in appropriate literature that regards marriage and sex as sacred.

Not only churches, but Christian schools and parachurch organizations need to address the sexual natures, thoughts, and behaviors of their students and leaders. Too often Christian leaders are not held accountable to each other for their moral lives. Their struggles with lust are ignored or glossed over till one day they erupt into immorality, and everyone is shocked and disillusioned about a sin that, with proper attention, could well have been prevented years earlier.

Few Christian colleges and even fewer Bible colleges and seminaries provide alternatives to the human sexuality courses offered on secular campuses across the country. As long as sex is spoken of by non-Christians and ignored by Christians, it will appear to be non-Christian, and Christians will continue to conform their minds to the secular drift with its disastrous consequences.

The church needs to develop a climate of openness about sexual struggles. Those who struggle with sexual temptation should feel the same freedom to come for help as those who battle depression or need marriage counseling.

Say It from the Pulpit

Such a climate of openness is not developed merely in the counseling office or small groups but from the pulpit. If those who preach never speak about sex or always speak of sexual sinners with wholesale condemnation—never as candidates for redemption and forgiveness—sexual sin will continue to grow and fester. Like a cancer it may surface in tumors here and there, but a large pocket of malignancy will exist—and breed—beneath the surface.

Sexual sin must be addressed not only directly and openly,

but in the context of Christ's offer of forgiveness, cleansing, and a transformed life.

Not long ago in our church another pastor and I preached a short sermon series on sexual purity. The response was phenomenal. The number of tapes ordered for each message was more than seven times the average number ordered for any Sunday in the previous six months. I still have six letters I received in the mail and numerous notes dropped in the offering boxes in direct response to this series. When this many people go out of their way to respond to a message, it's because it has touched an area of deep need in their lives. People are eager to hear what God's Word says about sex.

During this series, we also wrote Bible study lessons for discussion in our midweek small groups. Most reported exceptionally rewarding and helpful discussions. The church elders and small group leaders met regularly for their own discussions during the series, and shared honestly their own battles with lust. We were able to encourage and pray for each other—and together commit ourselves to sexual purity.

Biblical Counseling on Sex

Many people will come to the church for counseling in sexual matters. Whenever the subject is addressed publicly, however, many more will come out of the woodwork. They will acknowledge their sexual struggles and sins and often plead for help. When that happens, the church must be ready with wise biblical counseling that helps individuals in the nitty gritty of their lives, which often, by the time they come for counseling, resemble scrambled eggs.

Most pastors find it far easier to give answers from the pulpit than in counseling, where the principles cannot simply be broadly proclaimed but must be narrowly focused and brought to bear in the specific life, with all its unique history and circumstances. Whether pastors, counseling staff members, or lay counselors, the church must be sure its personnel are both biblically trained and sensitive to people's needs. They must themselves be morally pure, especially in light of the opportunity that is theirs to exploit the vulnerabilities of those seeking counsel. Too many counselors, even in the Christian community, have undertaken counseling with the morally weak and ended up being sexually involved with them rather than helping them.

Every church needs to have good premarital counseling that includes, among other things, careful and appropriate counseling as to sexual adjustment in marriage. In our situation, I meet privately with men and my wife with women, usually only a week or two prior to the wedding (because we speak explicitly, it would be unwise to fuel already strong sexual desires very long before marriage). Several couples have told us this was the single most helpful preparation for marriage they received.

In contrast, a thirty-year-old woman sat in my office, bitterly admitting her resentment of the pastor who performed her wedding five years earlier. He had felt uncomfortable discussing sexual matters and did not answer her questions or point her toward any other counselor or resource for help. Now she bore the scars of a miserable sexual relationship—one that might have been prevented with the right kind of counsel.

Churches can also establish fellowship and therapy groups for those who have suffered traumatic experiences such as abortion and rape. One church has a thriving ministry to incest victims, many of whom have suffered silently for decades, never having anyone to talk to they felt could understand. To protect confidentiality, group meetings are not publicly announced, and women seeking to join the group are carefully screened through an application and interview process with a church staff member.

ACCOUNTABILITY AND DISCIPLINE

John Donne was right. "No man is an island." We desperately need each other's presence, help, and support. Without them, we will never experience what our Father has for us.

Accountability: A Key to Sexual Purity

Accountability boils down to this: I need people to check up on me, to ask how I'm doing spiritually and to tell me when they see weakness or seeds of sin in my life. Nothing is more healthy in the body of Christ than a strong sense of accountability to each other. If I know I must answer to someone, it makes me more conscious and careful to do what is right. Through phone calls, notes, and regular meetings, we need to obey the biblical injunction to "spur one another on toward love and good deeds" (Hebrews 10:24).

Separated from the presence of accountability to his church and family, a college friend told me, "At first I resisted all the temptation everybody had warned me about. But I was so busy in school that I didn't get committed to a spiritual community soon enough. I went to church but didn't really have any other Christian to share with. I began to feel alone, and the things tempting me no longer seemed so bad. Finally, I just wore down and gave in." The result was three years of immorality, a lost witness for Christ, and scars that will remain the rest of his life.

Church leaders are in special need of accountability. Many pastors minister alone. Their position brings unique temptations and attacks from Satan. They need regular accountability to spiritual men in the church fellowship. Even when there is a plurality of pastors, it is easy for the business agenda to overshadow personal interaction at staff meetings. In one church a pastor repeatedly tried to bring up the subject of his personal sexual struggles. But there was never an opportunity; there was always too much business to be done. He finally managed to get the attention of his fellow pastors—*after* he committed adultery.

Other Christian leaders travel a great deal. They fly in and out of cities where they enjoy virtual anonymity. This lends itself to rationalizing: "Who would ever know if I went into this theater or bookstore, or watched this movie in my hotel room, or even if I had a few drinks with the woman I met on the plane?"

These men and women are in great need of accountability

to family and friends back home, and to Christians they are ministering to. They should ask and be asked to be accountable during their visit. Regardless of the expense, phone calls to spouse and children are important reminders of true and lasting values in contrast to the devil's tempting lies. Admitting sexual temptation to your wife over the phone gives you her encouragement, prayer, and accountability.

Prayer is a great way to support each other. But the sad truth is that many of us spend more time praying for our food than for our brothers and sisters. Perhaps many Christian leaders would have turned away from immorality had their people prayed for them. May God teach us what he did Samuel, who said to his brothers, "Far be it from me that I should sin against the LORD by failing to pray for you" (1 Samuel 12:23).

Public Confession of Sexual Sin

There is a place for the confession of sexual sin before the entire church body. It is in a church context that James tells us to "confess your sins to each other" (James 5:16).

But this good principle can be abused. In the case of sexual sin, it is possible to confess the matter, whether to one person or many, sharing unnecessary details that may stimulate others to lust. One group of believers struggling with homosexuality was told: "Describe your fantasies to one another, then renounce them." This sort of confession can easily prompt others to sin.

Confession to others is helpful to the degree that it develops accountability and to the degree that those confessed to are able to help the person live a more holy life. Confession to a pastor, elder, group of leaders, family member, or strong Christian friend, then, can be most appropriate. In some cases, particularly involving church leaders, confession of sexual sin to an entire church body may be necessary. Still, consideration should always be made for how the public confession will affect the person's spouse, children, and other members of the body. Certainly, in matters of sexual sin, details should always be avoided. I know of instances where homosexual behavior, adultery, and fornication have been specifically confessed to church bodies. In some cases, this has been good. In others, a more general confession might have been healthier.

Certainly, it is good for a whole church body to soberly examine itself, as normally happens when there is public confession of sin. I will never forget the expressions on the faces of our church family after a highly respected man confessed a sin (not a sexual one) in a church service. His confession—along with our explanation of the necessary disciplinary steps—was an effective deterrent to all of us as we faced our own particular temptations.

A Climate of Holiness

A spirit of accountability is cultivated in a climate of holiness in which worship is real, Christ is exalted, lives are transformed. In a climate of holiness, sin is hated—not tolerated, minimized, winked at, ignored, or mildly dismissed (Psalms 45:7; 97:10; 119:104; Proverbs 8:13; 13:5; Romans 12:9). In a climate of holiness the gospel is seen not as a call to happiness but to holiness. This kind of wholehearted commitment is as contagious in a church as is moral laxity.

The clearest sign of an unholy church (a phrase that is a contradiction in terms) is its high tolerance for sin. The church at Corinth is the primary New Testament example. It was a church full of knowledge and blessed with spiritual gifts, yet riddled with immorality. Paul addressed the issue of immorality in the Corinthian church with the strongest terms imaginable (1 Corinthians 5:1-13). Immorality must be tolerated—though never approved—in the world, but under no circumstances can it be tolerated in the church. Paul compares immorality and its effects on the church family to yeast that works its way through the whole batch of dough (1 Corinthians 5:6).

Paul is a realist. He acknowledges that sexual sin occurs in the church, but he refuses to concede that ongoing immorality is to be tolerated. It must be dealt with directly, decisively, and immediately.

John Stott tells us:

The Church's witness is impaired by its own low standards. The secular world is almost totally unimpressed by the Church today. There is a widespread departure from Christian moral standards, and unbelievers see no great difference between themselves and Church members. So long as the Church tolerates sin in itself and does not judge itself . . . and fails to manifest visibly the power of Jesus Christ to save from sin, it will never attract the world to Christ.[2]

How Holy Do We Look?

If the church is to be sexually pure, its members must appear sexually pure. At some point the church must address the controversial issue of proper clothing. Obviously it was an issue in the New Testament church since several writers address it.

It has been both ironic and disheartening to counsel men struggling with lust, then attend the church's July 4th picnic and see how some of the women and girls dress. One man told me every summer is a spiritual low point for him because he is surrounded by women, some of them fine Christians, wearing the latest swimsuits and summer fashions.

Many churches are now sponsoring women's aerobics programs that provide excellent opportunities for women to get exercise, fellowship, and bring in non-Christian friends. I greatly appreciate the thoughtfulness of the woman who directs this program in our church. Whenever men are invited, she instructs the women to dress in loose, nonrevealing outfits. (I saw another Christian group in a public place that did not take this care.)

Of course, men as well as women can be caught, innocently or deliberately, in the "let's be sexy" game. Sexiness should be reserved for the marriage bedroom. The church assembled should be a sanctuary to gain strength to resist the world's temptations, not a factory producing its own temptations. In its services, the church should be sensitive to modest and pure appearance.

This is a sensitive matter that requires an educational process as well as honest communication. Somehow, though, church members must be taught to give as much attention to preparing their hearts for worship as they do their bodies (1 Peter 3:3-4).

Confronting and Disciplining for Sexual Sin

If the church is to be a holy community, we must confront each other with the truth. Apathy or permissiveness disguised as love do no one a favor. We must remember that our primary objective is holiness not happiness. Our goal is not to help each other feel good but to help each other *be* good. Honesty, reproof, and discipline are a painful but essential part of the believing community. Whenever they are absent, immorality and a host of other sins will prevail.

In Ephesians 5:3-13 Paul affirms that the slightest suggestion of immorality is out of place among God's people. They are neither to act out nor even speak of immorality in a flippant, crass, or joking manner. The only justification for speaking of immorality is to expose its sinfulness and bring to bear the light of God's holiness. Part of being accountable in Christ's body is to lovingly confront each other when we speak and joke about what is sexually inappropriate.

A believer is never to consider his brother's moral life none of his business. The author of Hebrews says to a community of believers: "See that no one is sexually immoral" (Hebrews 12:16). We are both responsible and able to guard the moral purity of Christ's body.

How are we to respond when we believe a fellow church member is in sexual sin? The procedure of Matthew 18:15-17 specifically relates to offenses by one member against another. However, it seems an appropriate model for dealing with all sin, including sexual sin.

We are to confront in love the one guilty of sin—aware of our own frailties and never in a spirit of self-righteousness.

Often, such a confrontation will lead to repentance (Proverbs 12:1; 17:10). One man had lived in sexual sin for years until one brother confronted him on the matter. The guilty man said through tears, "Thank you. I didn't think anyone even cared what I was doing."

If the brother or sister does not repent, the procedure is to confront again, this time with one or two witnesses of good character. If there is still no repentance, the matter is to be brought before the whole church. If *this* does not work, Jesus states that the church is to no longer regard the offender as a part of the body. He or she is declared incompatible with the holy community and is put out of the church unless and until he repents, in which case he is to be accepted back (Galations 6:1; 2 Corinthians 2:5-11).

Many churches were frightened by the 1984 lawsuit won by an Oklahoma woman disciplined by her church for adultery. The elders and church were held liable for invasion of privacy and harassment. I've heard different accounts of how the situation was handled and will not attempt to state or defend whatever procedure was followed. It is clear, however, that despite the legal ramifications it could entail, churches are bound by Scripture to exercise discipline. Of course, we must be thoughtful, cautious, and never vindictive. But we are to exercise discipline nonetheless.

The Oklahoma woman's lawyer was quoted as saying this about her client, who was a member of the church at the time the sin was confronted: "It doesn't matter if she was fornicating up and down the street. It doesn't give [the church] the right to stick their noses in."[3] On the contrary, biblically speaking, the matter was very much the church's business. The church is responsible for itself, for all whom it comprises, for all associated with it. The immorality of one member affects the whole body and *must* be dealt with.

Disciplining the Church Leader

Those in positions of leadership are particularly subject to public discipline: "Those [elders] who sin are to be rebuked publicly, so that the others may take warning" (1 Timothy 5:20).

I know of pastors guilty of immorality who have quietly resigned from one church (everyone wanted to avoid a scandal), only to reappear at another church that was totally ignorant of their previous track record. Too often they repeat their sins, largely because they have been protected from sin's full consequences and never helped to overcome their problem.

Such an attempt to guard a leader's reputation amounts to an irresponsible endorsement of a man whose moral vulnerability should have required his stepping down from ministry, at least for a significant season. The leader, his family, his church, and his Lord's reputation all suffer when sin is covered up. The church must face the fact that the leader in sexual sin is neither a "one-woman man" nor "above reproach" (1 Timothy 3:2; Titus 1:6-7). He is therefore, for the present, disqualified for church ministry.

We must remind ourselves that lust is a sexual sin as well. A leader not guilty of physical immorality is nonetheless unfit for ministry if he has a roving eye or otherwise demonstrates an ongoing lust problem through his gestures, actions, or speech. It should go without saying (but unfortunately doesn't) that a man may express appropriate physical affection—such as a hug or a hand on the shoulder—without being guilty of lust.

Every church leader is human and therefore will experience temptation and at times be guilty of a lustful thought. Provided it is properly dealt with through confession and repentance, it does not disqualify him for ministry. It is the ongoing, persistent problem of lust (not just sexual temptation) that could spell disaster for the man and his ministry if it is not dealt with.

The goal of all church discipline is always restoration, not reprisal. The man guilty of the ongoing sexual sin addressed in 1 Corinthians 5 *did* repent, and as a result Paul tells the Corinthian church to welcome him back—the purpose of discipline had been fulfilled (2 Corinthians 2:7). Don Baker's book, *Beyond Forgiveness,* is a powerful account of one church's discipline of a leader in sexual sin, and God's grace in restoring him to a pure life and, eventually, to a new ministry.[4]

If the church is not to tolerate immorality, even less is it to tolerate those whose teachings promote or justify immorality (Revelation 2:20-23). One of the greatest weaknesses of the church today is her allowance of those who use their positions of authority to promote an antibiblical morality in the church.

The Church and the Homosexual

One of the most critical issues facing the church is homosexuality. But more important than the issue are the people behind it—those struggling with homosexual temptation and in need of the church's helping hand. We saw in a previous chapter the trend in churches toward accepting homosexual behavior in the name of Christian compassion. If this is the wrong approach, what is the right one?

The church must affirm that God created homosexuals—but not the homosexual orientation. When such orientation develops (for any of numerous reasons), it must be controlled, as must all urges and desires. Christians should not deny the reality and power of homosexual desires any more than they would heterosexual desires. But neither should they defend homosexual lust any more than heterosexual lust, or homosexual fornication and adultery any more than heterosexual fornication and adultery.

In many cases the homosexual actually has heterosexual desires that can be properly cultivated. In other cases this seems unworkable, and life-long celibacy may be the best or only option. Cruel? Paul does not think so (1 Corinthians 7:7, 25-28). Unfair? It may seem so to some. Yet innumerable believers have physical and mental handicaps that prevent full participation in many facets of life. And I know men and women with homosexual desires who have been greatly used of God in a life of obedience and sexual purity.

I'm not ignorant of the scientific and psychological studies done on homosexuality. And I have a number of good friends who struggle with homosexual temptations. I love and respect them. I have prayed with them, wept with them, rejoiced with them, and defended them—but never their homosexual actions. I refuse to accept the label "homophobic" or "self-righteous" simply because I'm committed to help them obey God's Word.

I too am disturbed by the vicious attacks of professing Christians who treat homosexuals with disdain, who refer to them as "human garbage," who call them names and make cruel jokes about their struggles. But I'm equally disturbed by the new breed of evangelicals who know how to express love to a person only by condoning his behavior.

The church *has* failed to meet the needs of those struggling with homosexual temptations. But we cannot atone for our sins against homosexuals by pretending the homosexual lifestyle is acceptable.

And surely we cannot endorse putting a homosexual lifestyle (a matter of moral choice) in a category with race, gender, age, and physical condition. I have never met a former white, former black, or former hispanic. But I do know a number of former homosexuals—those who have since chosen and lived out a life of sexual purity. Some (not all) of these have lost a significant degree of homosexual desire and have gone on to be happily married. I refuse to rob others of this hope by telling them their condition is unchangeable, their thoughts and behaviors uncontrollable, and that Christ is sufficient for everything *except* helping them in their area of deepest need.

To some readers this discussion of homosexuality is fairly academic. To others, it touches their very lives, their families, their friends, their churches—for they, or someone close to them, are homosexuals. The following are some of the many organizations devoted to ministering to the needs of those who struggle with homosexual temptation or have loved ones that do. Most offer helpful literature and support. I encourage you to write them for your personal help or for information in beginning an effective church or parachurch ministry to homosexuals.

Exodus International P.O. Box 2121 San Rafael, CA 94912	Love in Action P.O. Box 2655 San Rafael, CA 94912
Outpost 1821 University Ave. So. #S-296 St. Paul, MN 55104	Desert Stream The Vineyard Christian Fellowship 204 Santa Monica Blvd., #B Santa Monica, CA 90401
Spatula Ministries (for parents of homosexuals) P.O. Box 444 LaHabra, CA 90631	A Door of Hope (for wives of homosexuals) P.O. Box 295 Auburn, WA 98002
Reach Out P.O. Box 5817 Kansas City, MO 64111	Metanoia Ministries P.O. Box 33039 Seattle, WA 98133

CONCLUSION

As we will see in the next chapter, there is a great deal the church can do to influence the sexual standards of its community. But before she can say anything to the world, the church—created to be the spotless bride of Christ—must look to herself. "For it is time for judgment to begin with the family of God" (1 Peter 4:17).

Chapter 19, Notes

---

1. For instance, *The Gift of Sex* by Clifford and Joyce Penner; *Intended for Pleasure* by Ed and Gaye Wheat; and *The Act of Marriage* by Tim and Beverly LaHaye.

2. John R. W. Stott, *Confess Your Sins* (Philadelphia: The Westminster Press, 1964), 49.

3. Mark Starr, "Suing Over a Scarlet Letter," *Newsweek*, 27 February 1984, 46.

4. Don Baker, *Beyond Forgiveness* (Portland, Ore.: Multnomah Press, 1984).

Chapter 20

What We Can Do in the World

*T*he very title of this chapter raises a volatile issue. Can Christians in fact influence the morality of a world bent toward immorality? Is such an attempt simply rearranging the furniture on the *Titanic?* Is it compromising the church's mission and reducing the redemptive message to a mere social gospel?

Before all else, of course, we must tend to our own spiritual and moral lives. The world needs no more "Crusaders for Christ" who themselves are morally bankrupt. We must pursue a life of holiness and devotion to Christ, be feeding our minds on God's Word, be accountable to a holy fellowship, and be actively avoiding and resisting sexual temptation. Those of us who are married must be treasuring, guarding, and cultivating our sacred relationship with our spouse. This is where our moral responsibility begins. Contrary to what many Christians seem to think, however, it is not where it ends.

Otto Piper levels a strong indictment against this generation of Christians:

> Modern Christianity has incurred a grave guilt. Our congregations have failed effectively and articulately to protest against the widespread glorification

of sexual sins, and have been guilty of serious negligence by enduring degradation and scorn heaped upon the Christian virtues by the radio, the motion pictures, television, and the press. We have no right to plead excusable weakness. Our toleration is a sinful disdain of the divine insight granted us; and thus we are no less reprehensible than those who commit gross sexual sins. Our indifferent and tolerant frame of mind shows plainly that we do not only consider these portrayals of sexual sin unimportant but that we actually give them our inner approval, or even find them desirable.[1]

SALT AND LIGHT

This is not a time to be silent. It is a time to speak out with wisdom, tact, and compassion, yes, but also with strength and conviction. Otherwise, we will never be what Jesus called us to be:

"You are the salt of the earth. But if the salt loses its saltiness, how can it be made salty again? It is no longer good for anything, except to be thrown out and trampled by men.
"You are the light of the world. A city on a hill cannot be hidden. Neither do people light a lamp and put it under a bowl. Instead they put it on its stand, and it gives light to everyone in the house. In the same way, let your light shine before men, that they may see your good deeds and praise your Father in heaven" (Matthew 5:13-16).

In the sixties and seventies, American evangelicals were confident that Christ would return immediately. There was no need to change society. Only the humanists and liberals were trying to patch up a world we knew was destined for destruction and which we expected to leave soon anyway. We were so busy buying millions of books on the endtimes and listening to prophecy preachers tell us the details of the rapture, tribulation, and antichrist, our society's problems seemed dull and irrelevant.

In the eighties, it began to sink in with many of us that while Christ will come again, and he can come at any time, he may not choose to come in our lifetime (and there's nothing we can do either to predict or change his timetable). Meanwhile, we have neglected to speak out and become involved in issues that have produced an antimoral and anti-Christian social climate for which we, our children, and our grandchildren will pay dearly.

Many Christians are no longer content to stand idly by while their nation is sucked down a secularist drain they have not even attempted to plug. They have stopped labeling social-ethical issues "hands off." They are no longer content to spend their days blissfully listening to Christian radio, positioned for the rapture in their favorite recliner.

There is no end to the ways Christians can minister to the spiritual needs of people through addressing the problems created by the sexual revolution. We can reach out to the homosexual community, developing relationships with those that are open and making ourselves available in a time of crisis or need. We can address the rape problem by working for tougher laws and tougher enforcement. We can fight pornography, which feeds rape. We can also train or support training to increase mental preparation, self-confidence, and proper response to potential assaults.

A welcome change is taking place—Christians are taking seriously Jesus' call to be salt in a tasteless world and light in the midst of moral darkness.

PROVIDING ALTERNATIVES TO ABORTION

Most Christians agree that abortion is wrong. We grieve that one and a half million abortions are performed annually—that a full one-third of all pregnancies now end in abortion. But can we really do anything to save these precious lives? The answer is a clear *yes*.

We can speak out, write our congressmen, lobby against tax-supported abortions, together exert pressure that may one day result in the reversal of the Supreme Court's legalization of abortion on demand. We can write letters to the editor, picket abortion clinics, protest Planned Parenthood (proabortion) clinics in our community, vote for antiabortion congressmen, send letters and make phone calls to mobilize prolife forces and inform girls and women of the facts and alternatives.

We can read and distribute the fine literature that shows life in the womb and tells the truth about the unborn child's humanness and ability to feel pain.[2] We can open our homes to pregnant girls and adopt unwanted children. We can take out full page ads in local newspapers and say "There is no such thing as an unwanted child." We can print literature with our phone number offering help to pregnant girls. We can donate appropriate books to local public schools.

A good friend gave me a copy of a letter she wrote to her doctor. First, she thanked him for how sensitive and caring he had been when she had miscarried, and how excited he had been later at the birth of their now seven-year-old son (she even enclosed his picture).

Then she shared how disappointed she was to recently learn he sometimes performed abortions. She stated that, reluctantly, she would have to find another doctor because in good conscience she could not contribute to a practice that participated in abortion. Sharing some specific research on life before birth, she graciously but firmly challenged him to rethink his position. She ended by quoting Psalm 139:13-16. Regardless of his response, I'm sure her doctor will not soon forget that powerful letter.

You might wish to call your own doctor's office and—before identifying yourself—ask if they will perform an abortion. If the answer is yes, consider taking the same thoughtful step this woman did.

The most exciting and positive approach that Christians have taken to the abortion issue is in establishing Crisis Pregnancy Centers. Washington, D.C.'s Christian Action Council opened the first Crisis Pregnancy Center in Baltimore in 1981. Within a few years the number grew to dozens and soon it will be hundreds.

The Crisis Pregnancy Centers advertise free pregnancy tests to attract women, half of whom normally want abortions. After talking with trained counselors and viewing tasteful presentations of the alternatives, about 70 percent of those seeking abortion change their minds and decide to have the baby, either to raise it themselves or give it up for adoption (usually to Christian parents).

The Centers refer the girls to appropriate medical and legal professionals—usually Christians who volunteer these services at no cost—who can help them follow through with their decision not to abort. Many Crisis Pregnancy Centers provide housing with Christian families when needed, childbirth classes, maternity clothing, clothing and supplies for infant care, ongoing counseling and friendship, and adoption referrals when requested.

The Centers not only save human lives, but often provide women a direct exposure both to the gospel and to ongoing relationships with Christian families. Many women come to Christ through these Centers, and many who have already had abortions are offered forgiveness, compassion, and help.

My own experience with a Crisis Pregnancy Center has convinced me of what a positive and worthwhile ministry it can be. Nothing I know compares to walking into the church nursery and seeing a child whose mother was dissuaded from having an abortion. No community should be without a Center. Those interested in learning of, becoming involved in, or starting a Crisis Pregnancy Center in their own area should write: Christian Action Council, 422 C Street NE, Washington, D.C. 20002.

POLITICAL AND SOCIAL INVOLVEMENT

More believers than ever are becoming socially and politically active. There is a great need through mobilizing, lobbying, and voting, for believers to influence legislation in this country. Stiffer penalties for child pornography, for instance, have arisen only because concerned citizens pushed the issue. They will be enforced only if we continue to push.

We need tougher legislation applying to adult pornography, prostitution, and rape. But legislation is no better than its enforcement. For this reason we need better judges, better lawyers, more policemen, more prison facilities, and reformed jury and parole systems. We need to oppose antifamily and antichurch legislation, for the family and church are the moral fiber of the nation.

"But you can't legislate morality." No, but we can have moral legislation that protects the innocent and punishes the guilty. We can't make people behave morally, but we can legislate the consequences when they don't. That is precisely the purpose of laws.

Those Christians in government should be prayed for, helped, and encouraged to make biblical decisions, not politically expedient ones (a Christian politician can vote unbiblically, just as a non-Christian can vote biblically).

There is a desperate need for more Christians in government at the local, state, and national levels. We must not surrender this critical turf to those, both well-meaning and otherwise, living in spiritual and moral darkness. The church should encourage individual believers to be involved in the social and political arenas, even though the church itself must be careful not to become a political organization.

Churches should remember that much legislation—for instance that relating to abortion, infanticide, and capital punishment—is far more than a question of politics or partisan platforms. Sometimes these matters are clear-cut issues of biblical morality. To ignore them simply by saying, "Politics and religion don't mix," is morally irresponsible.

Churches and individual believers that refuse to get their hands dirty by being socially involved will have no grounds to complain when they wake up to a society that no longer allows them the personal and moral freedoms they have treasured—and taken for granted—for so long.

Becoming Informed and Involved

Effective community involvement requires a knowledge of the issues, local government structure, and the identity and sphere of influence of local officials.

Knowledge of the issues can come from the media and from personal contact. There is little value in knowing the issues, however, unless we are developing a firm grasp of the relevant biblical principles. Otherwise we will know what to talk about—but not what to say. Churches need to give their people a solid biblical education and an ability to bring Scripture to bear on moral and social issues.

Writing letters and making phone calls to local officials is the most basic means of involvement. Elected officials are particularly sensitive to this input because they are eager to please their constituencies.

When the opportunity arises, Christians can give public testimony at community hearings and forums on significant issues and proposals (e.g., on regulating cable television). A carefully written, concise statement shows deep concern when read at such meetings.

A woman in our church spoke out at a hearing about a proposed ordinance to permit nude dancing in her county. One of the public officials specifically stated it was this woman's testimony that changed her mind—and that official's vote kept the ordinance from passing. Had this Christian woman been too tired or too busy to attend that meeting, one more piece of ground would have been gained by the forces of evil.

The next level of involvement is volunteering time to serve on committees and task forces (e.g., on pornography or teen prostitution). Financial contributions are another significant means of involvement.

I served on a committee to evaluate and revise our local grade school's sex education curriculum (the committee was formed because parents expressed their disapproval of the materials and class content). Though the committee members came with significantly different perspectives, the dialogue proved very helpful, and the final product was a vastly improved course. With only a phone call to your local school, you can probably get involved in some significant parent-teacher group and influence the public education that largely determines our nation's future.

Concerned Christians can do a great service for others by compiling and distributing up-to-date lists of local projects worthy of involvement, with appropriate names and phone numbers. Circulating lists of local, state, and national officials can be very helpful. It is not enough for most people to be told to write their congressman. They need a name and address and at least a sample or outline of what they might say. Too many people do not get involved simply because they don't know an address or don't know what to say or how to say it.

How Much Can the Church Say?

As long as the church is careful not to recommend certain candidates over others, its tax-exempt status is not in jeopardy. It can even list the voting records of candidates on any issue it chooses. By simply informing its people—not persuading them to choose a certain candidate—the church can be responsible and effective.

A few years ago a prohomosexual bill was suddenly pushed to a vote in our state senate, with only a few days notice. Several area churches simply announced the matter on Sunday morning and gave a phone number for those who wished to call and give their opinion to their representatives. As a result of the calls (from forty people in our church and more from others), four legislators *changed their votes* and the bill was narrowly defeated.

In our church we have a Citizenship Committee that meets as a Sunday school class. It is not associated with any political group or party, but simply seeks to inform us of pertinent issues and remind us of our civic responsibilities. The committee encourages voter registration and provides the necessary forms, and offers petitions addressing strategic and clear-cut biblical issues (not secondary or gray issues).

While we recognize the risks of becoming or being labeled a "political church," we see the greater risk of hiding our light under a bowl. When positively and wisely done, the believer's social involvement can not only influence the tenor of society but open great doors for evangelizing people who otherwise would not have been reached.

One Church's Approach to a Social Problem

The experience of a nearby church provides a good model for social involvement. Prostitutes daily worked the streets outside of this Portland church, their customers sometimes even parking in the church's lot. Thinking their duty was to flush out this vice (which is one step ahead of many churches, who would simply ignore the problem), church members took out cameras to scare away business. When that didn't work, they picketed, carrying signs that read "Prostitution is illegal and immoral." That didn't work either. Soon the whole congregation made an antiprostitution march. They only succeeded in pushing the prostitutes further up the block.

When all else failed, one of the pastors took a different approach. He personally passed out business cards to the prostitutes, giving them a number to call if they wanted someone to talk with. When the weather turned cold, he and others took them coffee and doughnuts. At Easter, they gave them baskets filled with candy. They even gave them presents on their birthdays.

After a while, these young women began to come to the church for help. The pastor and others in the church opened their homes to them. Within two years fifteen women left prostitution, and several of these had come to Christ.

WHAT TO DO ABOUT TELEVISION

A script for an episode of a television situation comedy had the male star unwittingly seduce a man whose sex-change therapy was not quite complete. This program was used as an example in a *USA Today* article on TV censorship.[3] The article maintained that only 7 percent of viewers are likely to express objections to "unconventional" (read "immoral") programming; that the only reason television has gotten worse is that people have tolerated it.

For those of us becoming increasingly intolerant of programming content, here are five avenues we can call and write to express our support of good shows and our objection to bad:

The Networks. If the networks receive enough mail, they do pay attention. Don't forget to give them positive reinforcement for their good programs. Address your remarks to the president at each company:

American Broadcasting Company, Inc. 1330 Ave. of the Americas New York, NY 10019	Columbia Broadcasting System, Inc. 51 West 52nd Street New York, NY 10019
National Broadcasting Company 30 Rockefeller Plaza New York, NY 10020	Public Broadcasting Service 485 L'Enfant Plaza West S.W. Washington, DC 20024

Local television stations. You can get their addresses and numbers from the phone book. They're often more responsive to input than the networks. They care about their image in your city.

The Federal Communications Commission. The FCC governs what is transmitted over the air waves. Write to the FCC's chairman and tell him what you think about television programming using specific examples, including the network and program names, date, time, city, and local broadcasting station: Federal Communications Commission, 191 M Street, NW, Washington, DC 20050.

Your congressman and local representatives. Express your support for legislation requiring community accountability and strong local involvement and control in the programming of cable television franchises.

The sponsors. This may be the most effective means of improving not only television but most other media. Television, radio, magazines, newspapers—all are heavily dependent upon their advertisers or sponsors. The sponsors want their name to strike a positive note so that consumers will buy their products. They shun negative publicity.

Consequently, many companies are highly sensitive to consumer criticisms. For instance, when the Kellogg Company sponsored an offensive segment of NBC's "Saturday Night Live," some viewers wrote in protest. As a result, Kellogg apologized and immediately ordered its advertising agencies not to buy any more commercials on that program—ever.

The National Federation for Decency (NFD) has approached many sponsors with their criticisms and seen companies not only apologize and withdraw their sponsorship of certain programs, but establish fulltime staff positions just to monitor programs before the company's ads are placed.

Rev. Donald Wildmon, head of the NFD, has organized massive letter-writing campaigns to sponsors, beginning with a positive approach but moving to threatened boycotts if the input is not heeded. Sears bought commercial time for a sexually exploitive ABC series. The very day that the NFD began picketing Sears stores in thirty-six cities, Sears pulled its commercials. They responded when they saw how serious people were.[4]

In 1981 Proctor and Gamble, the largest buyer of television commercial time, stated it had pulled out of fifty television movies and series, including seven of the ten series the NFD had declared most sexually exploitive. In September 1983 NBC aired the television movie "Sessions" featuring the exploits of a high-priced prostitute. But they paid a high price themselves. As a result of the NFD and other concerned citizens, a dozen sponsors withdrew from the movie, costing NBC one million dollars. The networks may not understand morality—they *do* understand a million dollars.

The same approach applies to magazines. When I dropped our subscription to *TV Guide* because of the sexually exploitive ads that began appearing in 1983, I cited numerous examples to make my point. I stated I did not want my children raised to think of people as sex objects and sex as something cheap (I always try to make clear I am positive toward sex, and on that very grounds I oppose its misuse). *TV Guide* responded with a lengthy personal letter identifying with my concern and stating they were sending photocopies of my letter to each of the networks, who prepare and submit the ads.

Suppose ten thousand Christians dropped their subscriptions to *Sports Illustrated* to specifically protest the sexual exploitation of its annual swimsuit issue. Do you think this would leave an impression with the publisher?

As a result of a single letter of complaint from the editor of the *University of Colorado Daily,* the chairman of Coors decided to pull its entire nationwide use of one sexually suggestive beer ad that one student thought subtly promoted rape.[5]

You can obtain sponsors' names by checking the products they advertise, and their addresses from their local representatives (listed in the phone book) or *Standard and Poor's Dictionary* found in most libraries. Individuals and churches can help others by bringing sample letters, with current names and addresses, as models for others. The most effective letters, of course, are personal, not photocopies or verbatim duplicates.

The best long-term means for Christians to influence television and other media is for more to enter the field. If there were more skilled Christian screenwriters, directors, and producers—and actors who would not sell out their principles for "a good part"—the industry could be positively influenced from the inside. Unfortunately, many believers are avoiding these fields because they are becoming corrupt, thereby destining them to further corruption instead of possible reform. (On the positive side there is now an industry-wide organization devoted to supporting and uniting believers in the field, the Fellowship of Christians in the Arts, Media and Entertainment [FCAME].)

WHAT TO DO ABOUT PORNOGRAPHY

The clearest demonstration of what concerned individuals and communities can do is in the area of pornography. Whole cities have succeeded in banning its sale. They not only have no adult book stores, but their convenience stores do not even carry *Playboy*. They have also blocked efforts toward adult cable TV channels. All because concerned citizens spoke out with one voice.

Citizens for Decency Through Law provides experienced attorneys to combat the expert lawyers hired by wealthy pornographers (and the ACLU) to get them off the hook. The National Federation for Decency has fought pornography through its "pornographer of the month" award to companies doing the most advertising in magazines such as *Playboy* and *Penthouse*. As a result, more than twenty-five major advertisers, not wishing to win the award, have told the NFD they will discontinue advertising in pornographic magazines.

These organizations and others are dependent on financial support from the private sector. They provide informative newsletters detailing the war against obscenity, and how to make a difference in one's community. Write to them for details:

Citizens for Decency
    Through Law
450 Leader Building
Cleveland, OH 44114

National Federation for
    Decency
P.O. Box 1398
Tupelo, MS 38801

Morality in Media
475 Riverside Drive
New York, NY 10115

Another fine resource for waging war against pornography is *The Porno Plague,* by Neil Gallagher.[6]

Many fine antipornography laws exist. The major problem is their lack of enforcement. In a five year span, one Memphis attorney prosecuted sixty violators of federal pornography laws, and fifty-nine of the sixty were convicted. Yet they were given nine to eighteen months sentences and small fines (relative to their earnings). Most are never prosecuted at all or walk away with no more than a slap on the hand. Whenever there is a strong public outcry against pornography, the legislators and the courts respond. Whenever there isn't, they don't.

Specific Steps to Counter Pornography

When you see objectionable material sold in a store, ask to speak to the manager and courteously share your objections. I have found most managers are genuinely interested and concerned when they receive this kind of input. If the situation hasn't changed after a few weeks, speak to the manager again and tell him you feel so strongly about your objection that you will have to take your business elsewhere—and that you will recommend your friends do the same.

When I saw a store at a nearby family mall with lewd posters in its windows, my first response was to write letters to the store and to the mall owners. I took down the name but neglected to write. A week later a woman in our home Bible study group said she had also seen the posters and had called the store to protest. When she was told that the posters would stay, she called the central office two thousand miles away. She talked to a company executive who thanked her for her concern and told her he would see to it *immediately* that the manager took the posters down.

Quick and effective results often come from taking the time and trouble to get involved. The key is to be both congenial and firm. You may be amazed at the results. Two large grocery chains in the Pacific Northwest recently stopped carrying sexually exploitive magazines simply because some people cared enough to speak out.

Writing letters to the editor of local newspapers or picketing specific stores carrying pornography can be effective, but *only* if you have first talked to the store owners and there has been no change or intention to change.

In order to have broad effect on a whole community, it is necessary to organize and advertise a forum, then choose a task force to lay out a plan of action. (The resources listed previously will provide helpful material for this process.) Remember, whole communities and cities, such as Fort Wayne, Indiana, have succeeded in largely eliminating the pornography trade. Christians of many different denominations in Fort Pierce, Florida, met to oppose a new X-rated theater; before their fight was over they had eliminated *every* pornographic film in the whole city.[7] It is not an impossible task.

Forms to protest sexually exploitive material received through the mail are available in the Post Office. When you do receive such material, bring it to the Post Office and express your objection in person. One Los Angeles teenager sued a North Carolina company for $250,000 after receiving an unsolicited shop-by-mail catalogue advertising pornographic and sexual devices. That kind of action makes the sex merchants think twice.

There are many creative ways to attack the problem of sexually exploitive literature. For instance, a nearby college has a thriving paperback book exchange. One of the professors regularly takes the worst books off the shelf, throws them away, and replaces them with fine Christian literature—a double accomplishment.

Of course before we worry about the literature and viewing material outside our home, we must take care of that inside. To formally object to the sale and rental of materials that we ourselves buy, rent, watch, and read is the height of hypocrisy. To write letters objecting to television's sexually exploitive programs and then to watch these programs or permit our families to watch them is folly.

We must always have a positive attitude, uplifting and commending good literature and programming as much as we attack the bad. While the church stands against obscene practices and literature, it should be there to provide decent literature and a decent example that teaches a positive view of sex. Our image must not be that of vicious crusaders but of profamily and procommunity servants.

For every stand we take, whether it be antiabortion, antipornography, or antiprostitution, we must provide alternatives. We must not just say, "Get teen prostitutes off the street," but "We'll open our home to one of them."

A FINAL WORD

Early in this century, a great spokesman of the biblical faith, G. Campbell Morgan, saw clearly the church's responsibility to its society:

> The Church is responsible for the religious life of the city, for the moral standards of the city, for the social order of the city.
>
> If you can persuade me that we have no responsibilities, that the Church exists merely for the conserving of the life of her own members, then I will leave the Church, and join with others who have a keener sense of moral and religious responsibility; but it is impossible to persuade me to that conclusion in the light of the New Testament teaching. . . .
>
> The Church is against the city as it is, in order to make the city what it ought to be. The Church lifts her voice in protest against iniquity in the city or nation, because her business is to make the city and the nation what God would have them be.[8]

We cannot minister to those in bondage to spiritual Egypt by making Egypt a better place to live, but by offering a new and different citizenship, a radically different way of life. Our community needs not just reform but redemption; not just renovation but the Redeemer. We must take a stand for righteousness, yes, but always as a platform to share the one true Source of righteousness—the Lord Jesus Christ.

We must listen once more to Edmund Burke, whose words apply equally to the family, the church, and the nation:

> All that is necessary for the triumph of evil is that good men do nothing.

Chapter 20, Notes

1. Otto A. Piper, *The Biblical View of Sex and Marriage* (New York: Charles Scribner's Sons, 1960), 200.

2. For example, see Landrum Shettles and David Rorvik, *Rites of Life: The Scientific Evidence for Life before Birth* (Grand Rapids, Mich.: Zondervan Publishing House, 1983).

3. *USA Today,* March 1984, sec. D.

4. Harry F. Walters, "Does Incest Belong on TV?" *Newsweek,* 8 October 1979, 102.

5. *USA Today,* 16 December 1983, sec. B.

6. Neil Gallagher, *The Porno Plague* (Minneapolis: Bethany House Publishers, 1981).

7. *Christianity Today,* 2 January 1981, 52.

8. G. Campbell Morgan, *Living Messages of the Books of the Bible* (Old Tappan, N.J.: Fleming H. Revell Co., 1912), 123-25, 128.

Conclusion

Long ago Alexander Pope described the process of moral desensitization that has come to characterize not only America but the American church:

> Vice is a monster of such horrid mien,
> That to be hated needs but to be seen;
> But when seen oft, familiar with its face,
> We first endure, then fondle, then embrace.

Sexual immorality is so much a part of our environment that it is becoming no more remarkable than the air we breathe or the ground we walk on. It is rarely startling and seldom hated. Most believers are now enduring it, many fondling it, some embracing it. My prayer is that this book has helped to shake us from complacency and challenged us to take the scriptural steps to change ourselves, our families, our churches, our communities, and our nation—to change while there is still opportunity to change.

There are several kinds of readers I find myself concerned about as this book ends. First, the one who does not yet know the Lord Jesus Christ. To him or her I can only say that while the moral life is far superior to the immoral, no efforts toward moral reform can earn us God's favor. We must come to him on his terms, not ours. He offers love and forgiveness to all who swallow their pride and bend their knee to Christ, who died on a cross for our sins and offers us his own moral purity.

I am equally concerned about the reader, believer or unbeliever, who feels the concerns of this book are much ado about nothing—that sex outside of marriage is really not so bad and sometimes even acceptable, or that there is little or no harm done by an indulgence here, a compromise there, a little peek here, a slight indiscretion there, a bit of flirting here, an off-color joke there. He buries every twinge of conscience or conviction in a landslide of self-justification and self-deceit. His powers of rationalization are mighty, but they do not change the truth.

> There is a way that seems right to a man,
>   but in the end it leads to death (Proverbs 14:12).

Then there is the Christian who believes he or she is somehow above all this, that one so spiritual as himself would never indulge in sexual compromise like the moral weaklings around him. This pharisee looks down his nose at sexual sinners and prides himself in his own supposed righteousness.

> Pride goes before destruction,
>   a haughty spirit before a fall (Proverbs 16:18).

Other readers are not prideful but naive. They don't demean or write off sexual sinners but simply can't imagine they could ever join their ranks. Unaware of their own vulnerability, they are all the more vulnerable. "So, if you think you are standing firm, be careful that you don't fall!" (1 Corinthians 10:12).

Still other readers know only too well the tragedy of immorality. Some are now walking in purity, enjoying Christ's forgiveness and moral strength, but others are yet handcuffed by unconfessed sexual sin or suffering under a load of sexual temptation that repeatedly leaves them writhing in failure and guilt. To these brothers and sisters I offer the words of a friend who wrote this song to coincide with a sermon on sexual purity:

> Ask the miner underground "How do you feel?"
> Trapped by tons of earth and rock the tunnel home is
>   sealed.
> From the darkness the reply, a muffled hopeless
>   shout:

"The walls around caved in on me and there is no way
out,
The walls around caved in on me and there is no way
out."

Ask the diver in the sea, "How do you feel?"
Hopelessly his feet ensnared in weeds made out of
steel.
From the depth could he reply would come a frantic
shout:
"It seems the more I struggle here the more my
strength gives out,
It seems the more I struggle here the more my
strength gives out."

Ask the sad believer, "How do you feel?"
Ruled by passions ill-conceived lustfully he reels.
And from a mind that's torn in two his heart can
barely shout:
"God, I hate the trap I'm in, I hope no one finds out,
God, I hate the trap I'm in, I hope no one finds out."

Ask the God who made the man, "How do You feel?"
The Holy God who judges sin, in pain that's
unconcealed.
From a heart that breaks with love, He's always
crying out:
"Son, you're Mine, your battle's Mine and I have
heard your shout,
Son, you're Mine, your battle's Mine, please let Me
help you out!"[1]

Finally, I am concerned for the reader whose faith in Christ
and confidence in Scripture has been so undermined he feels the
church has no definitive answers, no clear moral standards to
offer a world sick with uncertainty. Whenever Scripture coun-
ters the prevailing winds of society (which is almost at every
turn), this hapless skeptic-saint finds himself uncomfortable
with his faith. He has heard so much about tolerance and

pluralism and open-mindedness that he is almost embarrassed by Scripture's no-nonsense declaration of right and wrong.

Taking his cue from some church leaders, he apologizes for, hedges on, and qualifies the Bible's position on sexual morality (and almost every moral issue). In a world offended by certainty, he dodges at all costs the sin of dogmatism and does penance by saying, "Of course, we Christians don't have all the answers." Harry Blamires responds to this approach:

> Let it be said firmly that the bogus humility represented by the "we haven't got all the answers" line is as far from Christian virtue as lust is from love. Whatever else our Lord was accused of, He was not charged with preserving a sage and mystical silence while the weary, the doubtful, dejected and oppressed threw their tragically unanswered questions at Him. Yet in every other religious journal one picks up today, one reads the amazing sentence, "We must not talk as if we've got all the answers."
>
> Why in God's name not? What is our Christian duty if not to make plain that in the Christian faith the gravest doubts and worries of men are richly answered? What do these prevaricators mean? Have we not got the answers in their eyes? Is our Lord untrustworthy, the church founded upon an eternal question mark, the faith a fog? It will be time enough to put this slogan on our banner when we have heard a dying martyr proclaim it as the surety of his hope.
>
> The scene is worth picturing. The flames gather around the stake, but the martyr's eyes are ablaze only with faith. "I die gladly. I die at peace with God. My last message to you is this: we must not talk as if we've got all the answers."[2]

The world is looking for answers to spiritual and moral questions. We *do* have the answers. They are not easy, but they are real. May God help his church not to doubt, hold back, apologize for, or dilute the answers he has given us.

Conclusion Notes

1. Paul Thorson, "Trapped." Used by permission of the author.
2. Harry Blamires, "The Tyranny of Time."

A Select Bibliography for Further Reading

Baker, Don. *Beyond Forgiveness*. Portland, Ore.: Multnomah Press, 1984. A moving account of one church's confrontation and gradual restoration of a staff member discovered in immorality; a brief but instructive portrait of sin's consequences, church discipline and forgiveness, and the potential of repentance and healing for the individual.

Blitchington, W. Peter. *Sex Roles and the Christian Family*. Wheaton, Ill.: Tyndale House Publishers, 1981. The author weaves together his research in psychology, sociology, and history to argue for God-created sexual identities and the purpose and necessity of clear male-female roles in family and society.

Court, John H. *Pornography: A Christian Critique*. Downers Grove, Ill.: InterVarsity Press, 1980. A succinct statement of the pornography issue; effectively dismantles the standard defenses for pornography.

Dobson, James. *Preparing for Adolescence*. Ventura, Calif.: Vision House, 1978. A personal, almost conversational book most beneficial to young people from ten to fifteen years old; though the sexual aspects of puberty are discussed, Dobson views adolescence from more than a sex-centered perspective, dealing with self-esteem, peer pressure, infatuation, emotions, and physical struggles ranging from awkwardness to acne; also exceptionally useful for parents.

Elliot, Elisabeth. *Passion and Purity*. Old Tappan, N. J.: Fleming H. Revell Co., 1984. An intimate and inspiring account of the author's first love relationship, with Jim Elliot; demonstrates that passion can be real and purity still maintained; a much-needed elevation of premarital virginity, especially helpful to young women.

Gallagher, Neil. *The Porno Plague*. Minneapolis: Bethany House Publishers, 1981. While forcefully exposing the dark side of pornography, Gallagher goes much further—he lays out a clear and proven civic and legal strategy to eliminate pornography from a community; specific, practical, and indispensable to those committed to the fight against porn.

Gilder, George. *Sexual Suicide*. New York: New York Times Book Co., 1973. A cohesive, insightful, and powerful secular analysis of the socially catastrophic results of gender dilution, especially among our young; decrying the current vogue of emasculating men and defeminizing women, Gilder sees differentiating between the genders as not only healthy but essential to the proper function and, ultimately, the survival of our culture.

Johnson, Lissa Halls. *Just Like Ice Cream*. Palm Springs, Calif.: Ronald N. Haynes Publishers, 1982. A romance novel for junior high and high school girls with a different twist—it demonstrates how dreams crash land into the stark realities of pregnancy, guilt, ruined plans, and shattered relationships when virginity is surrendered in the name of "love"; showing God's grace for those already in trouble, it includes a presentation of the gospel that naturally blends into the story line; must reading for adolescent girls.

Ketterman, Grace. *How to Teach Your Child About Sex*. Old Tappan, N. J.: Fleming H. Revell Co., 1981. A child psychiatrist, Ketterman sees sex education as beginning at infancy and stresses the importance of positive parental attitudes toward sex; sexual terms are defined and pertinent matters for discussion are provided for each level of a child's development.

Keysor, Charles, editor. *What You Should Know About Homosexuality.* Grand Rapids: Zondervan Publishing House, 1979. A careful Christian analysis of one of the central issues facing the church today; experts in each field address homosexuality in light of the Old Testament, New Testament, writings of the church fathers, biology and psychology, civil rights, and Christian ministry.

Leonard, George. *The End of Sex.* Los Angeles: J. P. Tarcher, Inc., 1983. Written by a former field general in the sexual revolution who, fed up with the emptiness of casual and promiscuous sex, has defected to the other side; far from being a Christian, Leonard argues on a humanistic and pragmatic basis for what he considers to be a radical concept—High Monogamy, the limiting of sex to a long term committed relationship.

Lutzer, Erwin. *Living with Your Passions.* Wheaton, Ill.: Victor Books, 1983. One of the best practical guides for resisting sexual temptation.

Menninger, Karl. *Whatever Became of Sin?* New York: Bantam Books, 1978. Named in 1984 "the greatest living psychiatrist" by his peers, Menninger examines the moral and social deterioration resulting from the virtual abolition of the concept of sin in some mental health circles; in calling for a recognition of the individual's responsibility and accountability for his behavior, Menninger implores church leaders to return to their historical role of calling sin by its proper name; while his understanding of sin is biblically inadequate, the author, along with several others in this bibliography, demonstrates how a perceptive non-Christian can arrive at many accurate—albeit incomplete—moral conclusions.

Penner, Clifford and Joyce. *The Gift of Sex*. Waco, Tex.: Word, Inc, 1981. A medically, psychologically, and spiritually sound examination of the total sexual relationship for married couples; specific yet appropriate, this is a needed and refreshing alternative to the writings of Alex Comfort, David Reuben, and the glut of secular sex gurus.

Petersen, J. Allan. *The Myth of Greener Grass*. Wheaton, Ill.: Tyndale House Publishers, 1983. A family counselor exposes extramarital affairs for what they are, and offers preventative advice and healing.

Rekers, George A. *Growing Up Straight: "What Every Family Should Know About Homosexuality."* Chicago: Moody Press, 1982. A university professor of child development eminently qualified to write on this subject; stresses the critical role of the father in the child's psychosexual development—must reading for all parents, especially fathers of young boys.

——————————. *Shaping Your Child's Sexual Identity*. Grand Rapids: Baker Book House, 1982. Another significant book by Dr. Rekers, in which he takes to task the unisex philosophy of the feminist movement; includes the author's firsthand account (as an expert psychological witness) of a widely publicized court case in which a lesbian mother was denied custody of her children; includes clear and helpful parenting guidelines.

Rueda, Enrique. *The Homosexual Network*. Old Greenwich, Conn.: The Devin Adair Co., 1982. Written by a Roman Catholic priest, this extensive and carefully documented work probes into the most important facets of the homosexual movement and subculture, including its character, ideology, and goals; Rueda's analysis of the relationship between organized religion and the homosexual movement is particularly significant and enlightening.

Shettles, Landrum B. and David Rorvik. *Rites of Life*. Grand Rapids: Zondervan Publishing House, 1983. A landmark work that calmly and objectively offers irrefutable scientific evidence of the reality and wonder of life before birth; Shettles is known worldwide for his pioneer studies in human reproduction—studies that, on a purely scientific basis, led him to make an about face from his activist proabortion stance; includes eight pages of breathtaking intrauterine color photos, most taken by Shettles himself; potentially persuasive to those who recoil at more emotional or polemic arguments against abortion.

Small, Dwight Hervey. *Christian: Celebrate Your Sexuality.* Old Tappan, N. J.: Fleming H. Revell Co., 1974. A fine historical, philosophical, and theological study of human sexuality; compares and contrasts the historical postures of the church and the Scriptures.

Smedes, Lewis B. *Sex for Christians*. Grand Rapids: William B. Eerdmans Publishing Co., 1976. An often quoted work that has much to offer discriminating readers desiring to understand human sexuality; unfortunately, the author is noncommital on many important issues, such as transvestism, transexualism, homosexuality, petting, and viewing pornography; Smedes asks excellent questions, yet seldom offers clear biblical answers.

Stott, John R. W. *Confess Your Sins*. Philadelphia: The Westminster Press, 1964. A superior little book that demonstrates the value and necessity of confession and examines three kinds: confession to God in secret, to others we have injured, and when appropriate, publicly before the church; includes a critical evaluation of the practice of confession to a priest, particularly helpful for those from Catholic and certain Protestant backgrounds.

Thielicke, Helmut. *Sex: Theological Ethics,* vol. 3. Grand Rapids: William B. Eerdmans Publishing Co., 1979. A scholarly examination of human sexuality in light of Christian anthropology, especially the doctrines of creation and redemption.

Trobish, Walter. *Living with Unfulfilled Desires*. Downers Grove, Ill.: InterVarsity Press, 1979. A well-known counselor's correspondence with high school and college students seeking to understand themselves, their relationships, and sex; with honest questions and sound helpful answers, this is an excellent resource for teenagers and their parents.

White, John. *Eros Defiled*. Downers Grove, Ill.: InterVarsity Press, 1977. A prominent evangelical psychologist's perceptive analysis of sexual appetites, problems, and sins; in many respects, the finest work on the subject.

Wilson, Earl. *Sexual Sanity*. Downers Grove, Ill.: InterVarsity Press, 1984. A Christian psychologist's examination of sexual obsession, its roots, and how to break free by learning to control personal habits.

Young, Curt. *The Least of These*. Chicago: Moody Press, 1983. A thorough study of abortion by the executive director of the Christian Action Council; includes a biblical development of the sanctity of preborn human life, an analysis of abortion procedures, and helpful guidelines for the church and the individual committed to opposing abortion and offering constructive alternatives.

Scripture Index

Subject Index